Tilting Cervantes

Tilting Cervantes

Baroque Reflections
on Postmodern Culture

Bruce R. Burningham

Vanderbilt University Press

NASHVILLE

© 2008 by Vanderbilt University Press
Nashville, Tennessee 37235
All rights reserved

12 11 10 09 08   1 2 3 4 5

This book is printed on acid-free paper made from
30% post-consumer recycled content.

Manufactured in the United States of America
Cover design by Gary Gore
Text design by Dariel Mayer

Publication of this book has been supported by a generous subsidy
from the Program for Cultural Cooperation between Spain's Ministry
of Culture and United States Universities.

Library of Congress Cataloging-in-Publication Data

Burningham, Bruce R., 1964–
Tilting Cervantes : Baroque reflections
on postmodern culture / Bruce R.
Burningham.
p. cm.
Includes bibliographical references and index.
ISBN 978-0-8265-1602-2 (cloth : alk. paper)
ISBN 978-0-8265-1603-9 (pbk. : alk. paper)
1. Mass media and literature. 2. Popular culture and literature.
3. Postmodernism (Literature) 4. Cervantes Saavedra, Miguel de,
1547–1616—Influence. 5. Cervantes Saavedra, Miguel de,
1547–1616. Don Quixote. I. Title.
P96.L5B87 2008
700.9'03—dc22
2007051879

For Cassie and Drew

Contents

Acknowledgments

As with many academic books, various segments of *Tilting Cervantes* started out as classroom lectures, then became conference papers, and later were published as journal articles, before achieving their final status as discrete chapters within a much greater critical whole. At each stage of the process, this book has been greatly improved by the support and feedback I have received from students, interested colleagues, congenial but incisive interrogators during the question-and-answer period of conference sessions, panel organizers who gave me the opportunity to rehearse my arguments in public, and journal editors who made it possible for me to formally disseminate parts of this project while it was still in progress. While I cannot possibly acknowledge by name every single person who has had a hand in shaping this book, I cannot fail to express my deep gratitude here to Luis Murillo, Jim Parr, Carroll Johnson, Michael McGaha, Fred de Armas, Meg Greer, Barbara Simerka, Ed Friedman, Roberto González Echevarría, María Rosa Menocal, Georgina Dopico Black, Chris Weimer, Bonnie Gasior, John Thieme, Francisco Caudet, Kerry Wilks, Kimberly Nance, Roberto Díaz, Maite Zubiaurre, Mario Saltarelli, Carmen Silva-Corvalán, Patrick Dove, Sofía Ruiz Alfaro, and Claudia Soria. Thanks as well to Mathew Klickstein for introducing me to *Fight Club* and to Andy McCutcheon for bringing *The Long Hard Road Out of Hell* to my attention. I also owe a special thanks to my research assistants, Kristen Kessell, Christy Stoller, and Molly Gleason, for all their hard work.

I wish to express my gratitude to the Instituto Cervantes of Chicago for sponsoring a symposium at which I first presented the nucleus of my Salman Rushdie chapter; to the Whitney Humanities Center at Yale University for sponsoring a Cervantes symposium at which I presented a version of my *Brazil* chapter; and to the College of Arts and Sciences at Illinois State University for providing me with a grant that allowed me to carve out a block of uninterrupted time to put the finishing touches on the book itself.

Of course, I cannot fail to acknowledge the wonderful people at Vanderbilt University Press. Thanks to Debby Smith and Dariel Mayer for helping me refine my rhetoric. And a special thanks goes out to Betsy Phillips not only for believing in *Tilting Cervantes* from the very beginning but also for doing such a masterful job of shepherding it toward publication.

Finally, thanks to Cassie and Drew for gathering dozens of books off library shelves, for helping me double-check my citations, and for not complaining too much when I would disappear into my office for days on end while I was finishing this project. And, as always, my deepest and most important thanks go to my wife, Toni, for supporting my work (and this project in particular) in more ways than I can possibly itemize here.

An earlier version of Chapter 1 was previously published as "Beleaguered Hegemony and Triangular Desire in Lope de Vega's *Las famosas asturianas* and John Ford's *Stagecoach*," in *Bulletin of the Comediantes* 56.1 (2004): 115–42; a version of Chapter 4 was previously published as "Walt Disney's *Toy Story* as Postmodern *Don Quixote*," in *Cervantes* 20.1 (2000): 157–72; an English-language version of Chapter 5 originally appeared as "Salman Rushdie, Author of the Captive's Tale," in *Journal of Commonwealth Literature* 38.1 (2003): 113–33; its Spanish-language equivalent originally appeared as "Salman Rushdie, autor del *Cautivo*," in *Estas primicias del ingenio: Jóvenes cervantistas en Chicago*, ed. Francisco Caudet and Kerry Wilks (Madrid: Castalia, 2003), 35–54; and a much-abbreviated version of Chapter 7 was published as "Cervantine Reflections on *The Matrix*," in *Don Quijote Across Four Centuries: 1605–2005*, ed. Carroll B. Johnson (Newark, DE: Juan de la Cuesta, 2006), 49–59. I thank the publishers of these journals and essay collections for permission to reprint this material.

Tilting Cervantes

Tinted Mirrors:

An Introduction

> Objects in mirror may be closer than they appear.
> —Anonymous

We inhabit a distinctly Cervantine world; which is to say, we largely see the world through a Cervantine lens. Idle readers, sipping decaf lattes at their corner bookstore-cafe (surely a Cervantine hybrid concept), cannot so much as browse the pages of the latest *New York Times* bestseller without unavoidably inscribing themselves within Miguel de Cervantes's textual universe. Movie enthusiasts who know the precise location of every cameo appearance Alfred Hitchcock inserted into his films—or television fans, for that matter, who delight at the notion of a stand-up comedian named Jerry Seinfeld who creates a sitcom on NBC in which he plays a stand-up comedian named Jerry Seinfeld who eventually creates a sitcom on NBC in which he plays a stand-up comedian named Jerry Seinfeld—are well-versed in the discourse of Cervantine meta-narrativity. Contemporary writers as diverse as David Lynch, Charlie Kaufman, Christopher McQuarrie, Christopher Nolan, Larry David, Neil LaBute, and Kathy Acker all use a Cervantine vocabulary that was literally unavailable before the seventeenth century and that they have inherited (often second- and third-hand) from writers like Miguel de Unamuno, Jorge Luis Borges, Julio Cortázar, Juan Rulfo, and Gabriel García Márquez, among others. Cervantes's baroque transformation in *Don Quixote* of the medieval romances of chivalry into an extended exploration of the limits of perception, the nature of reality, the slippages of language, and indeed the very intertextuality inherent in literary works themselves forever changed the way we view imaginative texts, whether as readers, writers, or critics. Postmodernism may very well be, in the words of Fredric Jameson, "the cultural logic of late capitalism" (1), but it is a cultural logic that is related to what José Antonio Maravall (*Culture*, 6) calls the "crisis economy" of the baroque and whose aesthetic origins can be traced to the literary revolution initiated by Spanish writers like Cervantes. As Michel Foucault famously argues, "Don Quixote's adventures form the boundary: they mark the end of the old interplay between resemblance and signs and contain the beginnings of new relations" (46). And these new relations are epitomized if by nothing else than by the kind of self-conscious, self-reflexive, mirror imagery Foucault analyzes in Diego Velázquez's *Las Meninas*. Indeed, Mieke Bal is entirely correct when she defines the baroque as not so much a "style" as a "perspective, a way of thinking which first flourished during a specific period and which now functions as a meeting point whose traffic lights make us halt and stop to think about (the culture of) the present and (some elements of) the past" (16).

In this regard, my aim in this book is to examine several contemporary cultural texts—some novelistic, some autobiographical, some musical, some cinematic—by reflecting them against a cluster of early modern Spanish literary works, principally *Don Quixote*. What I seek to accomplish with this series of cross-cultural, cross-epochal comparisons is to trace the ways in which each of these disparate texts illuminates its counterpart through a parallel critical reflection. Within a globalized consumerist and informational economy, where copies of *Don Quixote* (in the original Spanish and in English translation) occupy shelf space in megabookstores like Borders just steps away from copies of *The Matrix* (whose DVD format allows viewers to use embedded Spanish subtitles), I willfully examine what it means to read these texts side by side, especially for twenty-first-century readers who might not come to them in their "proper" chronological order. What do viewers of the Wachowski Brothers' landmark cinematic trilogy bring to a fresh reading of Cervantes's literary masterpiece? In a world where online shoppers can buy Marilyn Manson's latest concert video from Amazon.com while downloading the complete text of *Lazarillo de Tormes* into an electronic book or PDA, I explore the hermeneutic ramifications of the fact that for contemporary readers (as it has always been for each new generation of readers) the various texts I analyze in this book are ultimately coetaneous, regardless of the centuries that separate their actual moments of production. Taking seriously Borges's notion that literary works create their own precursors ("Kafka," in *Borges*, 243; "Kafka," in *Otras inquisiciones*, 109), I suggest that the collection of disparate texts I examine in this book can be read—in a very Borgesian fashion—as precursors of each other.

The central conceit of this book, as the title of this introduction implies, is one of mirroring and reflection. I employ the term "tinted" because it carries with it a double allusion to the Spanish word for ink, *tinta* (suggesting the long-standing critical recognition of literature as a type of mirror held up to life and up to nature, not to mention up to the other arts), and to the Biblical passage in First Corinthians 13:12, where Paul famously evokes the figure of seeing "through a glass, darkly" (highlighting the importance of temporal distance in viewing any object more clearly).

Yet, where Paul understands this clarifying temporality in a very linear, mono-directional fashion—now "through a glass, darkly"; then "face to face"—I take this temporal distancing to work in both directions simultaneously. Thus, I do not simply examine the ways in which two of Cervantes's exemplary novels inform our reading of Chuck Palahniuk's *Fight Club*, or the ways in which one of Lope de Vega's history plays affects our reading of one of John Ford's westerns; I also explore the ways in which contemporary cyberpunk literature necessarily colors our view of the Spanish picaresque, and the ways in which the Hollywood blockbuster affects the way we look at the Spanish *comedia*.

I employ the conceit of mirroring and reflection for two interrelated reasons. In the largest sense, this book demonstrates that the imperial culture of baroque Spain not only marks the boundary between what Foucault calls "classical" and "modern" epistemology but also reflects the culture of our own globalized postmodern era (xxii). In this regard, Spain and the United States can be said to represent "bookends" of Western colonial expansion, because the European invasion of the New World initiated by the Iberian conquistadores in the early sixteenth century came to its fruition some four hundred years later when scores of U.S. pioneers finally succeeded in stretching their nation from the Atlantic to the Pacific and beyond. These two societies have produced imaginative texts that mirror each other—as do bookends—in significant ways. Thus, what I offer in this book is my affirmative response to Gustavo Pérez Firmat's well-known question, "Do the Americas have a common literature?" by insisting that the whole concept of the term "Americas" must include more than just a geographical/hemispheric definition. The commonalities of the "Americas" cannot be fully comprehended without taking into account Spain's cultural impact on a world that changed radically and forever in the wake of history's first truly global empire.

At the same time, and within this wider juxtaposition, I also examine the function of mirrors and their reflective qualities as one of the central preoccupations common to both eras. Again, one need only think of the interplay of mirror imagery in *Las Meninas* or in Peter Greenaway's *Prospero's Books* (not to mention the role of mirrors in Lacanian psychoanalytic theory) to appreciate the pivotal status of specularity within the wider projects of the baroque and postmodern worlds. Indeed, as Angela Ndalianis argues in her own cross-cultural and cross-epochal study, "the seventeenth century and our own era are epochs that reflect wide-scale baroque sensibilities that, while being the product of specific socio-historical and temporal conditions, reflect similar patterns and concerns." Hence, most of the texts I examine in this book invoke some kind of mirror imagery, whether it be Cervantes's creation of the Knight of the Mirrors as a nemesis to Don Quixote or the Wachowski Brothers' frequent references to *Alice Through the Looking Glass* in their *Matrix* trilogy. My project is to tease out how these baroque and postmodern mirrors inter-reflect and to examine the function of specularity itself (as a primary theme or leitmotiv) within these texts.

I have written this book with two target audiences in mind. Because most of the "primary" works I examine consist of mass media texts produced in the United States and Great Britain during the latter part of the twentieth century, this book is directed to readers interested in contemporary popular culture. I seek to remind these readers that many of the more audacious literary and cinematic developments of the past several decades are not quite as novel as they may seem. I deliberately examine the ways in which these primary texts do not so much break new ground as simply rediscover terrain already explored by baroque writers like Cervantes, Lope de Vega, Francisco de Quevedo, and Sor Juana Inés de la Cruz. In this, I implicitly respond to the question—frequently posed by students and university administrators alike—Why should anyone bother to read *Don Quixote* (or *Celestina* or *Lazarillo de Tormes*) in this, the age of "media literacy"? Along the way, I hope to demonstrate with my methodology (and here the medium largely is the message) that popular culture can and should be examined from a variety of critical perspectives, not just those associated with the Birmingham Centre for Contemporary Cultural Studies.

A great number of scholarly works on popular culture all too often seem to view their objects of study as little more than points of departure for wider sociological and political arguments related to class struggle, postcolonialism, hegemony, and other such crucial issues. I read my primary texts, however, first and foremost as literary texts that may or may not provide documentary evidence of some larger social or political phenomenon. In exploring the intellectual, aesthetic, and philosophical intertextualities that exist between various works of contemporary popular culture and those of the "high culture" of the baroque, I expand the definition of cultural studies to include approaches besides those specifically related to Marxist literary theory. (And it is important to remember that many of the now-canonical "high-cultural" texts of the baroque were considered "popular" in their own age.)

At the same time, because many of the "secondary" works against which these "primary" texts are reflected have become the core of the Spanish literary canon, I have also written this book for readers interested in what has traditionally been called Spanish Golden Age literature. For this second target audience, I wish to help open up what has been a rather "self-enclosed" field of study by making critical connections that range far beyond the traditionally accepted parameters of Golden Age scholarship. Thus, in contrast to more traditional academic examinations that look backward (to classical antiquity, for instance) from the vantage point of the sixteenth and seventeenth centuries to trace the development of the Spanish baroque itself, this book looks forward from this baroque vantage point to trace the impact of these Spanish texts on the culture of the twentieth and twenty-first centuries. (The establishment of this "foundational" perspective is especially important given the increasing prominence of Latin American and U.S. Latino culture within the Anglo-American academy and contemporary global culture in general.) This book also proposes—again, through its very methodology—something of a novel approach to Golden Age literary study. While it is certainly true that many pioneering Hispanists have already reinvigorated Golden Age scholarship during the past two or three decades by bringing into the discussion ideas developed by such contemporary thinkers as Julia Kristeva, Jacques Lacan, Judith Butler, Jean Baudrillard, Homi Bhabha, and Stuart Hall (to name just a few), the central problem, to my mind, is that this importation of other theorists represents something of a losing game of "catch up" for Hispanism because it assumes that early modern Hispanic literature can be made relevant only by reading it through critical lenses established by scholars working in other fields. I am far less interested, however, in what French poststructuralist theory has to say about Quevedo's *Swindler* than what the thinkers of the Spanish baroque can tell us about Silicon Valley's latest best-selling video game (to name just one example among many). Because more people worldwide have probably seen John Lasseter's *Toy Story* than have actually read *Don Quixote* in its entirety (even in Spain and Latin America), this book offers a distinctive method for reading early modern Hispanic literature and contemporary popular culture that flows directly out of the Spanish and Latin American tradition itself.

Accordingly, a few caveats regarding my methodology are in order. First, I will freely admit that my choice of popular texts here is somewhat arbitrary; which is to say, I fully recognize that the kind of cross-cultural, cross-epochal analysis I undertake in this book can (and does) work equally well—as the scholarship of such varied critics as John Beusterien, Antonio Carreño Rodríguez, William Childers, Will McMorran, Barbara Simerka, Robert Stam, and Christopher Weimer clearly demonstrates—for any number of other texts and using any number of different approaches. My preference for this particular group of autobiographies, novels, songs, and films reflects my own idiosyncratic reading, listening, and viewing habits. At the same time, however, these texts do not stand in complete isolation from each other. As the reader will quickly discover, they are tied together not just by the various baroque elements I tease out of them but also by a cluster of contemporary issues that reflect back on those baroque components in significant ways. Second, because this book assumes a twofold readership—one Anglophone and one *hispanohablante*—I cannot presuppose that either group will be familiar with texts that might be considered "basic" by the other group of readers. For this reason, I frequently provide structural discussion and detailed plot summaries of the various texts involved to ensure that all readers are able to approach my analysis on a reasonably equal footing. I apologize to those readers who do not require such lengthy discussions of these details. Moreover, since I cannot automatically assume that those readers who are interested in contemporary popular culture will also be fluent in Spanish, I cite all texts in English translation. The original Spanish citations can be found in the endnotes that accompany each chapter.[1]

Chapter 1, entitled "Lope de Vega, John Ford, and the Beleaguered Hegemony of Empire," focuses on Lope de Vega's seventeenth-century play *The Famous Asturian Damsels* and John Ford's twentieth-century film *Stagecoach* and explores the representation of "national history" in the popular theater of Hapsburg Spain and the twentieth-century United States. Tracing the ways in which the success of the *Reconquista* and Manifest Destiny depend on the creation of an archetypal "national hero" (in the guise of the Caballero and the Cowboy) and of a subhuman "national enemy" (in the guise of the "Treacherous Moor" and "Wild Indian"), this chapter examines how each nation uses its popular theater to justify its imperialism while at the same time assuaging an underlying sense of national guilt associated with territorial domination and geopolitical hegemony.

Chapter 2, entitled "Johnny Rotten, Marilyn Manson, and the Limits of Picaresque Performance," closely examines John Lydon's *Rotten: No Irish, No Blacks, No Dogs* and Marilyn Manson's *Long Hard Road Out of Hell* and argues that "rock autobiography" is a quintessentially picaresque genre. Tracing the influence of the Spanish picaresque on Western narrative from its inception with the anonymous publication of *Lazarillo de Tormes* up through Daniel Defoe's *Moll Flanders*, Charles Dickens's *Oliver Twist*, and Anthony Burgess's *A Clockwork Orange*—with a corresponding examination of the picaresque aesthetic inherent in American and British popular music of the twentieth century from the blues to punk rock to hip hop—this chapter analyzes the ways in which these two interrelated picaresque strands flow together in the intertwining musical and literary production of two of rock music's most infamous "*pícaros.*"

Chapter 3, entitled "Chuck Palahniuk, Narrative Schizophrenia, and the Cervantine Picaresque," continues my examination of the postmodern picaresque—specifically, the duality inherent in all picaresque narrative—by focusing on Cervantes's exemplary novels "Rinconete and Cortadillo" and "The Dogs' Colloquy" and Chuck Palahniuk's novel *Fight Club* (which subsequently became a David Fincher film). Through a close reading of *Fight Club*—in which an autobiographical (and ultimately schizophrenic) narrator recounts the chance intersection of his life with that of an urban terrorist, only to realize in a moment of anagnorisis that both "biographies" are his alone—this chapter explores the ways in which this postmodern text functions as a very Cervantine critique of postmodernity by reinscribing Cervantes's split protagonist—who quite literally carries on a violent "dialogue" with himself—into a set of texts whose ultimate aim is to reintegrate a single discursive subject.

Chapter 4, entitled "John Lasseter's *Toy Story* as Postmodern *Don Quixote*," examines the ways in which *Toy Story* and its sequel, *Toy Story 2*, function as postmodern recapitulations of *Don Quixote*, principally through Lasseter's transformation of Don Quixote and Sancho Panza into Buzz Lightyear and Woody. Exploring the baroque elements *Toy Story* incorporates into its computer-generated world, this chapter culminates with an examination of *Toy Story*'s distillation of Don Quixote's encounter with his own reflection (in the guise of the Knight of the Mirrors): Buzz confronts his "mirror image" as it is multiplied countless times over on a television screen and in doing so loses his identity as an autonomous subject, becoming instead little more than a "sign" whose meaning depends on the "reader" who interprets him. Yet, while Don Quixote dies on the final pages of the novel, thus acquiring a supreme transcendence, the open-ended epilogue of *Toy Story* suggests that Buzz will simply become an "old toy" who will be supplanted little by little as his young owner slowly grows to adulthood. *Toy Story 2* follows up on this idea by exploring the choice Woody must make between "immortality" inside a Japanese toy museum and an inevitable—though far from immediate—"death" inside Andy's bedroom.

Chapter 5, entitled "Salman Rushdie, Author of the Captive's Tale," explores the Cervantine and Borgesian intersection of madness, captivity, and narrativity in Salman Rushdie's *Moor's Last Sigh*. Beginning with a discussion of the Ayatollah Khomeini's *fatwa* against Rushdie following the publication of *The Satanic Verses* (which led to his virtual "house arrest" at the hands of the Iranian government), this chapter explores the ways in which Rushdie's plight mirrors that of Cervantes as a captive in Algeria from 1575 to 1580. This chapter then traces the various ways Rushdie's novel can be read as a version of that segment of *Don Quixote* known as "The Captive's Tale," in which Cervantes revisits his own captivity through a diffused autobiographical tale told by his fictional alter ego, Ruy Pérez de Viedma. Moreover, by noting Rushdie's oblique allusions to Jorge Luis Borges's stories "Pierre Menard, Author of Don Quixote" and "The Garden of Forking Paths," this chapter argues that Rushdie's entire novel can be read as a version of Pierre Menard's abbreviated *Don Quixote*, whose center is a debate over arms and letters.

Chapter 6, entitled "Terry Gilliam's Apocryphal *Brazil*; or, Blame It on Dulcinea," continues my examination of the enduring impact of Cervantes's work on contemporary culture by exploring the relationship between Sam Lowry and Jill Layton as a reflection of the relationship between Don Quixote and Dulcinea del Toboso. Horrified to discover that Jill has been accused of being a terrorist by the Ministry of Information, where he works, Sam spends a great deal of energy trying to "disenchant" her from this serious charge. His ultimate solution to the problem is to "kill" Jill by declaring her "dead" within the government's database of vital records. The problem with this solution, however, is that it comes as part of Gilliam's well-known false ending of the film, and we are left to ponder the very real possibility that Jill has actually been killed (perhaps even "twice"). Teasing out the various "apocryphal" readings suggested by Gilliam's false ending, this chapter argues that *Brazil*'s narrative structure raises some very significant questions, the most crucial of which is, What if Alonso Quixano somehow managed to make Aldonza Lorenzo an unwitting accomplice to his lunatic assault on the Hapsburg empire and she wound up getting blamed for it all?

Chapter 7, entitled "*The Matrix*: Reflected," turns to an examination of perhaps the most baroque cultural text included in this book through an exploration of the function of Thomas Anderson/Neo as a figure of Alonso Quixano/Don Quixote in the Wachowski Brothers' trilogy. Arguing that the *Matrix*'s "Agents" serve as "inquisitors" whose function is the imposition of a single view of reality, this chapter culminates with an examination of the final encounter between Neo and Agent Smith. Turning Cervantes's battle between Don Quixote and the Knight of the Mirrors on its head, Neo vanquishes his reflective nemesis by allowing Smith to turn him into an exact replica of his chief inquisitor. However, because the film posits Neo as a "mathematical anomaly, the remainder of an unbalanced equation," this final baroque mirroring of Neo and Smith initiates a systemwide crash through which the *Matrix*'s virtual reality essentially "reboots" itself. In this, Neo proves not only that he is the "I" (as opposed to the messianic—and anagrammatical—"One" promised from the beginning of the trilogy), but also that his final status as a numerical cipher within a mathematically encoded text mirrors that of Don Quixote, whom Foucault has famously called "a long, thin graphism, a letter that has just escaped from the open pages of a book."

Chapter 1

Lope de Vega, John Ford, and the Beleaguered Hegemony of Empire

The Spain of the Hapsburg "Siglo de Oro" (literally, Century of Gold) and the United States of what has widely been called the "American Century" share remarkably coincidental historical trajectories. Both nations achieved unprecedented geopolitical prominence during their respective "golden ages," and both nations used this newfound status during the Counter-Reformation and the Cold War, respectively, to insinuate themselves into far-flung global ideological conflicts. Both nations were the product of the union of previously disparate political entities, and both had just recently completed a protracted geographical expansion—fueled in part by similar ideological notions of *Reconquista* and Manifest Destiny—through which the ethnically defined nation-state had subsumed and displaced two or more religious and racial groups.[1] Finally, the shift from the preceding epoch into the triumphant era was a surprisingly abrupt event in both countries. As J. H. Elliott remarks, the commencement of the Spanish Siglo de Oro virtually began on January 6, 1492, just nine months before Columbus's arrival in the Americas, when "Ferdinand and Isabella made their victorious entry into the city of Granada, wrested after nearly eight centuries from the grasp of the Moors" (45).[2] In the United States the beginning of the new American Century was formally marked on July 12, 1893, when Frederick Jackson Turner famously declared at a meeting of the American Historical Association that "the frontier has gone, and with its going has closed the first period of American history" (60).

Although the trajectories of these separate histories may be coincidental, at least one of the ways in which the dominating societies of these nation-states dealt with their novel superiority is not. One developed in the *comedia histórica* and the other in the Hollywood western, respectively, an immensely popular form of visual entertainment through which the so-called *cristianos viejos* (Old Christians) of the Iberian Peninsula (as opposed to the apologetic Moriscos and *conversos*, not to mention the recalcitrant Muslims and Jews, who were quickly expelled) and the so-called

WASPs of the United States (as opposed to the marginalized "Irish," "Italians," and "Mexicans," not to mention the still disenfranchised "Negroes" and "Indians") could actively participate in a grandiose morality play of national scale—what Sheldon Hall calls "history as spectacle" (259)—and could thus bear witness (seemingly first-hand) to their own greatness.[3]

These grand theatrical endeavors, along with the dramatic texts they engendered, depended to a great extent on the construction of a national myth of origin and identity that attempted to explain the success of the dominating culture in three convergent ways. First, these texts demonize the subjugated ethnic groups themselves—embodied in the "morally inferior" stereotype of the Treacherous Moor and Wild Indian—to rationalize the de facto territorial expansion all but complete at the time of their composition. The cultural demonization inscribed within these texts seeks to exclude the "national enemy" from full consideration as equal combatants in the geopolitical struggle by converting immediate territorial competitors into absolute—racially defined—Others who supposedly stand in moral opposition to everything the dominating culture holds dear. Second, these texts construct a national hero—embodied in the "morally superior" archetype of the Caballero and the Cowboy—to explain the inevitability of a historical trajectory that coalesced a previously "disunited" people and then catapulted them to world prominence. It is far from coincidental, for instance, that in some sectors of U.S. society John Wayne has become a kind of patron saint, similar in many ways to Spain's medieval Santiago Matamorros (Saint James the Moor Killer). And third, these texts deliberately invert the actual social hierarchies that existed in the wake of the territorial expansion in order to exonerate the triumphant ethnic groups by conferring upon them the a posteriori status of "beleaguered" victim fighting a "defensive" struggle against a militarily "superior" enemy. In essence, what these theatrical and filmic texts ultimately seek to accomplish is the self-justification of the ideology of *Reconquista* and Manifest Destiny to partially assuage the sense of national guilt associated with territorial domination and geopolitical hegemony.

While a great number of works are typical of this discursive strategy, Lope de Vega's *Famous Asturian Damsels* (written 1610–12; published 1623) and John Ford's *Stagecoach* (1939) are particularly illustrative. Lope's *comedia*, which is based on a well-known legend and set in the first century after the Islamic invasion, depicts a besieged Christian Spain that can avoid cultural dissolution only by remitting to the invading Muslims a hundred sacrificial damsels.[4] Tracing the way this dilemma plays itself out in the lives of its three main characters, Nuño Osorio, Doña Sancha, and her father, Don García, Lope's play shows the Asturians standing up for themselves and violently refusing to turn over its famous damsels to the Muslim horde. Ford's film, which is based on a short story entitled "Stage to Lordsburg" (written by Ernest Haycox and originally published in *Col-*

lier's magazine in April 1937), depicts the perilous voyage of a nearly defenseless group of late nineteenth-century American travelers as they make their way from Tonto, Arizona, to Lordsburg, New Mexico, under the constant threat of ambush by Geronimo's Apaches. Like *The Famous Asturian Damsels*, *Stagecoach* focuses on a very delimited set of characters—principally the Ringo Kid (John Wayne) and Miss Dallas (Claire Trevor)—who are proxies for a wider society that resolves its cultural conflict with the Apaches by taking a violent stand.

The Treacherous Moor emerges as a stock character in Western European literature beginning with such epic works as the *Song of Roland* and reappears in texts as divergent as Dante's *Inferno* and Walt Disney's *Aladdin*. Within the Spanish tradition, especially texts composed between 1100 and 1650, Treacherous Moors of various stripes can be found in the *Poem of the Cid*, *¡Ay, Jerusalem!*, Juan Manuel's *Count Lucanor*, Pedro del Corral's *Saracen Chronicle*, Miguel de Luna's *True History of King Don Rodrigo*, and Miguel de Cervantes's *Don Quixote* (to name just a few). In many instances, this Treacherous Moor is represented as the embodiment of absolute evil, symbolizing a level of villainy reserved in our time for mass murderers like Hitler, Stalin, and Pol Pot.[5] As Rafael Ocasio notes, a text like King Alfonso X's *Cantigas de Santa María* deliberately blurs the distinction between its Muslim characters and the devil himself (186–87). Likewise, Lope de Vega's *Last Visigoth* shows the Muslim commander Tarife ordering the execution of Abembúcar and Zara simply because the two have converted to Christianity and then shows him basking in the "astonishing spectacle" of their decapitated bodies (3:659; my translation).[6] The Treacherous Moor, if not the Antichrist, remains at the very least the epitome of anti-Christian. Indeed, as Edward Said argues, Western culture has largely defined itself since the Middle Ages against this contrived stereotype: "the European representation of the Muslim, Ottoman, or Arab was always a way of controlling the redoubtable Orient" (60).

As "Western" civilization pushed even farther west into the Americas it imposed this orientalist vision, ironically, on cultures geographically more "occidental" than itself. This is why a *Reconquista* play like *The Famous Asturian Damsels* (as opposed to more "American" plays like Lope's *Arauco Tamed* or *The New World Discovered by Christopher Columbus*) is such a crucial text for understanding the relationship between the Spanish conquest of the Americas and foundational myths of the United States. For, what ties Spain's imperial project in the New World to that of England is not the fact that both enterprises were staged in the Americas but that the fundamental concept of divine providence—what Manuel Alcalá calls a "messianic spirit" (xvi)—that undergirds these endeavors was first articulated during the eight-hundred year campaign by the Iberian Christians to expel the Muslim invaders in their midst.

For the Spanish conquistadores, the *Reconquista* was an omnipresent feature of their experience in the New World from start to finish. Patricia Seed notes, for instance, that the chief "protocol for conquest" in the New World—the *Requirimiento*—was itself inspired by the bureaucratic mechanisms that previously had been drawn up to subdue and integrate tribute-paying Muslim and Jewish communities (*aljamas*) on the Iberian Peninsula: "The status of Indians who surrendered to the Spanish crown was virtually identical to *aljama* status. Indians not enslaved by Christians were guaranteed life, liberty, and, in a modified sense, property" (85). Furthermore, it bears repeating, the Spanish conquistadores superimposed the very rhetoric of the *Reconquista* onto the reality of their own invasion of cities like Tenochtitlán by referring to the Aztec temples as "mosques" (Cortés, *Cartas*, 21) and to their own soldiers as heroic "Rolands" (Díaz del Castillo, 267).[7] In his *Short Account of the Destruction of the Indies*, Bartolomé de las Casas notes, for instance, that when Hernán Cortés and his men conquered Mexico they shouted "Santiago!" (the battle cry of the *Reconquista*) as they descended upon the Aztecs (110). In this regard, the Treacherous Moor and Wild Indian—the latter of which, in an ironic twist, leads back to a mistaken encounter with Asia—can be seen as two sides of the same orientalist coin. A pageant staged in Cuzco to commemorate the 1570 arrival of the viceroy recreated a mock battle between Christian knights and Moors, "casting the natives of the New World as the Islamic bogeymen of the Old" (Fuchs, 1). Likewise, a similar cultural conflation took place in North America when writers like José de Acosta "compared the nomadic life of the Central Plains Indians" with that of the Arabs, or when explorers like Francisco Vásquez de Coronado "repeatedly allied the Indian with the Turk" (Matar, 98).

The Wild Indian, for his part, emerges as a stock character in Western literature (broadly conceived to include such texts as chronicles, diaries, and histories) from the very first arrival of Europeans on New World soil and appears in numerous Spanish texts ranging temporally and geographically from Hernán Cortés's *Letters from Mexico* (1519–26) and Álvar Núñez Cabeza de Vaca's *Castaways* (1541) to Domingo Faustino Sarmiento's *Facundo: Civilization and Barbarism* (1845) and José Hernández's *Martín Fierro* (1872). In the Anglo-American context, the Wild Indian appears in such nineteenth-century texts as James Kirke Paulding's *Dutchman's Fireside* (1831) and Robert Montgomery Bird's *Nick of the Woods* (1837). In many instances, as with Cortés's idolatrous Aztec priest who cuts out the still-beating hearts of children (*Cartas*, 22; *Letters*, 35) or Bird's Wenonga who shouts, "I have fought the Long-knives, and drunk their blood" (320), the indigenous people of the Americas are broadly rendered as murderous as the "paynim" (pagan) Saracens of Zaragoza in the medieval *Song of Roland* (Sayers, 51).[8] They are represented—and, indeed, understood by their European authors (especially North Americans of a puritanical bent)—as diabolical figures whose native religions amount to little more than witchcraft (McDermott, 539–40; Simmons, 56).[9] The Wild Indian's primary defect—one he shares with the Treacherous Moor—seems to be his total lack of Christianity.

Yet, whereas the Treacherous Moor ultimately represents the heretical Other, the Wild Indian is seen from the outset not just as anti-Christian but "anti-human" as well. For the North American WASPs, the question of the aboriginal inhabitants of the New World was always bound up with the notion that Native Americans occupied a kind of Darwinian subhuman status. This is true even before Darwin elaborated his theory of evolution in the mid-nineteenth century. The basic "humanity" of the indigenous populations was a point of theological debate from the time when Columbus first landed on Hispaniola, when Europeans unexpectedly encountered people who did not easily fit into a Christian cosmology that insisted that all the earth's "human" inhabitants were descended from Noah's three sons and were representative of the three known continents: Europe, Asia, and Africa. Still, despite Bartolomé de las Casas's eloquent sixteenth-century defense of Amerindians, Anglo-American culture remained deeply suspicious of the basic "humanity" of the Wild Indian well into the twentieth century, and this suspicion profoundly informs many Hollywood westerns. Ford's *Searchers* (1956), to name just one prominent twentieth-century example, still portrays its Native Americans as little more than wild beasts. Says its central protagonist, Ethan Edwards (John Wayne): "A human rides a horse until it dies and then goes on afoot. A Comanch comes along, gets that horse up and rides him twenty more miles [...] then eats him."

This dietary criticism is a recurring theme of the western. As Jon Tuska notes, D. W. Griffith's *Battle at Elderbush Gulch* (1913) features an unspecified tribe of Indians who "have a ridiculous ceremony in which they eat their dogs and become delirious" (239). Likewise (although this is clearly meant to be taken ironically), *Hombre* presents us with a scene in which the passengers of a stagecoach debate the putative savagery of the natives by discussing their supposed habit of eating dogs. This preoccupation with the eating of dog meat also functions on a much deeper discursive level than merely presenting Anglo-American audiences with what amounts to a culturally unsavory menu. For, if the oft-repeated epithet "savage dog" carries any rhetorical force, having been used frequently in the negative description of both Moors and Indians, then these portrayals of Indians eating dog meat amount to a rhetorical accusation of cannibalism that dehumanizes these figures. And this accusation folds back on itself, since the word "cannibal" has its etymological origins in Columbus's first encounter with the Amerindian Other, the Caribs: "I also understand that, a long distance from here, there are men with one eye and others with dogs' snouts who eat men. On taking a man they behead him and drink his blood and cut off his genitals"; "The Indians aboard call this Bohío and say it is very large and has people there with one eye in the forehead, as well as others they call cannibals, of whom they show great fear" (Columbus, *Log*, 102, 113–15).[10] As Frank Lestringant notes in his excellent book on Western representations of New World cannibalism, the early modern notion of the Amerindian "cannibal" derives from the ancient myth of the dog-headed "Cynocephalus" and is ironically inflected through a false etymology that links the Arawak word "cariba" to the Latin "canis" (15–22).[11]

None of this is to say, however, that the Iberian Moor and the American Indian are always—and solely—refracted through the lenses of barbarism, savagery, and heresy. Both figures are often represented within what Barbara Simerka characterizes as a humanizing attempt to "stage the Other" (115) and what Renato Rosaldo calls an "imperialist nostalgia" (68) within which a maudlin backward glance converts the Treacherous Moor and Wild Indian into the "Exotic Morisco" and "Noble Savage" of the more sentimental literary genres. In Spain this post hoc romanticization took shape not only in the *comedia* but also in the *romances fronterizos* ("frontier ballads") and the Morisco novel where a lush orientalism blazes forth in a series of texts that depict the Moors as noble inheritors of a beautiful and exotic culture who fight valiantly to maintain this heritage against insurmountable odds. Novels such as *Ozmín and Daraja* or the well-known ballad "Abenámar" come to mind. But no text depicts this imperial nostalgia better than the ballad traditionally called "¡Ay de mi Alhama!"—famously translated by Lord Byron and which ultimately inspired the title of Salman Rushdie's 1995 novel *The Moor's Last Sigh*—in which the last Muslim king of Granada receives the news of the fall of the city Alhama (an echo that portends the coming fall of the Alhambra itself) with heavy sigh: "Woe is me, Alhama!" (Byron, 530). In the United States this backward glance—informed as it is by a profoundly Rousseauian romanticism—is conspicuously on display in such works as James Fenimore Cooper's *Last of the Mohicans* (1826), Buffalo Bill's Wild West Show, and such films as *Fort Apache* (1948), *Cheyenne Autumn* (1964), *The Mission* (1986), and *Dances with Wolves* (1990), where Native Americans are represented as sympathetic figures whose story is more tragic than heroic. Whether in *comedias* like Lope's *Bell of Aragón* (1622)—in which the defeated Muslim king of Zaragoza, echoing the "¡Ay de mi Alhama!" ballad, bids farewell to his beloved city with a heavy sigh (3:855–56)—or in films like John Farrow's *Hondo* (1953)—in which Hondo Lane (John Wayne) is seen lamenting the end of the Apaches' "good way of life"—this sentimentality becomes rhetorically indispensable once the territorial aims of the *Reconquista* and Manifest Destiny are complete. In both instances, the now-defunct national enemy cannot appear to be either too "unworthy" to have merited attention or too "inferior" to have ever stood a chance in the conflict, because otherwise the entire imperial enterprise will seem to lack legitimacy. In effect, as Israel Burshatin incisively comments, the total success of the *Reconquista* requires more than just military victory: "Moorish otherness exists as that which is to be (re)possessed in a Castilian universe of discourse" (570). Or, as Tuska rightly notes, by their very act of dying out the Indians give Anglo-American culture "their wholehearted blessing and wish it well in a future which cannot include them" (240).

Although critics have long viewed Lope de Vega and John Ford as cultural chauvinists whose work did much to advance the imperialism of their respective nations, their portrayals of the Treacherous Moor and Wild Indian in *The Famous Asturian Damsels* and *Stagecoach* are much more nuanced than one might expect.[12] Neither text contains explicit scenes of subhuman depravity (although *Stagecoach* admittedly does present the gruesome aftermath of this kind of depravity in the figure of a murdered woman lying among the smoldering remains of a ferry station); nor do they include any nostalgic images of the noble savage (there are no Ozmíns or Abenámars in *The Famous Asturian Damsels*; no Leatherstockings or Hiawathas in *Stagecoach*, although Yakima [Elvira Ríos] comes extremely close). Instead, the real "othering" that occurs in these texts functions at the level of language, a fact that takes us back to the semantic foundations of the word "barbarian," which, as the *Oxford English Dictionary* (2nd ed., s.v. "barbarous") reminds us, has its origins in notions of "stammering." Indeed, many early westerns establish the presumed "barbarity" of the Amerindians by portraying them as linguistically incompetent; that is, as people who can produce only such limited communication as "How" and "No can do." This barely intelligible communication is meant to be taken as a sign of a deeper alienation from the "civilized" English speakers who interact with them (not to mention the English listeners who "eavesdrop" on this conversation from the darkness of the movie house). And this lack of linguistic sophistication inexorably leads—again, as the *Oxford English Dictionary* notes—from an initial sense of "foreignness" to an ultimate condemnation of "inhumanity." Following this logic, *Stagecoach* literalizes the "barbarous" ethnicity of its Apaches by virtually representing them as a people entirely without language. For, although Ford's rampaging Wild Indians most certainly "vocalize" their homicidal intentions though a kind of undifferentiated war cry, none has any discernible lines in the film. In essence, the profound semiotic silence that surrounds Ford's Wild Indians provides a clear and pointedly negative response to Gayatri Chakravorty Spivak's famous question, "Can the subaltern speak?" (271). The only "signs" associated with Ford's Apaches are decidedly nonverbal: smoke signals seen in the distance, the leitmotiv of a drumbeat within the film's soundtrack, and the mute gesture of one warrior who points to the stagecoach as it crosses Monument Valley. In fact, it is this very absence of "signs" that not only "barbarizes" these Wild Indians but "bestializes" them as well. Says Gatewood (Berton Churchill) in response to an expression of relief voiced by Peacock (Donald Meek) that there has been "no sign" of the Apaches: "You don't see any signs of them. They strike like rattlesnakes" (01:05:10).[13] For Ford, the Wild Indians of *Stagecoach* are barely indistinguishable from the film's other desert mammals within a great chain of being atop which the white settlers occupy a position just below that of angels.

Significantly, *The Famous Asturian Damsels* employs a related, though clearly distinct, linguistic strategy in its differentiation of Christian and Muslim characters. To be sure, "barbarity" is linguistically marked in Lope's text. But, unlike the Pidgin English of many Hollywood Indians, it is the Spanish of Lope's Christians that stands out. In his dedication of the play to Don Juan de Castro y Castilla, Lope makes the following preliminary declaration:

> From Your Worship's ancient house and nobility I proposed this story to the Muses in the form of a *comedia* [...] and thus, among other things, I have sought to offer Your Worship this history, which I have written (not without significant study) in the *ancient tongue* in order to lend more weight and veracity to its enacted events through an imitation of Your native dialect. (1:336; my translation and emphasis)[14]

Despite Lope's claimed attempts at verisimilitude, however, only the Asturians speak this "ancient tongue."[15] The Moors of the play speak in a clear, elegant, seventeenth-century Spanish; Lope does not place in their mouths what Thomas E. Case calls the "Arabized pronunciation and broken Spanish syntax" of the traditional "Morisco clown" ("Lope," 204). Instead, this unmarked Spanish is meant perhaps to indicate that the Moors are actually speaking Arabic ("El morisco gracioso," 788), in much the same way the fluent English-speaking Indians of *Broken Arrow*—whose first-person narrator insists that the story happened exactly as portrayed, except that "the Indians will speak English" (presumably to facilitate the interpretive work of Anglo-American audiences but also to allow the Native Americans to communicate intelligently and thus on par with their real English-speaking counterparts)—are meant to be understood as speaking their own native tongues. Case is right, but what is important about this distinction between the archaic dialect of Lope's Asturians and the presumably classical (albeit translated) "Arabic" of his Moors is that the linguistic division underscores the Asturians' status as "*Old* Christians," which—at a time when *pureza de sangre* (blood purity) is of paramount concern—underlines the ethnic superiority not just of the "ancient" House of Don Juan de Castro y Castilla but also of the seventeenth-century Spaniards who stood in the *corral* listening to the ethnically charged interplay between dialects.[16]

Despite these similarities, however, there are significant differences between *The Famous Asturian Damsels* and *Stagecoach* that should be acknowledged. The most important distinction between the two texts relates to the inherent differences between the notions of *Reconquista* and Manifest Destiny from which they emerge. For Christian Spain during the Middle Ages, the *Reconquista* was just that: a "re-conquest," the *recovery* of territory lost to an invading culture that (no matter how "infidel" it might have been considered by the retreating Visigoths) was clearly a "civilization," often more advanced and refined than the Christian one that sought to re-displace it. In contrast, for the United States of the eighteenth and nineteenth centuries, the westward expansion was a "conquest" of supposedly "virgin" territory; which is to say, European settlers in North America inherited—or at least, shared—the Spanish assumption that they were actually "taming" a "wild" geography previously unclaimed by any (recognizable) "civilization." (Compare this to Viviana Díaz Balsera's astute observation that Lope's *Arauco Tamed*, a text that also deals with the Americas, "positions the colonizer as the tamer of wild, terrifying natives" [30]). In essence, what Charles Mann calls "Holmberg's Mistake"—in honor of Allan Holmberg, whose *Nomads of the Longbow* codified for an entire generation of anthropologists the notion that "the indigenous peoples of the Americas floated changelessly through the millennia until 1492" (9)—turns out to be a recurring motif in European attitudes toward Amerindians. The Indians of popular myth and legend cannot be considered anything but "savage" without compromising the entire ideology of Manifest Destiny. For, if the original inhabitants of the American landmass are indeed allowed a definable "civilization," they would have had a legitimate claim to the disputed land that in turn would have vacated the need to "tame" this "wilderness" as part of the Anglo-American "civilizing" mission; just as recognition of the legitimacy of Amerindian religions would have vacated the need to Christianize the Indians by setting up a system of "missions" in the Americas, including the twenty-one California missions that span the distance from San Diego to San Francisco.

Thus, the notable divergence in linguistic approach between *Stagecoach* and *The Famous Asturian Damsels*—between an essentially "voiceless" enemy and one that is "super-voiced"—can be attributed perhaps to the essential differences between the American and Iberian experiences of conquest and re-conquest. *Stagecoach* depends on a view of the American West as a kind of tabula rasa waiting to be written on by European settlers who bring to the untamed wilderness everything civilization represents: agriculture, art, religion, laws, literature, and—of utmost importance—language, since all these previous elements derive from this one alone. As Anthony Pagden comments, "the struggle for political and cultural control in America was also, at a crucial level, a struggle for linguistic supremacy" (118). For, if one assumes that the indigenous languages of the Amerindian populations have already been written upon the landscape, then European culture must necessarily "erase" these traces before it can begin to write its own narrative palimpsest on the geographic tabula. But, on the one hand, unlike the Spanish conquistadores and missionaries, who had few qualms about razing Aztec temples in order to build Catholic churches on their smoldering foundations, Anglo-American immigrants have steadfastly resisted the notion that their presence in the New World constitutes a conquest of any kind. *The Famous Asturian Damsels*, on the other hand, has no reason to deny the one-time presence of an Arabic-speaking civilization on the Iberian Peninsula. For Christian Spain, the *Reconquista* was the most important military endeavor of the Middle Ages, with the fall of Granada in 1492 representing the culmination of a long national struggle. The architectural, scientific, artistic, and linguistic traces of Muslim occupation that had been written upon the Iberian Peninsula over the course of eight hundred years reminded—and continues to remind—Spanish Christians of their ultimate victory over the invading culture. To erase these traces from the "national" narrative would be to erase the glory of the *Reconquista* itself.[17]

These differences notwithstanding, *The Famous Asturian Damsels* and *Stagecoach* demonstrate the supposed perfidy of their Treacherous Moors and Wild Indians in two strangely lyrical sequences that, although written hundreds of years apart, uncannily mirror each other. Both scenes involve the abrupt suspension of the narrative to allow for the insertion of a nocturnal lament sung by characters who play virtually no role in the text other than to enter and perform these pieces. And both scenes end with acts of cattle rustling—one forestalled and one successful—apparently included solely to demonstrate the thievery of the national enemy. The first song, performed by a troupe of Lope's minstrels, takes place the night before Nuño Osorio has promised to deliver the one hundred Asturian damsels into the possession of Mauregato, after which they will presumably become sexual slaves to the Muslim infidels.[18]

> My mother gave birth to me / on a dark night, / she covered me with mourning, / I lacked fortune. / When I was born, / the hour had waned; / not even a dog was heard, / not even a cock crowed; / not even a cock crowed, / not even a dog was heard, / only my fortune, / which cursed me. (1:355; my translation)[19]

The second song, performed by Yakima (the Apache wife of the Mexican station owner, Chris [Chris-Pin Martin]), occurs when Ford's travelers have stopped for the night at the oasis of Apache Wells, a Mexican settlement where the Spanish invasion of western North America overlaps in time and space with that of the United States (Figure 1).

Figure 1: As an Apache woman married to a Mexican man and living in the now-U.S. oasis of Apache Wells, Arizona, Yakima (Elvira Ríos) embodies the linguistic, cultural, and ethnic hybridity of the American West. (*Stagecoach*, United Artists, 1939)

> As I think of you, / land where I was born, / what nostalgia my heart feels. / In my solitude / with this song / I console myself and alleviate my pain. / (*Now, boys, get going!* [whispered aside]) / The notes of this sad song / evoke memories of that love. / As I think on it / the happiness of my sad heart / is reborn. (00:45:33; my translation)[20]

To set the tone for the scenes that follow, both pieces exude a profound melancholy, a particular variety of "Spanish melancholy" that, Roger Bartra argues, connects Mexico to Spain ("Maybe the Spanish colonizers planted the seeds of melancholy in America" [70]) and that also has been seen as a partially "Arabic" disease ultimately stemming from the "deep aftertaste" of the *Reconquista* (69). Lope's imagery of darkness, of mourning, of lonely silence, and of unlucky births is undoubtedly intended to presage the impending misfortune of his star-crossed "Asturian damsels," whose unhappy fate is about to make them "famous." Ford's evocation of a faraway "homeland"—which is ironically filtered through the voice of the Apache enemy, and thus articulates perfectly Rosaldo's notion of "imperial nostalgia"—underlines the lonely plight of his travelers, characters who might also be thinking nostalgically about "home" as they spend a sleepless night contemplating their own impending doom at the hands of a murderous tribe of "savages" who have no respect for human life. Unlike Lope's song, however, Ford's ends on a "happy" note with Yakima recalling a former lover and resolving to slip away unnoticed with the Mexican *vaqueros* who steal the Americans' horses. (Of course, Lope's song could also be said to end "happily," since Laín and Tomé's defeat of the Muslim cattle thieves can be read as an omen of the Asturians' ultimate success.)

This melancholy, however, whether mitigated or not, is not the only link between the two songs. Both are originally sung in Spanish. For Lope, this linguistic fact is unremarkable. But for Ford, the sudden change of linguistic code bespeaks a deliberate discursive strategy. Yakima's Spanish serves two purposes in the film. First, it maintains the Apaches' lack of recognizable speech. In ways similar to the elegant Spanish of Lope's Moors (which is intended to be understood as Arabic), Yakima's Spanish here is perhaps meant to be read as Apache by monolingual Anglo-American audiences who simply hear it as just another incomprehensible tongue emanating from the mouth of just another dark-skinned speaker. Second, and despite its function as a stand-in for Apache, the sudden insertion of Spanish into the film also reminds audiences that the Hispanic culture of the American Southwest functions in the borderlands as a kind of bridge between Amerindian and Anglo-American societies. Mexicans who suddenly found themselves within the territory of the United States in the wake of the 1848 Treaty of Guadalupe Hidalgo (somewhat like the Moriscos before them who suddenly found themselves inside Christian Spain following the fall of Granada) were expected by the territory's new overlords to act as sociopolitical mediators in large measure because of their cultural and racial hybridity.[21] Yet, it is this hybridity—what Homi Bhabha would call their very "in-betweenness" (127)—that makes them suspect. By occupying the open space between European and Amerindian societies, they are free to shift alliances at will, as *Stagecoach* so flawlessly demonstrates when its travelers arrive at Apache Wells and are suddenly confronted by a very alien *mestizaje* (miscegenation):

> Peacock: Savages!
> Chris: That's my wife, Yakima, my squaw.
> Peacock: Yes, but she's . . . she's . . . savage!
> Chris: Sí, señor. She's a little bit savage, I think. [...]
> Gatewood: There's something funny about this. That woman's an
>   Apache.
> Chris: Sure. She's one of Geronimo's people. I think, maybe not so
>   bad to have an Apache wife, eh? Apache don't bother me, I think.
>   (00:44:20)

A "good" Mexican—like Chris, whose deliberately anglicized name suggests his relative "Americanness" and his redeeming Christianity—allies himself with the WASP travelers and thus provides for their protection. A "bad" Mexican—like Yakima, whose pointedly Indian name suggests her lack of conversion to European civilization—allies herself with horse thieves and ultimately escapes the bonds of Christian matrimony to return to the company of "savages." In either case, their usefulness is a product of their loyalty—or lack thereof—to the Cowboys who defend "civilization" on the frontier, just as the best Moriscos of the Spanish *comedia* are those who willingly convert to Christianity and then help to further the religious and territorial aims of the Caballeros in the *Reconquista*.

Standing opposite the Treacherous Moor and Wild Indian, then, are the Caballero and the Cowboy, both of whom vaunt notable literary pedigrees.[22] José Antonio Maravall argues that such a focus on the individual, rather than the collective, reflects the fact that the whole chivalric system of warfare requires a "private" and "personal" enemy (*Utopía*, 65). For early modern Spain, this genealogical line of hero/warriors begins with Rodrigo Díaz de Vivar, a character peerless among Reconquest caballeros (despite the historical precedence and prominence of other, earlier figures), and one who remains the clear prototype of Iberian feudal honor.[23] María Eugenia Lacarra notes that Rodrigo's cultural elevation to this heroic status began very early on with his appearance in such Latin texts as the eleventh-century *Carmen Campidoctoris* and the twelfth-century *Historia Roderici* (15–16). Nevertheless, the Cid really develops his archetypal personality in the popular, vernacular realm. In addition to the *Poem of the Cid* (unavailable to early modern writers because the only surviving manuscript remained buried in the Archivo del Concejo de Vivar until the sixteenth century, and no published version of the poem appeared until the late eighteenth century), Rodrigo appears in numerous *romances* and several of the most prominent *comedias* of the Golden Age, where he is portrayed time and again as a figure possessing such a keen sense of ethics that he would rather affront his natural sovereign than ignore possible injustice, accepting whatever consequences arise from his ethical stance with honorable resignation. A ballad like "The Oath of Santa Gadea," for instance, portrays a Rodrigo who forces King Alfonso to swear that he had nothing to do with the untimely death of his [the king's] brother (Menéndez Pidal, 167).[24] Likewise, the ballad that inspired Lope's play *The Battlements of Toro* (1620) depicts a Cid who countermands a direct order by Alfonso to his men to kill his [again, the king's] sister, the *Infanta* (3:771). In both episodes Alfonso banishes the Cid for his temerity, and in both episodes his punishment is portrayed as a badge of honor that demonstrates the inherent superiority of this caballero hero who—as the symbol of the Spanish nation—perhaps constitutes a more genuine patron saint than Saint James.

This same cultural elevation of a historico-literary character to national symbol recurs some three hundred years later in the Anglo-American context through an analogous secular beatification of the Cowboy. This profoundly iconic figure is often portrayed in both mythic and epic terms: he is the nameless "Marlboro Man," the anonymous "Lone Ranger." Rita Parks calls this ubiquitous western hero an "American Ulysses" whose "quest for both independence and community" in the mythic wilderness is symptomatic of the American spirit (124), while Wallace Stegner, perhaps the twentieth century's most acute literary observer of the American West, argues that the Cowboy, whose "knightly sense of honor and [...] capacity to outviolence the violent" (110) typifies an American national character deeply ambivalent toward settlement and wilderness, order and anarchy (105–6). In all cases, this knightly Ulysses remains a larger-than-life figure. His ethical superiority is established in a film like *The Man from Laramie*, for instance, by being depicted in scene after scene in which he is beaten, shot, and tortured for his attempts to discover the identity of the men who have been selling rifles to the Apaches, and who are thus indirectly responsible for the death of his brother. Like the Cid, Will Lockhart (James Stewart) must respond to this injustice with honor and resignation. His heroic stoicism is the quintessence of both caballero and cowboy ethics.

Still, although the Caballero and the Cowboy—as political emblems— share a number of significant traits, they again differ from each other in significant ways. And these differences can be attributed, again, to the distinct social contexts within which they perform their symbolic function. The Caballero is quintessentially a feudal paladin who rightfully owes his fealty to the hierarchical military order in which he serves. During his lengthy campaigns into Muslim territory, for example, the Cid maintains his feudatory relationship with King Alfonso, neglecting at no time to remand to his estranged sovereign what is rightfully due (i.e., the "quinta," the fifth part of all the booty won), because he cannot place himself outside the established order and still maintain his archetypal status. Conversely, the Cowboy of American myth is much more like the semi-independent knight-errant associated with Arthurian legend and such texts as *Amadís de Gaula* or *Don Quixote*.[25] He is a solitary figure who owes his allegiance solely to God, to himself, and to the downtrodden, and who applies a rigorous, though largely self-imposed, moral code to every situation. Hence, the Lone Ranger, commanded by conscience alone, vigorously defends the poor widow against the scheming rancher because to do otherwise would be to deny the very essence of his heroism.

Montesquieu, perhaps better than any other political theorist, shrewdly predicted these differences in national archetype by arguing that the driving principle behind aristocratic government is "honor," while the pivotal rationale for democracies is "virtue" (22–26). Thus, although both the Caballero and the Cowboy exhibit virtuous as well as honorable traits, the Spanish hero, as a symbol of the Hapsburg monarchical order, moves through his environment motivated chiefly by *pundonor* (a self-motivated sense of personal dignity), demanding "preferences and distinctions" for himself and rendering them to others when due, because it is his "ambition" within the hierarchy that "gives life to that government" (Montesquieu, 27). Likewise, the western hero of the United States, as a symbol of Jacksonian democracy, must remain untainted by vice if the nation is to endure: "In a popular government when the laws have ceased to be executed, as this can come only from the corruption of the republic, the state is already lost" (Montesquieu, 22). In each instance, the strength of the nation-state can be effectively measured by testing the "honorable" or "incorruptable" actions of its prime champion, and this "test" of national character is nowhere better performed than on the *corral* stage and the silver screen, respectively, where the whole process can become part of a collective, national catharsis.

This said, however, the Caballero and the Cowboy are not entirely dissimilar, especially when viewed from a material perspective. As Lacarra notes, the primary purpose of the Cid's military campaigns is not really that of promoting the *Reconquista*—not the genuine conversion of the "infidel," nor even the actual expansion of Christian territory—but the acquisition of material goods and the upward social mobility that results from this acquisitive pursuit (37). Likewise, the "sooners" and "forty-niners" who rushed headlong into Oklahoma and California were motivated not really by "Manifest Destiny" (although they most assuredly justified themselves through this doctrine) but by a desire for the same kind of material wealth and social mobility Lacarra ascribes to Rodrigo Díaz de Vivar and his three hundred men. Since the drive for personal aggrandizement represented in both instances a zero-sum enterprise, the invaded peoples of the frontier necessarily found themselves on the losing end of the landgrab. Thus, to reinforce the importance of the honor/virtue paradigm in the national myth, as a way of rationalizing the rather naked aggression of the (re)conquest, it is not enough for the *comedia histórica* and Hollywood western to merely "represent" the paramount national hero for the benefit of those who sit in the gallery watching the morality play unfold. The subjugated Treacherous Moors and Wild Indians must be seen to confess the clear ethnic and ethical superiority of their conquerors. They must willfully confirm, as Antonio Gramsci argues, that "force and consent are simply equivalent" (*Prison Notebooks*, 271).

Hondo, for instance, shows Vittorio (Michael Pate), the chief of the Apaches, praising his Cowboy aggressor's integrity in no uncertain terms immediately after the eponymous protagonist has refused to lie on his behalf. "You have a good man here," he says to Hondo's female companion, "treasure him." Guillén de Castro's *Youthful Deeds of the Cid*, for its part, pointedly displays the defeated Muslim king praising the Cid: "You have, Sir [King Don Fernando], a vassal / equal to four kings. [...] The great Rodrigo arrived, fought, broke, killed, / and vanquished me first and foremost" (137; my translation).[26] His speech, which clearly, though inversely, echoes Caesar's famous *veni, vidi, vici*, ties a triumphant Cid to one of history's greatest conquering heroes. Yet, what is more important than the Caesar/Cid connection here, or the lofty esteem in which Vittorio holds Hondo above, is that the purveyors of these flatteries are decidedly not Old Christians or plainspoken pioneers who presumably would have a stake in painting these heroes in such glowing terms; rather, this glowing praise comes from the "national enemies" who would seemingly prefer that Rodrigo and Hondo were not quite so valiant. In both instances, this deliberate rhetorical inversion makes the flattery all the more appealing to its intended *corral* and movie house audiences by making their own dominance seem "common sense" (Stuart Hall et al., 154).

And this brings us to Nuño Osorio and Ringo Kid, the knightly heroes of *The Famous Asturian Damsels* and *Stagecoach*. Though clearly members of the same heroic coterie that includes Amadís and the Lone Ranger, Nuño and Ringo are far from perfect archetypes. They do not overtly exhibit the kinds of heroic traits we see in the Cid or the Man from Laramie; nor are there any particular scenes in either text that fully capture their status as quintessential Caballero or Cowboy. Unlike the Cid, for instance, who acts decisively when provoked (and occasionally even when unprovoked), Nuño spends much of *The Famous Asturian Damsels* stranded in a kind of Hamletian universe of inaction as he struggles to decide whether he should comply with the demand to supply the sacrificial damsels or fight the Moors in defiance of his own king. What Lope does in this play—as he similarly does in *Fuenteovejuna*, in which he problematizes the whole notion of *honra* by contrasting the Comendador's "honor" with that of the local townsfolk—is to astutely pit Nuño's chivalric sense of honor (the notion that a man's word is his bond even to those not worthy of the gesture) against his chivalric sense of duty to protect the weaker elements of society (in this instance the "famous Asturian damsels"). So important is this inner conflict that Lope underlines it through a poetic leitmotiv uttered several times by Don García as he prepares to deliver his daughter, Doña Sancha, into Nuño's temporary care: "I give her to Osorio, and he takes her to the Moor" (1:357; my translation).[27] Ringo, for his part, is an escaped convict who throughout most of *Stagecoach* remains a virtual prisoner of Tonto's town marshal. And like Nuño before him, Ringo—the tainted heroic vessel—struggles with competing chivalric urges: between fully embracing his heroic pedigree on the one hand, and taking the coward's way out on the other. Lacking the kind of verbal leitmotiv so prominent in Lope, *Stagecoach* is imbued with a visual leitmotiv that is just as effective in underlining Ringo's inner turmoil. Ford's penchant for turning his camera to the horizon to create framing shots of the little stagecoach moving across the vast expanses of the desert Southwest provides viewers with the kind of spectacular vistas that made the western popular. But these shots also give the audience an unmistakable view of Ringo's "freedom" calling him from a distance, a freedom easily reached by simply abandoning the

Figure 2: By setting his stagecoach (see lower right quadrant) against the backdrop of Monument Valley, John Ford not only underlines the precarious isolation of the coach's travelers but emphasizes how easy it would be for Ringo (John Wayne) to escape prison, if only he were willing to abandon the stagecoach to its fate at the hands of the Apaches. (*Stagecoach*, United Artists, 1939)

stagecoach to its unhappy fate (Figure 2; note the miniscule stagecoach in the lower right quadrant).

The turning point of these texts occurs when each hero finally decides to embrace his status as hero, when each is finally forced to accept his archetypal role as defender of the defenseless. For Nuño, this crucial moment comes late in the third act when he finally decides to fight the Moors rather than simply turn over the damsels as he has been ordered, even if it means deliberately disobeying his sovereign, even if it means execution at the hands of King Alfonso. For Ringo, this decisive moment arrives when he is offered a brief opportunity late in the film to escape to Mexico. (And here, by the way, the entire nation of Mexico functions as a "good" Mexican by providing a safe haven for the Anglo Cowboy.) When the Apaches menacingly appear on the horizon, however, Ringo decides to return to the stagecoach, and from this moment on there is no question that he will remain with the beleaguered group (in exchange for which loyalty he receives little more than the promise of dying in the stagecoach's defense or returning to prison). In both instances, Nuño's and Ringo's conscious decisions to put themselves at personal risk represent the ultimate gesture of heroic self-sacrifice within the discursive world of these texts.

That Nuño and Ringo become heroes by choice emphasizes the centrality of "free will" for both Catholic Spain, champion of the Counter-

Reformation, and Protestant America, paragon of "Western individualism." That women lie at the core of these choices is even more important. Had the Moors merely demanded one hundred chests of gold coins, or had the stagecoach simply been carrying the deposits of a local bank, who can doubt that Nuño would have easily handed the treasure over to Mauregato, or that Ringo would have sped off to Mexico without looking back? These heroes' archetypal masculinity is constructed largely through their relationship to women. The Caballero and the Cowboy of *The Famous Asturian Damsels* and *Stagecoach* are defined not merely by their opposition to the villains they fight but also by their connection to the women they protect. In other words, what must play out for these characters to exist at all within the confines of these melodramatic morality plays is not a binary relationship but a trilateral one in which the hero, the ingénue, and the villain depend on each other for their defining roles. For, without the ingénue, there is nothing for the hero to protect; without the hero, the ingénue remains completely undefended; and without the villain there is no need for her protection.

René Girard argues that this interrelationship is a manifestation of what he calls "triangular desire," the aspiration to possess an object based on the perception that someone else—a "mediator"—also wants it (2).[28] Girard's quintessential example of this can be found in *Don Quixote*, whose knightly protagonist, Girard says, "has surrendered to Amadis the individual's fundamental prerogative: he no longer chooses the objects of his own desire—Amadis must choose for him" (1). Following this line of reasoning, we might say that Nuño and Ringo decide to defend the Asturian damsels and American travelers (three of whom, including a newborn baby, are female) only because the Treacherous Moors and Wild Indians of these texts—that is, Lope's and Ford's "mediators"—have clearly expressed a desire to capture them. (In this regard, the question of "desire" does not depend on what the mediators plan to do with these "objects" once they have them in their possession.) Such an interpretation, however, would misread Girard in two ways. First, his theory depends on the mediator's function as a "role model" for the "subject," which it would be difficult to ascribe to either Lope's Treacherous Moors or Ford's Wild Indians. Second, Girard's "triangle" assumes its "subject" from the outset and only later discovers its "object" and "mediator" in the interplay that occurs between them. He speaks of the "metamorphosis of the desired object" (23) and of the way in which the mediator is "brought into existence *as a rival*" (7; my emphasis). But in *The Famous Asturian Damsels* and *Stagecoach* it is not the hero who transforms the other characters into objects of desire and mediators; rather, it is the latter two groups that actually transform the hero into a subject.

Ringo, for instance, is differentiated from the other men in the stagecoach through his relationship to the women of the coach, and to one

woman in particular, Miss Dallas. Though the film never explicitly desig-
nates her as such, Miss Dallas is clearly a prostitute, and this fact seems to
be known and disapproved of by most of the passengers in the coach, all
of whom treat Dallas as a kind of pariah, particularly the respectable Lucy
Mallory (Louise Platt), whose local women's group is largely responsible
for running Dallas out of town. (In this sense, Dallas functions as a very
poor object of Girardian desire, since no one but Ringo seems to want her
there in the first place.) Despite her reputation, however, Ringo accords
Dallas as much respect as he does to every other woman in the film, even
to the point of proposing marriage to her. Various critics have sought to
explain Ringo's unusually generous treatment of Dallas through his apparent ignorance of her past. He seems either to be baffled by the others' behavior toward her or attributes these deliberate slights to his own
status as an escapee: "Looks like I got the plague, don't it? [...] Well, I
guess you can't break out of prison and into society in the same week"
(00:29:10). Yet this reading of Ringo's ignorance is untenable, I think, unless we define it not as a naive ignorance but as a willful one. For, what
ultimately distinguishes Ringo from all the other masculine characters in
the film (many of whom are as "manly" as the next), what confers on him
the status of quintessential Cowboy, despite his lack of many of the other
obvious archetypal qualities, is his heightened sense of chivalric respect
toward women—all women—who represent civilization itself precariously
situated on the dangerous frontier. And civilization, however imperfect,
cannot be left undefended, as Edward Buscombe shrewdly notes: "The
Western is constructed in such a way that the hero cannot choose what
the woman offers and still live with himself. [...] In the moral world of
the West, civilisation depends on there being men who will not choose the
seductive comforts the woman offers. A society without violence, a society fit for women, can only be established *through* violence" (59; original
emphasis).

The Famous Asturian Damsels, not coincidentally, could be said to
perform this very hypothesis, since what is at stake is whether Nuño will
or will not become the kind of archetypal hero found in other *comedias
históricas*, an issue that again turns not only on his relationship to the
"famous Asturian damsels" as a group, but to one "Asturian damsel" in
particular: Doña Sancha. Here, however, Doña Sancha (who pointedly
does not share Miss Dallas's social stigma) turns out to be a far superior
representative of masculine valor than Nuño himself. For, when he initially complies with the king's order to deliver the hundred virgins to the
Moors, these celebrated Asturian women—led by Doña Sancha—remove
their clothing during the journey (much to the dismay of the Asturian men
who accompany them) and replace it only when they arrive in the presence
of the Muslim soldiers who have come to take them into custody. When
Nuño demands an explanation for this clearly aberrant behavior, Doña

Sancha answers him with a taunting rebuke that underlines the fact that her gesture is fully intended to call his archetypal manhood into question:

> Listen, coward Osorio, / affront to men, listen / so that you will under-
> stand the reason / even if you do not wish to understand it. / Women
> have no shame / among other women; / she who walks among you / can
> surely disrobe herself, / because you are like us women: / cowardly, frail,
> and feeble, / feminine, womanly, and ladylike. / Thus, there is no reason
> for me not / to disrobe in front of you, / as happens among women. / But
> when I saw the Moors, / who are indeed men, strong men, / I got dressed
> because it is not right for them to see my nudity. (1:363; my translation)[29]

So powerful is this rhetorical rebuke in questioning the masculinity of the Asturian men that it spurs Nuño on to immediate violent resistance. More-over, it also causes King Alfonso "the Chaste" to strangely defend his own self-imposed phallic impotency:

> [...] we are all / men, by the grace of God. / I am no woman; yes, by God,
> / they call me Chaste, / but "Chaste" because of my virtue, / not because
> I lack vigor. (1:367; my translation)[30]

Melveena McKendrick has shown that the multifaceted persona she calls the "manly woman" (*mujer varonil*) appears frequently in the Span-ish *comedia* (ix–xiii), particularly the *comedia histórica*. And Lope is sim-ply repeating here the basic plot of his own play *The Damsels of Simancas*. Yet, this powerful character is no less prominent in the history—both fac-tual and fictional—of the American West, where much of what McKend-rick says about the Spanish "Amazon" (174–217) or "bandolera" (109–41) might equally apply to such figures as Calamity Jane or Annie Oakley (or even Miss Dallas herself, whose vaguely "masculine" name and blatant disregard for respectable "feminine" virtue also make her a bit "manly"). Calamity Jane (a.k.a. Martha Canary) spent most of her short life living and working in the West and is conspicuously famous for wearing men's clothing during her career as a female "frontiersman." Annie Oakley, for her part, whose actual contact with the West was limited to what could be called infrequent tourist visits, and who pointedly "refused to wear trou-sers or other masculine attire, even when riding a bicycle" (Riley, 103), achieved national fame as a member of Buffalo Bill's Wild West Show and later as a quasi-historical character in the Broadway musical *Annie Get Your Gun*, where she defiantly sings to her leading man, "Anything you can do I can do better."

Lope's Doña Sancha can be seen as a rhetorical mixture (*avant la lettre*) of these two American women. Like Annie Oakley, Doña Sancha insists on maintaining her "feminine" social persona, even in the face of what can only be considered the ultimate attack on that very "femininity." What I mean by this is that in stark contrast to Lope's Solmira from *The Last Visigoth* (1617), whose combat skills behind enemy lines inspire the Moors to call her "fury," "death," and "lightning" (3:662), or the "damsel warrior" of the well-known Spanish ballad who so badly desires to represent her family honor in defense of her country that she impersonates a male soldier in order to join the fray (Menéndez Pidal, 198–202), Doña Sancha steadfastly refuses to allow herself the "masculine" option of directly confronting her enemies.[31] Because she is unwilling to fight her own battles, her only recourse is to shame her male protectors into coming to her defense. Like Calamity Jane and the damsel warrior, however, this recourse manifests itself in a defiant—although (in this instance) inverted—deconstruction of her society's culturally imposed dress code. Where the presence of "male" clothing for both "Calamity Jane" and "Don Martín el de Aragón" (as the balladistic damsel warrior calls herself) masculinizes Martha Canary and the unnamed damsel warrior, thus discursively elevating them to the same plane as the men with whom they compete, the absence of "female" clothing in *The Famous Asturian Damsels* (that is, the unapologetic presence of the exposed female body) feminizes Nuño, thus reducing him to Sancha's level of self-imposed inaction.[32] This feminization of the male archetype—Sancha's rhetorical diminution of the "masculine hero" into "feminine coward"—provides the impetus for the *comedia*'s triumphant conclusion when Nuño finally reasserts his manly valor and embraces the masculine violence necessary for the protection of feminine civilization.[33]

And this brings us back to the question of beleaguered hegemony. From the start, *The Famous Asturian Damsels* and *Stagecoach* have allegorized their respective "national" histories as a kind of precarious journey from darkness into light. (It is perhaps not rhetorically coincidental that Ford's travelers move from "Tonto" to "Lordsburg," from a place of "stupidity, ignorance, and folly" to the very "City of God.")[34] The "famous Asturian damsels" physically conveyed by Nuño and his men to Mauregato travel the symbolic route of the *Reconquista* south from the northern mountains into hostile Muslim territory, where the invading overlords are eventually defeated. Likewise, the lone stagecoach traveling through Monument Valley evokes the westward migration celebrated in Walt Whitman's poem "Pioneers! O Pioneers!" (although, in truth, the actual geography demands an eastward trek) through which its passengers conquer the untamed wilderness. But these symbolic re-enactments of the *Reconquista* and Manifest Destiny do not merely extol the virtues of the "ancient" Iberian Old Christians (Vega, 1:336) or the "youthful sinewy races" (Whitman, 194) of the United States. Instead, these symbolic journeys trace a deliberate arc, taking their beleaguered passengers from a point of safety through a profoundly dangerous territory before depositing them once again back in the safe haven of the nation-state. They are constructed in such a way as to remind their audiences—regardless of the actual historical circumstances or the real state of geopolitical affairs when they were produced—that there was a time when the nation was very much under siege, when there still existed the very real threat of complete cultural dissolution at the hands of an enemy who very much wanted to destroy everything the nation valued and stood for. And through this allegory *The Famous Asturian Damsels* and *Stagecoach* invert Girard's triangle one last time.

For Girard, the "subject" perceives that a "mediator" desires a particular "object" and through this perception begins to desire it as well. The inherent jealousy attached to this process then causes the subject to convert the mediator into a "rival" who must be defeated. (Girard points to the inevitable friction between Anselmo and Lotario in Cervantes's "Tale of Inappropriate Curiosity" as a perfect example [49–52].)[35] The logic of *The Famous Asturian Damsels* and *Stagecoach*, however, suggests a different sequence of psychological events. The "subjects" of this inverted triangle are not the Caballero and the Cowboy but the Treacherous Moors and Wild Indians themselves who initially perceive the value of Hispano-Iberian and Anglo-American culture with growing interest. In this regard, these European societies function as "mediators"—that is, as Girardian "role models"—whose very "civilization" inspires the barbarians in their midst to covet this distinctly feminine object. Yet this barbarian desire is not constructive (as it is for Don Quixote with regard to Amadís), nor is the relationship between role model and subject positive (again, as it is for Don Quixote and Amadís). Instead, the Treacherous Moor and Wild Indian jealously vow to capture European "civilization" in order to inflict as much damage as possible. They covet the object only to obliterate it. Theirs is a negative and destructive desire that must be opposed at all costs by the Caballero and the Cowboy who are transformed from mere "mediators" into "rivals." And, in rising to a triangular occasion they did not invite, the Caballero and the Cowboy prove themselves worthy to possess the object they are forced by circumstance to defend. This insistence on Hispano-Iberian and Anglo-American besiegement justifies the expansive geopolitical power inscribed in these texts. Nuño and Ringo are positioned not as rapacious subjects who jealously covet someone else's object but as protective mediators who must safeguard that which is ignobly coveted by others. Their very beleagueredness vindicates their prodigious hegemony. They become heroes by demurring their own heroism; they become worthy of greatness by apparently seeking to avoid it.

Chapter 2

Johnny Rotten, Marilyn Manson, and the Limits of Picaresque Performance

In 1994, sixteen years after the Sex Pistols broke up in San Francisco during their first and only American tour—and fifteen years after the sudden death of Sid Vicious—John Lydon (a.k.a. Johnny Rotten) published his autobiography, *Rotten: No Irish, No Blacks, No Dogs.* Four years later, in 1998, Marilyn Manson (a.k.a. Brian Warner) published his autobiography, *The Long Hard Road Out of Hell,* a work strikingly haunted by Lydon's earlier publication.[1] Lydon's work, whose paperback cover revealingly touts the book as "Dickensian," depicts the author's childhood in the slums of North London during the 1960s and describes the rise and fall of what the Sex Pistols' manager, Malcolm McLaren, would later call (in another telling turn of phrase) his "little Artful Dodgers" (*The Filth and the Fury,* 01:42:24). Manson's autobiography, in contrast to Lydon's, traces Brian Warner's middle-class childhood in Canton, Ohio, and his subsequent metamorphosis into "Marilyn Manson" and then marks the triumphant culmination of four meteoric years during which Manson and his band released four albums and toured the United States, Canada, Japan, Portugal, Brazil, and Mexico. Like the autobiographies of many other rock stars before them, these narratives by John Lydon and Marilyn Manson function simultaneously as salacious confessions of their authors' outrageous lifestyles, as personal histories of particular movements or eras in British and American popular music, as public relations devices carefully designed to sell CDs, DVDs, T-shirts, posters, and other memorabilia, and as revenue-generating products in their own right. Unlike other rock autobiographies, however, *Rotten* and *The Long Hard Road* are remarkably literate (and, in fact, self-consciously literary) documents that inscribe themselves within an aesthetic tradition far richer than that of the kind of exculpatory autobiography generally published by other public figures. This is especially true of Manson, whose autobiography demonstrates a literary self-awareness that befits a frustrated writer whose intellectual capacities are appreciable, despite the fact that these capacities are often obscured by the grotesque persona he has created to give voice to his intentionally unorthodox ideas.

As the title of Manson's book suggests, the most obvious intertext for

The Long Hard Road Out of Hell is Dante's *Inferno* (although, in truth, Manson's evocation functions as a kind of inverse homage, because he claims to emerge from hell rather than descend into it). Manson's journey of self-discovery, like that of the *Divine Comedy*, is divided into three parts. Embedded within the book's sixteen chapters, however, is a separate (and often unrelated) subdivision in which Manson takes his reader through Dante's nine circles of hell.[2] Each circle of Manson's own literary hell parallels a different moment of his life, and each category of sin corresponds to one of his own perceived deficiencies. Yet, whereas Dante conceives of his journey as a progressive movement from hell to purgatory to paradise, Manson conceives of his own progression as a kind of monstrous metamorphosis: "When I Was a Worm" gives way to "Deformography," which in turn gives way to "How I Got My Wings" (vii). Thus, the climax of Manson's downward spiral—which he simultaneously suggests is also an upward escape from the banal, middle-class existence into which he had been born—arrives at the precise moment when his album *Antichrist Superstar* succeeds far beyond the expectations of nearly everyone involved in its production. In short, the release of this album marks the point at which Manson's transformation was complete (206).

Woven into this overtly Dantean superstructure are several other explicitly literary citations ranging from Dr. Seuss to Stephen King to George Orwell to the Marquis de Sade to Bertrand Russell to Roland Barthes. Chapter 1, for instance, begins with an epigraph from *Histoires Prodigieuses* (1561) in which Pierre Boaistuau claims that "nothing is seen that arouses the human spirit more, that ravishes the senses more, that horrifies more, that provokes more terror or admiration than the monsters, prodigies and abominations through which we see the works of nature inverted, mutilated and truncated" (Manson, 3). Added to this, and throughout his book, Manson also intersperses a series of anatomical drawings that simultaneously evoke *Gray's Anatomy* and the anatomical sketches of Leonardo Da Vinci. When coupled with Boaistuau's epigraph, these drawings visually underline the fact that Manson conceives of his autobiography not just as an itinerary through hell but also as a kind of anatomy of monstrosity. But within this very baroque conception of a "monstrous autobiography," especially one whose tone is confessional, the book's third major literary intertext comes into view, shedding light on *Rotten* as well by explaining the Dickensian references I cited earlier. Whether Lydon and Manson (or their ghostwriters) intended these books to be read as such, *Rotten* and *The Long Hard Road* exist as nothing less than picaresque novels in and of themselves that uncannily mirror the best-known mock autobiographies of baroque Spain.

The picaresque novel originated in 1554 with the simultaneous publication in Burgos, Alcalá de Henares, and Antwerp (then a Hapsburg possession) of the anonymous *Lazarillo de Tormes*. Eventually listed on the

Index Librorum Prohibitorum because of its scandalous content, this brief but ground-breaking book exists as a short "autobiographical" narrative recounting the personal history of its eponymous protagonist presented through a formal epistle written to his employer—an unnamed narratee denoted merely by the honorific title of "Your Honour" or "Your Grace" (*vuestra merced*) (Alpert, 24–25)—within which Lazarillo seeks to explain his difficult journey from childhood to maturity.[3] The work consists of seven chapters, each focusing on Lazarillo's experience with a series of abusive or unethical "masters," one of whom, a priest, sexually abuses Lazarillo (hence the work's censorship at the hands of the Inquisitor Fernando de Valdés). Over the course of the narrative, Lazarillo matures into manhood as he rises in social station from virtual orphan to blind man's boy to painter's assistant and, finally, to town crier in the employ of the aristocratic figure to whom he directs his autobiography.

Scholars have long debated the origins of the picaresque novel and have frequently quarreled over the parameters that mark its defining characteristics as a literary genre.[4] Indeed, Daniel Eisenberg argues that the wide range of texts to which critics have applied the term "picaresque novel" necessarily vacates any "exact meaning" we may wish to attach to the concept, and that its only real value, therefore, is as a "convenient modern label" (210). This is not the place to provide a detailed history of these debates, but since I apply the term "picaresque" analogically to the autobiographies of Johnny Rotten and Marilyn Manson, it is worth remembering—Eisenberg's well-argued dissent notwithstanding—that the whole notion of "genre" is not just a temporal construct but a dialectic one as well.[5] As Ralph Cohen correctly points out, generic change is often the product of "different genres that combine, contrast, challenge, and oppose one another" (87). Alastair Fowler, for instance, argues that the picaresque itself functions as an "antigenre to romance" (175). Hence, many scholars note that *Lazarillo*'s first chapter is obviously borrowed from a widely circulated medieval story known as "The Boy and the Blind Man," while recognizing that Fernando de Rojas's 1499 *Celestina* (as *The Tragicomedy of Calisto and Melibea* is generally known) contains "proto-picaresque" elements. At the same time, others argue that we cannot really speak of a "picaresque" tradition until 1599 when Mateo Alemán—the first author to actually use the term *pícaro* in a literary text—repeats *Lazarillo*'s performance in *Guzmán de Alfarache*.[6] Whether or not Alemán's recapitulation of *Lazarillo* does indeed represent the true moment of the picaresque's inception as a genre, it is perhaps useful here to briefly summarize the characteristics I consider crucial to any notion of "picaresque," if only as a starting point for a wider discussion that leads back to *Rotten* and *The Long Hard Road*.

First among these characteristics is the presence of the *pícaro* (a term of disputed origin roughly meaning "rogue" or "knave") who sits at the center of the picaresque novel and drives its movement with his "auto-biographical" narration. This antiheroic protagonist is almost always depicted as an orphan whose family origins, usually outlined in a kind of brief genealogical summary in the first chapter, clearly place him at the very margins of society, where he tenaciously struggles for survival. The second crucial characteristic is the ubiquitous narratological presence of "Your Grace," the narratee to whom the *pícaro* directs his epistolary autobiography. A third essential component is the episodic structure of the epistle, created by the sequence of masters—often priests, petty noblemen, and schoolmasters—who provide easy targets for the *pícaro*'s social satire. And finally, these texts usually reveal what could perhaps best be characterized as a "picaresque aesthetic," a darkly pessimistic view of life—closely related to the visual representations depicted in baroque chiaroscuro painting—through which the grotesque, the scatological, and the violent all assume an unprecedented literary centrality designed to call into question the exuberant and conservative ideology of the sixteenth- and seventeenth-century ruling classes.

Lazarillo was such an influential work, despite early attempts to censor it, that it established the model on which all future picaresque novels would in some way be based and launched an explosion of imitators in Spain and abroad. Within the Hapsburg empire the first such imitator, as I note earlier, was Alemán's *Guzmán de Alfarache*, published in two parts in 1599 and then 1605. Francisco López de Úbeda significantly modified the genre in 1603 by creating a female protagonist in *The Picara Justina*, a novel that quickly generated its own imitators, including Alonso Jerónimo de Salas Barbadillo's *Daughter of Celestina* (1612) and Alonso de Castillo Solórzano's *Teresa de Manzanares* (1632). In 1613 Miguel de Cervantes published "Rinconete and Cortadillo" and "The Dogs' Colloquy" as part of his collection of short narratives entitled *Exemplary Stories*.[7] Vicente Espinel added his own contribution to the corpus in 1618 with his publication of *Marcos de Obregón*. And, while numerous picaresque novels continued to be published throughout the seventeenth century, Francisco de Quevedo's 1626 satiric masterpiece *The Swindler* marks both the pinnacle and the outer perimeter of the picaresque in Spain, at least until the publication of Camilo José Cela's *Family of Pascual Duarte* (1942) and the release of Pedro Almodóvar's *What Have I Done to Deserve This?* (1984).

Outside the Iberian Peninsula, the picaresque novel found just as many imitators as it did within Spain itself. Across the Atlantic, in what would eventually become Latin America, Carlos de Sigüenza y Góngora, Calixto Bustamante Carlos (a.k.a. Concolorcorvo), and José Joaquín Fernández de Lizardi updated and adapted the genre for a distinctly New World context in *The Misfortunes of Alonso Ramírez* (1690), *El Lazarillo: A Guide for Inexperienced Travelers Between Buenos Aires and Lima* (1773), and *The Mangy Parrot: The Life and Times of Periquillo Sarniento* (1816), respectively. In France, where dramatists such as Pierre Corneille and Molière were already busy turning Guillén de Castro's *Youthful Deeds of the Cid* into *Le Cid* and Tirso de Molina's *Trickster of Seville* into *Don Juan*, French translations of *Lazarillo*, *Guzmán*, and *Justina* were widely available and provided the impetus for a whole series of French originals, including Charles Sorel's *True Comic History of Francion* (1622) and Alain-René Le Sage's *Gil Blas* (1715). In Germany, where the Spanish *auto-sacramental* would be respected and remembered long after Spain had deliberately pushed it out of public view, Martinus Freudenhold's "sequel" (which is to say, his own original "third" part) to *Guzmán de Alfarache* (1626), Hans Jakob Christoffel von Grimmelshausen's *Adventurous Simplex* (1668), and Daniel Speer's *Hungarian or Dacian Simplicissimus* (1683) would figure prominently in the history of German picaresque literature. In the Anglo-American context, however, the Spanish picaresque novel would have its greatest impact. The four centuries following the appearance of *Lazarillo* saw the publication of Richard Head and Francis Kirkman's *English Rogue* (1665), John Bunyan's *Life and Death of Mr. Badman* (1680), Daniel Defoe's *Colonel Jack* (1722) and *Moll Flanders* (1722), Tobias Smollett's *Adventures of Roderick Random* (1748), Charles Dickens's *Oliver Twist* (1837–39), a work profoundly indebted to Cervantes's "Rinconete and Cortadillo," Herman Melville's *Confidence Man* (1857), Mark Twain's *Huckleberry Finn* (1885), George Orwell's *Down and Out in Paris and London* (1933), and Anthony Burgess's *A Clockwork Orange* (1962).[8]

A Clockwork Orange—particularly through Stanley Kubrick's well-known cinematic adaptation—marks an important intersection in the history of picaresque narrative. In the first place, it seems to have had more than just a passing influence on the development of punk rock. At least two of Lydon's "cast of contributors" point to Kubrick's film as one of the prime influences on the rise of the punk aesthetic: "When *Clockwork Orange* came out, we used to wear white boiler suits. Some wore bowler hats"; "Punk was an antidesign movement. Isn't the movement from punk just an extension of the *Clockwork Orange* film by Stanley Kubrick that came around a bit before that period?" (75). Indeed, in describing the genesis of his own shock rock band, Alice Cooper insists that in the 1960s he was "more of *Clockwork Orange* than *Clockwork Orange*" (00:06:44). In the second place, *A Clockwork Orange* paved the way for a whole series of science fiction and picaresque films—some based on original screenplays, some based on previously published works that were already indebted to either Burgess's novel or Kubrick's film—that were released in the wake of the punk revolution. These include Ridley Scott's *Blade Runner* (1982), Robert Longo's *Johnny Mnemonic* (1995), Danny Boyle's *Trainspotting* (1996), David Fincher's *Fight Club* (1999), and the Wachowski Brothers' *Matrix* trilogy (1999–2003). In fact, the rise of what came to be known as "cyberpunk" literature (in all its manifestations) amounts to little more than a postmodern permutation of picaresque narrative under the influence of the punk movement of the 1970s and the "hacker" culture that emerged in the wake of the Internet revolution of the 1990s. As Bernadette Wegenstein rightly notes, cyberpunk is nothing if not a "fusion and interference of codes," ranging from "the musical codes of synth-rock and heavy metal to the film languages of film-noir and private-eye fiction," which imbues it with a "dark, pragmatic, and paranoid urbanism, an underworld of social marginality" (338).

This is not to say that Kubrick's film—much less the novel on which it is based—is singularly (or even primarily) responsible for the rise of punk rock, or that there is nothing particularly picaresque about popular music before the rise of Alice Cooper, the New York Dolls, or the Sex Pistols. Lydon is absolutely correct when he says that the "*Clockwork Orange* connection to the early punks is too easy" (76), at least by itself. Indeed, while Fredric Jameson argues that punk rock stands in postmodern opposition to the "high-modernist" music of the Beatles and the Rolling Stones (1), one could make an equally strong claim that rock and roll itself—from Chuck Berry, Bill Haley, Buddy Holly, and Elvis Presley on—stands in postmodern opposition to the high modernism of jazz. Having evolved out of the African American blues traditions of the early twentieth century, rock music (broadly defined to include such contemporary subcategories as heavy metal, reggae, punk, grunge, and gangsta rap) has always functioned as a picaresque literary form, whether recounting the harsh realities of life as a sharecropper in the Jim Crow South, the harsh realities of life as a working-class immigrant in London, or the harsh realities of life in what hip hop music has come to call "the 'hood" in such metropolises as New York, Chicago, and Los Angeles. And just as there is a clear line of literary provenance tying *Lazarillo* to Irvine Welsh's *Trainspotting*, there is an equally profound musical genealogy that connects Robert Johnson's "Cross Road Blues" (1936) to Muddy Water's "Hoochie Coochie Man" (1953) to John Lee Hooker's "No Shoes" (1960) to The Who's "Behind Blue Eyes" (1971) to Tupac Shakur's "Dear Mama" (1995). Indeed, when read alongside such texts as *Celestina*, *Lazarillo*, *Guzmán*, and *The Swindler*, the Rolling Stones' 1968 single "Jumpin' Jack Flash" emerges as a quintessentially picaresque text that encapsulates nearly all the requisite generic markers, from its oblique allusion to stormy waters in the opening line (which recalls Lazarillo's own impoverished birth in the Tormes river) to its reference to the "toothless, bearded hag" (which uncannily evokes the witchy Celestina whom various characters refer to interchangeably as "mother," "old whore," and "bearded old woman" [Rojas, *Celestina*, 45, 53]) to its notion of being "schooled" with a strap across the back (which suggests both the daily violence visited upon these *pícaros* by their masters and the boarding school setting where they are often abandoned to the

Figure 3: As a deliberate attack on the stadium rock and disco of the 1970s, the Sex Pistols cultivated a caustic aesthetic that reaffirmed rock music's fundamental role in challenging authority. The notorious punk band's most infamous members, Johnny Rotten (left) and Sid Vicious, did so by building on a picaresque tradition of social criticism that can be traced to baroque Spain. (*The Filth and the Fury*, Fine Line Features, 2000)

whims and cruelties of dictatorial schoolmasters and adolescent bullies). But where traditional picaresque narratives revolve around the theme of redemption (through which the *pícaro* eventually overcomes the circumstances of his birth), "Jumpin' Jack Flash," with its thinly veiled references to a heroin rush, demonstrates that for postmodern *pícaros* the quickest way out is often not through art but through pharmacology. When considered within the context of other rock songs like the Kinks' "Father Christmas" or Pink Floyd's "The Wall" (both of which incorporate their own Dickensian themes) it is clear that the punk revolution—within which the Sex Pistols played such an integral role—was not so much a reaction to the proto-cyberpunk aesthetic inherent in *A Clockwork Orange* as it was a parallel development within what was already a rather picaresque performance tradition (Figure 3).[9]

Neither *Rotten* nor *The Long Hard Road* was written specifically, of course, to mimic a picaresque novel, much less constitute one. Each autobiography has its own agenda and each appeals to a different (though related) readership. For this reason there are any number of nonpicaresque components within these texts. These distinctions notwithstanding, both works contain recognizably picaresque or baroque elements, including strong anticlerical and anti-educationalist themes. Of these picaresque elements, perhaps the most important relate to what can only be called a "scatological exuberance." A great many readers will naturally associate the narrative preponderance of bodily fluids in *Rotten* and *The Long*

Hard Road with Mikhail Bakhtin, whose influential work *Rabelais and His World* explores the medieval carnivalesque culture around which the discourse of *Gargantua and Pantagruel* (1532–62) revolves. But despite Bakhtin and Rabelais's interrelated association in this regard, these same carnivalesque elements are already present in the Spanish picaresque novel and its immediate precursors. They are an essential part of what Hispanists frequently call the incipient "realism" inherent in the picaresque. For instance, Rojas's *Celestina* contains several "scandalous" scenes of implied lovemaking between Sempronio and Pármeno and their respective paramours, Elicia and Areusa; which is one of the reasons it too was placed on the list of prohibited books. For its part, *Lazarillo*—written at the same time Rabelais was composing the five books that make up *Gargantua and Pantagruel*—contains a very memorable scene describing the moment in which Lazarillo vomits in the face of his blind master after the old man has stuck his protruding nose deep into his servant's throat in order to gauge whether the young boy has eaten a purloined sausage: "the deed and my greed were revealed and my master received his property back; for, before he could get his trunk out of my mouth my stomach was so upset that I brought it all up, and his nose and the half-digested sausage came out at the same time" (Alpert, 34).[10] And Quevedo's *Swindler* contains a scene in which his autobiographical protagonist, Pablos, recounts his status as the victim of a hazing ritual at a boarding school where his fellow students launch such a heavy volley of globs of phlegm on him that he is left "slimy" from head to toe: "From what they threw up at me from their stomachs I thought they were trying to save on doctors and chemists by giving themselves a good clean-out on the new students" (Alpert, 107).[11]

In this regard, Lydon's autobiography contains lengthy discussions on the amount of spittle and phlegm launched at the Sex Pistols by their fans, and vomit makes an appearance in an anecdote on how the Sex Pistols got so sick on alcohol that they threw up in the parking lot of their record label. Urine becomes the central topic in a description of Nancy Spungen (Sid Vicious's infamous girlfriend) who "had piss stains all down her tights" because she "could never be bothered to clean herself, and her legs were so dirty that you could see the white marks where the piss dribbled" (144). Moreover, blood figures prominently in a story about Sid Vicious casually cutting open his own hand and letting the blood drip into his steak and eggs (while he continued to eat) in order to outdo some American cowboy who had put out a cigarette on his own hand as a way of trying to demonstrate his masculine superiority over the singer (248). And as far as excrement and semen go, few texts can surpass the following passage:

> I was with a couple of mates, and Nora was foolish enough to let us cook the food. Now Nora would never eat anything we cooked in the kitchen,

so we served it to Nora's friends. It was literally a shit in the frying pan cooked in olive oil. Then we all wanked into this fucking omelet—one egg and at least four good doses. They all thought it was the best food they ever ate. The shit sandwich was the killer. It was deep fried and put between two toasted slices of bread. They ate it and thought it was corned beef. (277)

The Long Hard Road is even more preoccupied with bodily fluids than *Rotten*. It includes talk of enema bags (3), of "gushing blood" (178), and of an exchange of "thrown" vomit—what Manson drolly calls a "post-food fight" (198)—between various members of his band and its producer, Trent Reznor. (This is not to mention one of Manson's concert videos that includes a backstage scene of a transvestite urinating onto the floor in front of the camera to demonstrate the existence of a working penis, despite the otherwise female-gendered body.) Given Manson's apparent delight in graphically describing the various sexual encounters he relates throughout his book, however, bodily fluids seem always to be connected with sex acts, whether real or imagined, interrupted or completed. These include a scene of adolescent romance that ends abruptly when the girl accidentally spews a huge wad of thick, lime-green snot into Manson's hand ("When I pulled away, a long string of it hung between my fingers and her face like apple taffy" [21]); a scene describing the loss of his virginity, following which he obsesses over the smell of the girl "permanently stained" on his hand (37); and a scene describing the clandestine moment when he accidentally caught his grandfather masturbating. Manson's description of this sordid scene surpasses even Lydon's for sheer shock value, and as it does, it begins to approach the limits of picaresque scatological discourse, even for a culture that prides itself on no longer being shocked by anything:

> After several excruciatingly slow minutes, a gruesome noise leapt from his throat, like the sound a car engine makes when someone turns the key in the ignition when it's already on. I turned my head away, too late to keep from imagining the white pus squeezing out of his yellow, wrinkled penis like the insides of a squashed cockroach. When I looked again, he had lowered his handkerchief, the same one he'd been using to wipe away his phlegm, and was sopping up his mess. (Manson, 15)

In his well-known work *Renaissance Self-Fashioning*, Stephen Greenblatt traces the important connection between "estrangement" and the invention of modern subjectivity: "Self-fashioning is achieved in relation to something perceived as alien, strange, or hostile. This threatening Other [...] must be discovered or invented in order to be attacked and destroyed" (9). I mention Greenblatt's book here because it raises the whole issue of the self-fashioning function of autobiography in general, and specifically the way *pícaros* tend to use their texts to carve out a new identity by positing an alienation so profound that not even family ties can bind them to their pasts. Readers will remember that one of the most important components of the picaresque novel is the *pícaro*'s problematic genealogy. Lazarillo's thieving father, for instance, is sentenced to serve as a mule driver on a military expedition against the Moors, where he is soon killed in action. His mother, having been left poor and widowed, finds herself with no choice but to become the mistress of a North African slave named Zaide who, in exchange for sexual favors, provides sustenance for her, for Lazarillo, and (eventually) for Lazarillo's mulatto stepbrother. Later, when Zaide is also caught stealing—and subsequently "whipped and basted with hot fat" (Alpert, 26)—Lazarillo's mother abandons her young son to the care of the blind man (the first in a series of injurious masters).[12] And so it goes for Guzmán and Pablos, both of whom stem from immediate families also riddled with thieves, moneylenders, Jews, Moors, bawds, whores, and witches. Faced with such "insalubrious" genealogies, Lazarillo and Guzmán initiate the process of self-fashioning by attacking family identity itself: Lazarillo takes as a surname the name of the river in which he was born (i.e., the Tormes); while Guzmán, conspicuously aware of his status as a bastard, takes the name of his place of origin. Pablos, for his part, who discovers much to his horror that his own uncle—his last remaining relative—has served as executioner to his father, deliberately turns his back on his past forever: "In the morning I got up before he was awake and went off to an inn. I shut my uncle's door, locked it and threw the key down a hole used to let the cat in and out. [...] In the room I left him a sealed letter in which I told him why I had gone and that he shouldn't try and find me as I had made up my mind I never wanted to see him again" (Alpert, 146).[13] The first step on the road to picaresque subjectivity is orphanhood.

And thus it is in this alienation from family and society that the autobiographies of Lydon and Manson most profoundly reflect the initial chapters of the Spanish picaresque novel. Consider, for instance, Lydon's narration of his own early years in Finsbury Park, North London:

> I was raised in a tenement, working-class slummy. I was brought up to about the age of eleven in a two-room flat. No bathroom. Outside toilet. It would be a slum in anyone's language. There was an air raid shelter outside next to the toilet. It was infested with rats, and that used to thrill me. It was totally open, and you could go in and play in it.
>
> The building was a Victorian dwelling that held forty or fifty families. I've got three brothers. I'm the eldest, and we were all born relatively close together. I don't know how old they are, to be quite frank. Don't know when their birthdays are, and they don't know mine. We're not

that kind of family. We don't celebrate that kind of thing. Never had any interest in it. Until recently, I wasn't close to my father at all. I don't think I ever seriously spoke to him until the day he kicked me out of the house. (10)[14]

Though Lydon ultimately establishes a good relationship with his father, he cannot undertake the story of his life as a Sex Pistol without cutting his family ties first. "Johnny Rotten" simply cannot exist as anything less than an "orphan" of sorts.

Manson's discursive act of "patricide" is even more deliberate than Lydon's. For, although Manson certainly dedicates his book to his parents ("May God forgive them for bringing me into this world" [xi]), and although there are several family pictures of the Warners interspersed among the book's various photographs and drawings, Manson's parents are very marginal figures indeed, even by picaresque standards. Six chapters into the text, Manson devotes roughly three pages to his relationship with his parents from the age of six ("the first time I realized something was wrong with our family" [46]) up through the moment during his teens when the family moved from Ohio to South Florida. These three brief pages rehearse all the standard complaints about how his father abused him ("He constantly threatened to kick me out of the house and never failed to remind me that I was worthless and would never amount to anything" [46]); how he, in turn, began to abuse his mother ("I lost the temper my father had handed down to me and threw the bottle at her face, opening up a bloody gash over her lip" [48]); and how, in the end, he was left "bitter and angry" not just at his parents but "at the world" (48). Still, the purpose of Manson's discussion of his dysfunctional childhood and adolescence seems designed not so much to support his burgeoning picaresque narrative as to "introduce" the interpolated story that follows, a previously unpublished manuscript on incestuous necrophilia entitled "All in the Family" (51).

None of this is to suggest, of course, that Manson begins his picaresque narrative without a requisite nod to questions of pedigree and familial marginalization. In fact, unlike Lydon (who begins and ends his text with the "demise" of his picaresque alter ego), Manson properly begins with his genealogy, even if this means skipping a generation backward. His first chapter, entitled "The Man That You Fear," commences with what appears to be Manson's earliest baby picture taken in the hospital minutes after he was born. Having visually announced his birth—and in this way, paid homage to all those picaresque narrators before him whose first utterance includes some formulation of Lazarillo's "I was actually born on [in] the River Tormes and that's why I took that surname and this is how it all happened" (Alpert, 25)—Manson immediately turns to a description of his paternal grandfather, Jack Angus Warner, a man he deliberately conflates with the space he inhabits:[15]

Hell to me was my grandfather's cellar. It stank like a public toilet, and was just as filthy. [...] Dangling unconcealed from the wall was a faded red enema bag [...]. To its right was a warped white medicine cabinet, inside of which were a dozen old boxes of generic, mail-order condoms on the verge of disintegration; a full, rusted can of feminine-deodorant spray; a handful of the latex finger cots that doctors use for rectal exams; and a Friar Tuck toy that popped a boner when its head was pushed in. Behind the stairs was a shelf with about ten paint cans which, I later discovered, were each filled with twenty 16-millimeter porno films. (3)

Manson's strategy of beginning his autobiography with memories of his grandfather serves two crucial discursive purposes. First, by painting this very grotesque picture of Jack Angus Warner—a man with a tracheostomy, a collection of bestiality magazines, and a penchant for masturbating in the basement even when there is a chance his grandchildren might catch him in the act—Manson accounts genetically for his own grotesque metamorphosis. "The man you fear" is both a description of Manson's childhood reaction to Jack Angus Warner and a description of the rock god he will ultimately become. Appropriately, then, this first chapter begins with the epigraph by Pierre Boaistuau on "monsters, prodigies, and abominations" (Manson, 3). Second, by focusing on this generational link to his monstrous grandfather—by deliberately eliding his more immediate connection to the all-too-bourgeois Barb and Hugh Warner—Manson effectively orphans himself for the remainder of his narrative, even if he occasionally includes pictures of his parents among the text's various images, even if he eventually brings them into the narrative.

Manson's shift in genealogical focus away from his parents and toward his grandfather is significant because picaresque orphanhood is actually quite difficult to achieve in the twenty-first century (at least in first-world countries). Adoption agencies, foster care programs (however imperfect), child labor laws, and all the other social mechanisms created by the industrial world during the twentieth century to prevent the kind of exploitation of children depicted in the picaresque novel have made it extremely difficult for any child in the United States or the United Kingdom to suffer the kind of life described by Lazarillo and his successors. While poverty and homelessness remain substantial problems in the United States, there are very few homeless orphans running around the streets of New York, Chicago, or Los Angeles—let alone Canton, Ohio—eating out of garbage cans. In this regard, the social criticism inherent in the picaresque novel—principally through Dickens—has largely helped ameliorate the negative social forces that gave rise to the picaresque genre in the first place. For better or worse, globalized multinational capitalism has successfully shifted the impoverished milieu of the picaresque novel from European and North American urban spaces to third- and fourth-world locations like Mexico City and Kinshasa. Nevertheless, orphanhood—however difficult to achieve—is an essential component of picaresque narrative; which is why contemporary authors who undertake the creation of a picaresque narrative must find new ways of cutting the *pícaro*'s family ties. It is not coincidental, therefore, that Burgess releases Alex from prison two-thirds of the way through *A Clockwork Orange* only to have him discover that his parents (quite unaware that he would be home so soon) have sublet his room to someone named Joe, a stranger who claims to have been treated "more like a son [...] than like a lodger" (134). Without this moment of parental abandonment, which forces Alex to seek "HOME" elsewhere (152), he cannot actually become the *pícaro* he has been aspiring to be from the first page of the novel.[16]

The reason this moment of abandonment is so crucial in any picaresque narrative is that it marks the point at which the protagonist realizes he is entirely alone in the world. For, it is at this moment when the alienation Greenblatt refers to becomes the catalyst for picaresque self-representation. It marks the point at which the narrator ceases to be a child and starts down a path that will eventually lead to his status not just as an adult but as a narrator as well. Lazarillo's mother, for instance, sends her young son off with the blind man, saying, "I've raised you as best I know and I've put you with a good master. Now you must look after yourself" (Alpert, 27).[17] This "look after yourself" moment comes at different times and in different ways for each *pícaro*. For Lazarillo (despite his mother's advice), it doesn't actually come until the blind man—in one of the best-known scenes in the novel—bashes the young boy's head against a stone statue of a bull after tricking him into putting his ear against it to hear a loud noise. In response to the old man's admonition that a blind man's boy must learn to be "sharper than a needle," Lazarillo makes the following confession to the reader: "At that moment I felt as if I had woken up and my eyes were opened. I said to myself: 'What he says is true; I must keep awake because I'm on my own and I've got to look after myself'" (Alpert, 27–28).[18] This crucial moment of recognition doesn't come for Pablos until nearly six chapters into *The Swindler*, when, shortly after the "barrage and shower" of phlegm he suffers as part of the hazing ritual described earlier, his young master, Don Diego (echoing both *Lazarillo* and *Guzmán*), says: "Pablos, you've got to wake up. Watch out for yourself. You know your father and mother can't do it for you" (Alpert, 108).[19] In other words, it is precisely in his most profound moment of alienation that the protagonist becomes the *pícaro*.

Since neither Lydon nor Manson is literally orphaned, these explicit "look after yourself" moments do not occur within the same context as they do in the traditional picaresque novel. Nevertheless, they do exist as crucial turning points in the texts. For Lydon, this alienated recognition is bifurcated into two crucial moments. First, following nearly a year of hospitalization and recuperation from meningitis, Lydon begins to see himself as something of a free-floating signifier, detached from its original context: "Once I came back to school after twelve months, I didn't recognize anyone. A year in a comatose state at that age tends to take some of the memory away. *My perspective shifted, and I saw myself as apart*" (18; my emphasis). This sense of social detachment is solidified later when he comes to appreciate the strategy behind his father's calculated indifference to him: "What he's done all my life, which I never understood until the day I left home, was to deliberately make sure that *I would always be my own man and not be led or fooled by anyone*. He never gave me an easy time about anything. No matter what I did, he called it crap" (23; my emphasis). Manson also experiences his "look after yourself" moment in two installments, the first of which is also connected to his school life. Having spent the better part of several months trying to get himself expelled from his religious school through a series of pranks, the last of which involved planting one of his grandfather's giant dildoes inside his teacher's desk, Manson suddenly realizes that such passivity ("passive-aggressive" though it may be) is not only insufficient but actually "unworthy" of him:

> That's when I realized that I would never be expelled. Half the kids at Heritage Christian School were from lower-income families, and the school received a pittance from the state to enroll them. I was among the children who could pay, and they wanted the money—even if it meant dealing with my dildoes, heavy metal cassettes, candy, dirty magazines and smut-filled recordings. I realized that if I ever wanted to get out of Christian school, I would have to exercise my own free will to walk away. And two months into tenth grade I did just that. (30)

The second moment occurs some years later when, after establishing himself as a local rock journalist in South Florida, Manson grows tired of this passivity as well: "Each successive interview I did, the more disillusioned I became. Nobody had anything to say. I felt like I should be answering the questions instead of asking them. I wanted to be on the other side of the pen" (74). At this crucial moment the author finally decides to shed his "Brian Warner" skin and replace it with the mask of "Marilyn Manson": "The next time Trent Reznor came to town, I was his opening act" (74).

The Long Hard Road acknowledges the writerly significance of Brian Warner's premeditated creation of a new picaresque identity: "Marilyn Manson was the perfect story protagonist for a frustrated writer like myself. He was a character who, because of his contempt for the world around him and, more so, himself, does everything he can to trick people into liking him. And then, once he wins their confidence, he uses it to destroy them" (79). In an ironic nod to Saint Augustine's *Confessions*,

Manson's autobiography traces his conversion from "protagonist" to "author." And because he occupies a space on both sides of the same pen, Manson—like Augustine before him—necessarily flows from that pen as well. In other words, like "Johnny Rotten," who exists as Lydon's alter ego for purposes having solely to do with the Sex Pistols, "Marilyn Manson" is a character created by Brian Warner through which he can vicariously live a picaresque lifestyle explicitly connected to defrauding the public. In this one sentence, Marilyn Manson succinctly captures the essence of the picaresque as have few other authors before him. The *pícaro*, whether in seventeenth-century Spain or the twenty-first-century United States, is an actor whose entire performance—from beginning to end—is a theatrical or literary construct.

The importance of "performance" in the life of the *pícaro* cannot be underestimated, and a number of critics have devoted considerable attention to an examination of the relationship between theatricality (broadly conceived) and the discourse of the picaresque. Helen Reed, for instance, in her study of theatricality in Cervantes's picaresque narratives, insists that *pícaros* often "play out their lives on the world's stage self-consciously— imitating scripts set by previous picaresque tales" (72). As I argue elsewhere, however, the *pícaro* is essentially an "improvisational actor" whose various tricks and con games are inherently theatrical; which is to say, the *pícaro*'s most important talent is not the ability to mimic other rogues but rather a capacity for protean self-representation (95).[20] Nina Cox Davis takes this notion even further in her study of *Guzmán* when she suggests that the picaresque autobiography is perhaps the rogue's greatest trick (*burla*). As even a cursory reading of the most notable Spanish picaresque novels will demonstrate, the *pícaro* almost always winds up connected in some way or another to the theater: Guzmán finds himself working as a kind of court jester at two distinct points during his career as a *pícaro*; Teresa de Manzanares marries an actor and subsequently joins his troupe; and Pablos not only joins a theater company but becomes one of its most successful dramatists. For the poverty-stricken orphans who inhabit the urban spaces of the picaresque novel, the theater is one of the few professions in which they can secure gainful employment.

The same is apparently true of the picaresque world of rock music— at least according to the Rolling Stones, whose "Street Fighting Man" contains the lyric, "But what can a poor boy do / except to sing for a rock 'n' roll band?"[21] Moreover, it is through the act of performing that these postmodern *pícaros* create for themselves the mechanism for achieving upward social mobility. Indeed, as B. B. King boasts in "Riding with the King" (the title cut from his collaborative album with Eric Clapton), his entire life—from the moment he first stepped out of Mississippi as a child—has been inextricably bound up with his guitar and his music. Or, as Ian Christe says of the members of the heavy metal group Black Sabbath, "They were prophets bred from the downside of English society, the unemployed—people regarded as morally suspect and of negligible social worth. [...] In the world they inherited, the only action worthwhile was to become professional misfits and adventurers" (1). Given the relative paucity of strolling theater companies in our contemporary major cities (there really are no "garage theater troupes" comparable to the numerous "garage bands" that have found success in the music industry), rock bands have become the primary engine of picaresque performative escape. The music business, despite its increasing corporatization in the past fifty years, has been the gateway to upward social mobility for three generations of working-class performers, from the early bluesmen of the Depression era to the hip hop artists of the twenty-first-century. And the most successful— and sustained—performance for these singers across the decades has not been a single song (much less a single performance) or even a collection of songs. These singers' most important performance is the invented persona they present to the world, one conceived in picaresque terms. This is true even for singers whose backgrounds are far from marginalized, even for singers who eventually find themselves on the Forbes list. As several critics have noted, Mick Jagger's public persona—with his affected combination of a "mock-Cockney" accent borrowed from Kubrick's *A Clockwork Orange* (Nehring, "Shifting Relations," 92) and his African American "blues argot" borrowed from Muddy Waters (Hellmann, 367)—reflects a social alienation unlikely to come from the middle-class son of a physical therapist.[22]

This centrality of "performing a persona" (even when the musical performance associated with this persona is just as powerful) is crucial to the picaresque narration of both *Rotten* and *The Long Hard Road*. Lydon and Manson each admit that their self-fashioning of a public persona to front their bands was influenced as much by their respective sense of theater and spectacle as it was by any musical ambitions they may have had: "The punk thing started pretty much nonmusically" (Lydon, 74). Or, as Dick Hebdige notes in his influential work *Subculture: The Meaning of Style*: "The punks wore clothes which were the sartorial equivalent of swear words, and they swore as they dressed—with calculated effect, lacing obscenities into record notes and publicity releases, interviews and love songs" (114). The Sex Pistols represented a Brechtian "Theater of Rage" (Lydon, 78), a "musical vaudeville," an "evil burlesque" (Lydon, 114).[23] Thus, despite Lydon's frequent attempts to minimize (or even dismiss) the memories of his "cast of contributors," and despite his claims that "the music you make should reflect your real personality, your real self" (158), his oral history of the Sex Pistols makes it clear that the aesthetic self-representation performed by Johnny Rotten and Sid Vicious owed much (if only as a negative reaction) to the equally artificial personas created by such precursors as Mick Jagger, Gary Glitter, David Bowie (as Ziggy Stardust), and even Laurence Olivier:

> Johnny Rotten definitely has tinges of Richard III in him. I saw it a long time before I conceived Rotten. No redeeming qualities. Hunchback, nasty, evil, conniving, selfish. The worst of everything to excess. Olivier made Richard III riveting in his excessive disgust. Having seen it aeons ago, I took influences from Olivier's performance. I had never seen a pop singer present himself quite that way. It wasn't the norm. You're supposed to be a nice pretty boy, sing lovely songs, and coo at the girlies. Richard III would have none of that. He got the girls in other ways. (Lydon, 154)

Indeed, the primary leitmotiv of Julien Temple's documentary *The Filth and the Fury* can be found in the repeatedly interspersed footage of Laurence Olivier's cinematic performance as Richard III, which culminates in the juxtaposition of the "death" of the Sex Pistols and the death of Olivier's Richard.

"Marilyn Manson" is an even more audacious and more deliberately theatrical creation than either "Johnny Rotten" or "Richard III." Manson tells us that the genesis of this persona occurred in 1989 through the confluence of several interrelated events arising from the censorship of 2 Live Crew's album *As Nasty as They Wanna Be.* As a writer of fiction and poetry, as a theater student, and as a sometime performer at an open-mike night at a South Florida club, Brian Warner decided to engage in what he calls a "science project" designed to test whether "a white band that wasn't rap could get away with acts far more offensive and illicit than 2 Live Crew's dirty rhymes" (80). But because he did not want to compromise his budding career as a rock journalist, he needed an alter ego who could occupy the space on the other side of the pen. Marilyn Manson was the perfect literary and theatrical solution. In addition to the obvious nomenclatural connection to Charles Manson and Marilyn Monroe (she, herself, the theatrical persona of Norma Jean Baker), Warner's self-fashioned persona reflects images established earlier by David Bowie, Alice Cooper, Gene Simmons, Ozzy Osbourne, and even Johnny Rotten (who screamed "I am an Anti-Christ" two decades before Warner self-consciously became "Antichrist Superstar," a name that itself is intertextually linked to Andrew Lloyd Webber's well-known rock opera *Jesus Christ Superstar*).[24] In this regard, Marilyn Manson represents the ultimate postmodern pastiche of all the punk rock *pícaros* who came before him. Indeed, as Alice Cooper admits, "Marilyn Manson understood what Alice was, looked at it, and said 'I'm just going to up the ante'" (00:42:00). And like Johnny Rotten before him, Marilyn Manson deliberately and directly ties his pub-

Figure 4: Updating the anticlericalism of the Spanish picaresque for contemporary audiences, Marilyn Manson's performances during 2000–2001 vividly derided what Harold Bloom calls the American Religion's obsession with the flag and the fetus. (*Guns, God, and Government World Tour*, Eagle Vision, 2002)

lic persona to the aesthetics of baroque literature, thus arriving full circle at the very origins of the picaresque novel. But where Rotten invokes one of Shakespeare's best-known diabolical characters, Manson is much more interested in Milton's ultimate hero/villain:

> The words *Marilyn Manson* seemed like an apt symbol for modern-day America, and the minute I wrote it on paper for the first time I knew that it was what I wanted to become. All the hypocrites in my life from Ms. Price to Mary Beth Kroger had helped me to realize that everybody has a light and a dark side, and neither can exist without the other. I remember reading *Paradise Lost* in high school and being struck by the fact that after Satan and his angel companions rebelled against heaven, God reacted to the outrage by creating man so that He could have a less powerful creature companion in his image. In other words, in John Milton's opinion at least, man's existence is not just a result of God's benevolence but also of Satan's evil. (85)

Taking Milton's baroque notion of God's less powerful "image" as a direct challenge, Manson turns himself into what he calls the "reflecting god" (209): "I believe I am God. I believe everyone is their own God. I dreamt I was the Antichrist, and I believe it" (213).

Figure 5: The costumes and sets of Marilyn Manson's *Guns, God, and Government* concert tour—which mirror the visual aesthetic of the Nazi Third Reich—are intentionally designed to accuse contemporary U.S. culture of fascism. (*Guns, God, and Government World Tour*, Eagle Vision, 2002)

Statements such as these—along with the deliberately shocking visual imagery Manson has cultivated to accompany them—are designed to provoke American evangelical Christians to fits of near hysteria. Manson's success in this endeavor, as he so proudly documents in his final chapter of *The Long Hard Road*, is demonstrated in the sheer number of Christian groups that have organized protest movements against him. As Robert Wright notes: "Manson's messianic complex is animated by his remarkable fluency with the concepts and especially the jargon of conservative evangelicalism, which helps to explain why the religious right finds him 'dangerous' and 'evil'. Indeed, Manson's 'Antichrist' persona is chilling— and brilliant—because he has so thoroughly appropriated the language of the New Testament" (377). In fact, as the set design for Manson's *Guns, God, and Government* world tour strongly suggests, Manson spent the greater part of two years (2000–2001) enacting a performance of what Harold Bloom describes as the twin fetishes of American evangelical Christianity—"the flag and the fetus" (*American Religion*, 270)—by staging his concerts on a set whose red, white, and black colors are deliberately designed to tie evangelical Christianity to the visual discourse of the Nazi Third Reich (Figures 4 and 5). Manson's total assault on the religious sensibilities of conservative Christians—up to and including the release of his sexually charged cover of the song "Personal Jesus"—approaches the limits of the "anticlericalism" embedded within the picaresque tradition.[25] *Lazarillo*'s Erasmian critique of the avarice and penury of Spain's early modern clerics has become *The Long Hard Road*'s "Satanist" attack on Christianity itself:

> What nearly everybody [...] had misunderstood about Satanism was that it is not about ritual sacrifices, digging up graves and worshipping the devil. The devil doesn't exist. Satanism is about worshipping yourself, because you are responsible for your own good and evil. Christianity's war against the devil has always been a fight against man's most natural instincts—for sex, for violence, for self-gratification—and a denial of man's membership in the animal kingdom. The idea of heaven is just Christianity's way of creating a hell on earth. (164)

At the same time, however, the discourse of Manson's anti-Christian philosophy demonstrates why his performance—including that of writing his autobiography—marks yet another set of limits within the picaresque tradition. Throughout this chapter I refer to the author of *Rotten* as "John Lydon" and to the author of *The Long Hard Road* as "Marilyn Manson." My reasons for doing so are not simply bibliographical (not simply because these are the two names listed on each book's respective copyright page); my reasons are conceptual as well. Every picaresque text—and indeed, every autobiography—inscribes within it a split protagonist: the *pícaro* who lived the tale, and the reformed *pícaro* who narrates that tale once he has moved on to what Manson characterizes as "the other side of the pen" (74). John Lydon's *Rotten* exemplifies this traditional picaresque bifurcation perfectly. "Johnny Rotten" is able to write his "authorized" history of the Sex Pistols only when he has ceased to be Johnny Rotten; that is, when Lydon has stopped being a musician and become an author instead. (I do not mean to suggest that John Lydon no longer performs music; almost immediately following his unceremonious exit from the Sex Pistols he formed Public Image Limited [PiL] and has had a very successful post-Rotten musical career. What I mean is that he writes *Rotten* not as a current member of PiL but as a former member of the Sex Pistols.)[26] *The Long Hard Road*, in contrast, attempts to have it both ways by collapsing the traditional boundaries separating the various components of Manson's picaresque performance. Ultimately, Marilyn Manson's picaresque autobiography is not a reflection on his "former" self, despite the fact that *The Long Hard Road* is nothing if not the story of Brian Warner's metamorphosis into Marilyn Manson. Rather, it is the narcissistic act of a "performer" who wants to sit on both sides of the pen simultaneously. In this regard, *The Long Hard Road* is the autobiography of a *pícaro* so infatuated with his own mirror image that his picaresque narration threatens to drown him in a pool of immediate and unrepentant "self-adoration."

Karen Pinkus in her examination of what she calls punk "self-representation" reads the Sex Pistols song "God Save the Queen" (whose lyrics include the refrain "no future for you" and which has thus been generally viewed as an ironic attack on the British monarchy) as a prescient omen related to the punk movement itself, portending the very demise of the avant-garde aesthetic on which it is based: "Punk has no future, not because of any specific condition exterior to the movement, but because it is intrinsically impossible to remain a Punk" (191). What Pinkus means by this is that once the punk movement is "named, known, read, and textualized, it has ceased to live"; that "as soon as the Sex Pistols are, they are finished, even if traces of their presence remain inscribed in photographs, records, accounts of their performances, merchandise, or even in post-Punk bands like PIL" (191). Her analysis of this particular song is extremely insightful—even if it does not specifically mention Lydon's autobiography among the various "traces" left behind by the Sex Pistols—because it highlights the differences between *Rotten* and *The Long Hard Road* (although perhaps not in a way anticipated by Pinkus herself). Johnny Rotten has "no future" because he cannot exist outside the discursive world of the Sex Pistols any more than Lazarillo de Tormes can exist outside the rhetoric of the picaresque text that—like Lydon's—bears his name. As Pinkus rightly notes, it is impossible to remain a punk (just as it is impossible to remain a *pícaro*). Ironically, however, this very fact demonstrates that Johnny Rotten does indeed have a future, even at the moment of articulating this nihilistic "no future" refrain. Johnny Rotten's future lies in becoming the picaresque protagonist of John Lydon's autobiographical backward glance.

The same cannot be said of Marilyn Manson, however, whose narcissistic autobiography strands him within the circular limits of a kind of eternal present. Because Manson sits on both sides of the pen, staring into his own reflection, there is simply nowhere for him to go once his narrative is completed. Johnny Rotten gets up and dusts himself off and then goes on to become (or, better yet, re-become) John Lydon, working-class kid from North London, front man for PiL, and author of *Rotten: No Irish, No Blacks, No Dogs* ("*The Authorized Autobiography* [*of*] *Johnny Rotten and the Sex Pistols*"). At the end of *The Long Hard Road Out of Hell*, however, Marilyn Manson can only become Marilyn Manson. Should he decide at some future date to reclaim his identity as Brian Warner (which his narrative takes great pains to erase), his picaresque autobiography will already have been published by his alter ego, thus depriving him of his own backward glance. Brian Warner may have a future; Marilyn Manson does not. His very performance (as both protagonist and author of *The Long Hard Road*) has stranded him inside a house of mirrors from which he cannot escape. Marilyn Manson has "no future" because the culmination of his narrative is the recounting of his own narrative; a fact that, as Jorge Luis Borges notes in connection to Scheherazade's accidental self-narration in *The Thousand and One Nights*, can strand a storyteller within an infinite narrative loop ("Garden," 97; "El jardín," 111).[27] As soon as he gets to the end, he is immediately back to the beginning. In the last chapter, having clawed his way up out of hell, Manson finds himself right back where he started: at the bottom of Dante's ninth circle (243–44), a place he associates with his childhood bedroom:

> At night my mind struggles desperately to take me back there, to make me feel as if I've never left there, as if my whole life has unfolded in that basement. It places people I've met since then and will meet in the future in that room, and once there, they twist and contort, become monstrous and malevolent. Then my mind blocks the exit, making the crooked wooden staircase impassable. I try to run up the stairs but never make it to the top because hands are grabbing my legs through the slats between steps. (210)

Here, trapped in this hellish subterranean bedroom, this self-proclaimed Antichrist comes to realize—deliberately invoking Friedrich Nietzsche's *Genealogy of Morals* and John Lennon's claim that the Beatles were bigger than Jesus Christ—that he had become "even bigger than Satan" (244). Where Dante finds Lucifer in hell's ultimate pit, Marilyn Manson narcissistically finds himself in the guise of a figure he calls the "reflecting god" (209).

As a "reflecting god," however, Manson does in fact become his own infinite mise-en-abîme. Sensing the metaphysical circularity of this autobiography, Manson and his co-writer, Neil Strauss, attempt to break this vicious (ninth) circle by appending to the text a chapter entitled "fifty million screaming christians can't be wrong" (245–69). This chapter consists of various affidavits, protest letters, and panic-stricken posters juxtaposed (on facing pages) with a "tour diary" of Manson's 1996–97 world tour. However, the problem with this appendix—aside from the fact that it calls itself a "chapter," despite being nothing like the previous fifteen chapters—is that it merely reinscribes the very narrative circularity it is intended to circumvent. It does so in two ways. First, it attempts to articulate a new circle of hell, one not mentioned by Dante ("circle zero: enlightenment" [269]). But since this new Mansonian circle represents the numerical point right before circle one, *The Long Hard Road*'s appendix manages to take us back to the text's point of origin in spite of itself (and despite the fact that the following page attempts to contradict Jean-Paul Sartre's well-known title *No Exit* by recreating the "infernal" diagram from Manson's table of contents page and then appending to it the sentence "There is an exit here" at the deepest point of hell [270]). Furthermore, the "tour diary," like the main body of the text to which it is appended, plots a chronological course that leads inevitably up to the book's point of narration. In fact, the final word of the book's narration (discounting the acknowledgments, photo credits, and fan club address that are appended to the appendix) is "beginning" (269).

Unlike Johnny Rotten, Marilyn Manson is entirely self-contained. And in this crucial distinction we can detect, I think, the difference between Renaissance self-fashioning and its baroque counterpart. (And I say this despite having defined both *Rotten* and *The Long Hard Road* as baroquely postmodern texts throughout this chapter.) Greenblatt's Renaissance man fashions himself through "submission to an absolute power or authority situated at least partially outside the self—God, a sacred book, an institution such as church, court, colonial or military administration" (9); hence, the centrality of "Your Grace" within the narratological structure of the picaresque novel. In other words, *Rotten* reaffirms Michel Foucault's "old interplay between resemblance and signs" by acknowledging a clear distinction between its author and his self-fashioned protagonist (46). *The Long Hard Road*, however, offers no such solace to its author, to its protagonist, or to its reader. Because Manson has untethered himself from his own history—in a rhetorical move not unlike that of the self-imposed "absence" of *Lazarillo*'s anonymous author, or of Quevedo's subtle shift of narratee from "Your Grace" to "the pious reader" over the course of *The Swindler* (209)—he exemplifies Jameson's summation of postmodernism as "an attempt to think the present historically in an age that has forgotten how to think historically in the first place" (ix).[28] Ultimately, Marilyn Manson is perhaps the most postmodern of all *pícaros*; he is a baroquely self-fashioned rogue who exists nowhere except within his own self-inscribed text.

Chapter 3

Chuck Palahniuk,
Narrative Schizophrenia,
and the Cervantine Picaresque

S
ince its first iteration in the middle of the sixteenth century, the discourse of picaresque narrative has filtered its social criticism through the lens of "autobiography." As I note in the previous chapter, works like *Lazarillo de Tormes*, *Guzmán de Alfarache*, and *The Swindler* assume the stance of a written "confession" through which the picaresque narrator apologizes for—and yet at the same time seeks to justify—his prior social deviancy to an authority figure whose capacities seemingly include the power to "absolve" the narrator's youthful indiscretions, allowing the *pícaro* to reintegrate himself fully into an imperial society from which he had once been alienated. This confessional relationship between the first-person narrator and the nameless narratee—vocatively denoted by the term "Your Grace" or other such formal titles—accounts for the basic narratological structure of the picaresque novel. These texts exist from the outset not just as fictional works (similar to any number of stories whose plots are purely imaginative) but as fictitious entities: the picaresque novel masquerades as a genuine "real-world" document (usually a letter) produced by a writer whose words just happen to have been disseminated to a readership far more extensive than the anonymous narratee inscribed within its epistolary parameters. In other words, these texts are self-conscious of their own status as texts and come into being (along with modern literature itself) by drawing the reader's attention to the constructed interrelationship that must necessarily exist between what Martin Buber calls the constitutive "I" and "Thou" of existence. The picaresque "I" cannot exist as a character—much less as a narrator—without the "Thou" to whom it directs itself. This complex interdependence is certainly evident in postmodern texts like John Lydon's *Rotten*, in which the epigraph page pointedly instructs the reader to "Enjoy or die" (xiii), and Marilyn Manson's *Long Hard Road Out of Hell*, which contains a chapter giving the reader sets of rules useful to determine "whether you are a user or an abuser of cocaine, pot and other substances"

(132), or if "you are gay" (134). But it also holds true for a standard baroque text like Francisco de Quevedo's *Swindler*, where a clearly discernable slippage occurs over the course of the novel, as the *pícaro* who starts out addressing himself to the epistolary "Your Grace" ends up speaking directly to the novelesque reader (giving rise to the disquieting suspicion that the voice we hear in the final chapter does not belong to the same discursive entity as the voice we initially heard at the beginning).

Yet even without such authorial slippages, this discursive duality is inherent in all picaresque novels (and indeed, all autobiography), since the rogue who "confesses" the tale is no longer the same rogue who "lived" it. The picaresque has always grounded itself on an essentially divided subjectivity by which the "autobiographical" narrator and his self-recollected protagonist exist as discursive constructs of each other. Thus, the Pablos who innocently goes off to school with Don Diego at the beginning of *The Swindler* is a vastly different person from the effective "cop-killer" who on the final page warns the reader: "But [things] went worse [in America], as they always will for anybody who thinks he only has to move his dwelling without changing his life or ways" (Alpert, 214).[1] Likewise, the Lazarillo we meet in chapter 1 is a child utterly incapable of writing to "Your Grace" (much less understanding the significance of the events he describes), while the Lazarillo who pens this "letter" is a married adult who not only feels compelled to revisit his former childhood self but does so (strangely) to somehow explain away rumors that his wife is having an affair with a local priest. They are simply not the same Lazarillo any more than the teenage Kevin Arnold played by Fred Savage in the television show *The Wonder Years* is the same Kevin as that of the ethereal grown-up voiceover provided by Daniel Stern.

It might be argued, at least in the case of *The Wonder Years*, that hiring two actors to play the same character at different stages of life is simply one of the material exigencies of theatrical, cinematic, or television production. Were Savage to have provided his own voiceover, audiences and critics alike would surely have had difficulty accepting so adolescent a timbre emanating from the throat of an adult supposedly looking back on his childhood. Our willful suspension of disbelief would most certainly have been challenged by this performative singularity. Yet, this is precisely the point. The fact that the producers of *The Wonder Years* felt obliged to employ two different actors—one a preteen and one an adult—demonstrates their recognition that the show actually contained two different Kevins, each discretely separated from the other by a temporal gap that exists within the narrative itself. Somewhere between Kevin's junior high experience and his nostalgic moment of its recollection he becomes a different person, even if Kevin-the-Autobiographer later chooses to elide the events that have transformed Kevin-the-Character into a narrator capable of creating just such a self-portrait. The same is true for the picaresque novel (despite the fact that this inherent duality is not quite as visible or audible as it is on television, where real bodies exert genuine semiotic force). As Roberto González Echevarría notes, "the memorialist must undergo a conversion, must become another to be able to have enough distance from his former self" (60). Each picaresque text contains two simultaneous, yet temporally distinct *pícaros*.

Miguel de Cervantes, who delighted in drawing our attention to the artifices of literary convention (if only to subvert them as a way of underlining their very artificiality), also recognized the inherent duality of the picaresque nearly three hundred years before anyone else even took notice. Thus, in his two picaresque exemplary novels, "Rinconete and Cortadillo" and "The Dogs' Colloquy," Cervantes shrewdly splits his *pícaro* into two distinct characters, each of whom tells his life story not to some external narratee but to his own Borgesian doppelganger. In the first story—which, for reasons that will shortly become apparent, Cervantes has rendered as a traditional third-person narrative—two teenage rogues named Pedro del Rincón and Diego Cortado run into each other one hot summer afternoon at an inn, where they spend a siesta sharing abbreviated versions of their life stories with each other. Immediately following this brief picaresque exchange, they decide to join forces and then proceed to Seville, where they are ultimately inducted into a local crime syndicate whose leader gives them the famous nicknames documented in the story's title. In the second of the *novelas*—which, again for reasons that will become apparent, Cervantes has rendered as a Renaissance dialogue—two dogs named Scipio and Berganza suddenly find that they have acquired the power of speech. To avoid letting such a miraculous gift go to waste, these dogs decide that each should take a turn recounting his life story to the other. Berganza goes first, with Scipio agreeing to take his turn the following night (although we are never actually privy to the second dog's narration because Cervantes suspends this colloquy at the very moment when Berganza finishes his tale at dawn). In both stories, the embedded narrators of these framed autobiographies remain remarkably true to picaresque form—Rinconete, Cortadillo, and Berganza each recount an episodic narrative that focuses on questions of geography, genealogy, deceit, and social criticism—though Cervantes has seen fit to modify the first-person narratological structure so characteristic of the picaresque novel.

By having his picaresque narrators deliberately talk to each other, rather than write an epistle to some extra-textual reader, what Cervantes realizes (in both senses of the word) in each of these innovative texts is not only that the narratee of the traditional picaresque novel—"Your Grace"—is a superfluous entity but that the picaresque narrator should not stoop to address himself to someone so unqualified to judge his autobiography as a nobleman who knows nothing about surviving life on the streets. For the most influential writer of the Spanish baroque, the *pícaro* can be judged only by a jury of his peers, one that turns out to be a singular reflection of himself. In this way, Cervantes's two picaresque exemplary novels subtly suggest that the rogue's "confession" is an entirely self-contained discursive mode; that the "I/Thou" relationship most crucial to this exchange does not exist between servant and master (much less between penitent and priest) but exists between the narrator and himself. In other words, "absolution"—and hence, social reconciliation—can come about only through a symbolic exchange between both halves of the same bifurcated subject. "Rinconete and Cortadillo" and "The Dogs' Colloquy" offer up (albeit obliquely) the radical notion that the *pícaro* actually absolves himself through a narrative act that merely codifies an absolution that has already taken place in the gap between the living of the tale and the telling of the tale; which brings me to Chuck Palahniuk's *Fight Club*.

Published in 1996, *Fight Club* was such a tour de force that plans to option it for a possible feature film began while the novel existed only in galley proofs. The film, directed by David Fincher and based on a screenplay by Jim Uhls, was released by Fox Studios a short three years later. The novel and the film both open with a scene of the autobiographical protagonist (played by Edward Norton in the film) sitting with the barrel of a gun in his mouth. From this point of departure, both texts present a series of flashbacks—and often flashbacks within flashbacks—that explain exactly how this first-person narrator (whom I will call "Jack") came to be in such a precarious situation.[2] Jack, we learn, is an unmarried yuppie who lives in an elegant high-rise apartment decorated with IKEA furniture and who works for a major automobile corporation as a kind of cost/benefit analyst. Jack's job is to determine whether it is cost-effective to recall any given model of defective car by calculating the costs of a recall versus the costs of settling all the liability suits brought by people either injured or killed in crashes.

Jack's major problem in both the novelistic and cinematic texts is that he suffers from terrible insomnia. When Jack complains to his doctor about his plight, the doctor suggests that if Jack wants to see some real suffering he should visit a local support group for victims of testicular cancer. Jack does this and finds the experience so therapeutic that he begins a nightly regimen of visiting all kinds of support groups, where he pretends to suffer from one condition or another, from sickle cell anemia to brain parasites. Along the way, he meets Marla (played by Helena Bonham Carter in the film), who is also a support group addict and who also pretends to have diseases she does not have. (This character—who dresses herself in clothes stolen from a local laundromat and who eats food stolen from Meals-on-Wheels—is a genuine *pícara* worthy of taking her place alongside the female protagonists of *The Picara Justina* and *Teresa de Manzanares* in the pantheon of picaresque heroines.) When Jack confronts Marla about her attendance at all these support groups (calling her a "tourist" without the slightest trace of irony), they agree to divide up the various groups so that neither has to face the other. Jack's statement, "Marla's lie reflects my lie" (23)—which is followed shortly thereafter by a comment regarding the mirror that hangs in Jack's bathroom—is only one of many Cervantine components of Palahniuk's novel and Fincher's film.[3]

The first turning point in the plot occurs when Jack meets a soap sales-man named Tyler Durden (played by Brad Pitt in the film) shortly after waking up from a nap. (In the book Jack meets Tyler on a nude beach; in the film Jack meets Tyler on an airplane during one of his many mind-numbing business trips.) When Jack arrives home from the airport, he dis-covers that his apartment has mysterious exploded (possibly because of a natural gas leak), leaving Jack homeless. In an effort to find a place to spend the night, he first calls Marla but hangs up the moment she answers the phone. He then calls Tyler Durden. The two meet at a local bar, where they drink beer for hours while Jack obliquely tries to elicit an invitation and Tyler patiently waits for Jack to ask the obvious question. When Tyler finally does force Jack to ask if he can move in with him, Tyler responds with a friendly "Yeah" but asks Jack for something in return: "I want you to hit me as hard as you can" (46), a request followed up in the film by a rhetorical question: "How much can you know about yourself if you've never been in a fight?" (00:34:15).

Jack moves into Tyler's rotting, dilapidated Victorian house located on the outskirts of town in what has become a highly industrialized zone. Shortly thereafter, Marla also moves into Tyler's house and becomes Ty-ler's lover, much to the dismay and disgust of Jack. Jack and Tyler's initial fight soon blossoms into a weekly "fight club" whose ever-growing mem-bership of disillusioned young men must follow a set of strict rules written up by Tyler. This seminal fight club, which spawns a whole series of fight clubs across the country, is founded on the ethos of the "Iron John" men's movement of the early 1990s.

> You aren't alive anywhere like you're alive at fight club. When it's
> you and one other guy under that one light in the middle of all those
> watching. Fight club isn't about winning or losing fights. Fight club isn't
> about words. You see a guy come to fight club for the first time, and his
> ass is a loaf of white bread. You see this same guy here six months later,
> and he looks carved out of wood. This guy trusts himself to handle
> anything. (51)

Later, when Tyler transforms this franchise network of fight clubs into what he dubs "Project Mayhem," these Iron Johns (or, better yet, Wooden

Jacks) become the backbone of an underground, anarchistic organization of "service industry terrorists" and "guerrilla waiters" (84) who engage in such subversive activities as urinating in the soups of fancy restaurants, de-magnetizing (and hence erasing) the entire inventory of video rental stores, and placing department store mannequins in compromising positions.

Project Mayhem, like fight club before it, outgrows its modest beginnings and soon becomes a genuine terrorist organization of the first order whose headquarters is located in Tyler's Victorian house, and whose ultimate goal is to blow up several major banks and credit agencies in an attempt to cause the total collapse of the U.S. economy by erasing the debt record and thus returning every person back to some kind of precapitalist square one. The second major turning point in the story occurs when Jack, who has more or less been left out of the loop, finally discovers Tyler's terrorist intentions. He heroically attempts to thwart Tyler's elaborate designs but soon finds himself sitting with a gun in his mouth, as Tyler insists that his goals are worthy, his methods necessary, and his plans unstoppable—a scene that then returns us to the opening segments of the narrative.

Fight Club is both picaresque and Cervantine in a number of overlapping ways. In its broadest conception—as with both *Rotten* and *The Long Hard Road Out of Hell*—it is thematically and aesthetically picaresque if what one refers to with this term is a literary work that focuses primary attention on the most disreputable or marginalized figures in society and that filters its social criticism through the pessimistic lens of dark satire. As José Antonio Maravall rightly notes, the picaresque emerges largely in relation to an "extreme form of antisocial protest and deviant conduct" that "grew at an alarming rate" in the seventeenth century, a social phenomenon whose origins lie in an "increase in misery, vagabondage, and banditry" (*Culture*, 47). In this regard, there is an aesthetic element of chiaroscuro to the picaresque that is as easily discernible in *Fight Club* as it is in *Blade Runner, Trainspotting, Memento*, the *Matrix* trilogy, and any number of other recent postmodern films. Moreover, this dark visual aesthetic parallels what could only be called an "excremental" view of life. As I note in the previous chapter, these squalid texts ooze bodily fluids left and right. In one particularly memorable episode from Quevedo's *Swindler*, Pablos shoots the discharge of an enema that has been forced upon him into the face of the offending nurse who applied it (Alpert, 98). *Trainspotting* contains an unforgettably surrealistic scene in which a heroin addict literally (and I do mean "literally") climbs headfirst into a toilet bowl full of a very opaque brown liquid searching for the hit he dropped; the film shows him fully submerged swimming beneath the surface of the water until he finally comes up—again, headfirst out of the toilet bowl— with the missing object in hand. *Fight Club* itself contains so much visible blood, spittle, and human cellulite (which Tyler Durden renders to make both soap and explosives) that one particularly bloody fight scene had to be trimmed in the film so as not to incur the wrath of British censors. (And this is not to mention all the invisible urine, semen, and other bodily fluids that permeate the text thanks to Palahniuk's cleverly worded innuendos.)

In ideological terms, *Fight Club* can also be called picaresque in large measure because of its function as a platform for its author's social satire. But where texts like *Lazarillo* largely target a morally bankrupt class of priests who seem less interested in caring for their flocks than they do in sexually abusing their young protégés or in defrauding the population of entire villages in order to sell them worthless indulgences, *Fight Club* focuses its criticism on the morally bankrupt class of bourgeois social climbers who spend their mindless days pushing paper back and forth from one corporate cubicle to another and who spend their nights sleeping in tony apartments decorated with all kinds of "global" trinkets. The anticlericalism of baroque Spain has given way to the anticonsumerism of the contemporary United States. Says Jack: "The people I know who used to sit in the bathroom with pornography, now they sit in the bathroom with their IKEA furniture catalogue" (43). In fact, furniture really is the metaphor for the nexus between vacuous consumption and identity in Palahniuk's postmodern world:

> You buy furniture. You tell yourself, this is the last sofa I will ever need in my life. Buy the sofa, then for a couple years you're satisfied that no matter what goes wrong, at least you've got your sofa issue handled. Then the right set of dishes. Then the perfect bed. The drapes. The rug.
>
>   Then you're trapped in your lovely nest, and the things you used to own, now they own you. (44)[4]

In an effort to escape the kind of consumerist entrapment figured above, *Fight Club* demolishes this ethos first by literally blowing up Jack's perfect bourgeois apartment (a rhetorical move reminiscent of the physical destruction that occurs in Egon Wolff's provocative *Paper Flowers* and second by moving Jack into Tyler's decaying house within which he must return to a kind of primal existence bereft of most, if not all, the modern conveniences sold to the American public since the turn of the twentieth century.[5] *Fight Club* thus explores the delicate asymmetrical balance between order and chaos, cleanliness and squalor, soap and explosives (both of which can be made from the same initial recipe). Says Jack: "Maybe self-improvement isn't the answer. [...] Maybe self-destruction is the answer" (49). Or, in the words of Tyler Durden, "Soap and human sacrifice go hand in hand" (75); which is why the ultimate goal of Project Mayhem is the total destruction of civilization: "It's Project Mayhem that's going to save the world. A cultural ice age. A prematurely induced dark age. Project Mayhem will force humanity to go dormant or into remission long enough for the Earth to recover" (125).

If hunger is the prevailing theme of *Lazarillo* and *The Swindler*, cancer is the primary leitmotiv of *Fight Club* (exemplified by the notion of "remission" in the previous quotation). The problem with this leitmotiv, however, is that it is difficult to determine whether Palahniuk thinks it is the Church or the State or the Multinational Corporation that is a cancer on society— with the *pícaro* serving as a kind of subaltern oncologist whose anarchy functions like a radiation treatment designed to challenge the dominance of the parasitical cells—or whether he thinks it is the *pícaro* himself who is the cancerous parasite that must be eradicated to save the body politic. It is no wonder that *Lazarillo*'s unknown author wisely chose to remain anonymous during the time of the Spanish Inquisition, or that critics on both the left and the right have called *Fight Club* "dangerous" either because of its direct attack on consumerism (and hence on capitalism) or because its "vision of liberation and politics relies on gendered and sexist hierarchies that flow directly from the consumer culture that the film claims to be criticizing" (Giroux, 16).

Moving beyond these aesthetic, thematic, and ideological questions, *Fight Club* also engages the Spanish picaresque in its narrative structure. That *Fight Club* exists (in the original novel and the subsequent film) as a first-person autobiographical narrative is hardly enough to label it "picaresque." Still, because *Fight Club* is a story of identity whose narrator essentially says *"I am what I am because of what I was, what I did, and what happened to me"* (Friday, paragraph 8; original emphasis) and because the secondary leitmotiv in this text (after cancer) is the notion of "orphanhood, neglect, and disjunction" (Friday, paragraph 29), it is very hard not to link Jack's autobiography to those of Lazarillo, Pablos, Guzmán, or Marilyn Manson, all of whose narratives invariably begin with a scene of parental abandonment. Consider Jack's description of his early childhood: "Me, I knew my dad for about six years, but I don't remember anything. My dad, he starts a new family in a new town about every six years. This isn't so much like a family as it's like he sets up a franchise. [...] What you see at fight club is a generation of men raised by women" (50). The novel and the film strongly suggest (each in its own way) that Tyler and Marla function as surrogate parents for Jack. The film in particular underlines this parental role at the same time that it reinforces the notion of abandonment by staging a scene reminiscent of the night Jack alludes to when his father left home to set up a new franchise family in some other town. As Jack slips in and out of sleep, Tyler strokes his head and says, "Take care, Champ," and with this, he walks out of the bedroom, not to be seen again until almost the end of the film. As Kevin Alexander Boon argues, the key to *Fight Club*'s nostalgia for violence "is a longing for the father, the source of masculine legacy. Fight club and Project Mayhem seek to recapture the function of the father as the primary male mentor and model for manhood" (273). And this nostalgia for the absent father underpins one of the central philosophical constructs of Palahniuk's text:

> If you're male and you're Christian and living in America, your father is your model for God. And if you never know your father, if your father bails out or dies or is never at home, what do you believe about God? [...] What you end up doing [...] is you spend your life searching for a father and God. (141)

Is it any wonder that Lazarillo has so many masters? Is it any wonder so many of them are priests? Is it any wonder he tells his entire life story to "Your Grace" just for the sake of explaining his wife's sexual indiscretions? Is it any wonder Marilyn Manson becomes a "reflecting god" (209)? The narratee of the picaresque novel ultimately turns out to be God himself.

Where Fincher's film diverges from Palahniuk's novel in this picaresque narrative structure, it does so in a particularly Cervantine way (uncannily mirroring "Rinconete and Cortadillo" and "The Dogs' Colloquy") by splitting its picaresque narrator into two speakers, each of whom tells his story to the other. In the novel, Jack's discussion of his father's abandonment of the family—regularly interrupted by a kind of writerly "voiceover" in which Tyler announces the various rules of fight club—is directed to the reader and hence closely follows the conventions established by Lazarillo, Pablos, and Guzmán. In the film, this discussion takes place during a strangely homoerotic scene in which Jack and Tyler exchange their life stories in the bathroom. Shortly thereafter Jack ironically notes, "Most of the week we were Ozzie and Harriet," unmistakably evoking one of the most heteronormative sitcoms of the twentieth-century and the one perhaps most grieved for by social conservatives who lament that we have become a society "slouching towards Gomorrah" (Bork).[6] Nevertheless, the issue of fathers and sons is prominent in *Fight Club*, as is the notion that the problem with this current generation is that it has been raised by "single mothers," a criticism that could easily have come from the mouth of Robert Bork or William Bennett.

> Tyler: If you could fight anyone, who would you fight?
> Jack: I'd fight my boss, probably.
> Tyler: Really.
> Jack: Yeah, why? Who would you fight?
> Tyler: I'd fight my dad.
> Jack: I don't know my dad. I mean I know him, but he left when I was like six years old. He married this other woman, had a lot of

> kids. He like did this every six years; he goes to a new city and
> starts a new family.

Tyler: Fucker's setting up franchises. [Pause.] My dad never went to
         college so it was real important that I go.

Jack: That sounds familiar.

Tyler: So I graduate. I call him up long distance. I said, "Dad, now
         what?" He says, "Get a job."

Jack: Same here.

Tyler: Now I'm twenty-five. I make my yearly call again, and said,
         "Dad, now what?" He says, "I don't know. Get married."

Jack: I can't get married. I'm a thirty-year-old boy.

Tyler: We're a generation of men raised by women. I'm wondering if
         another woman is really the answer we need. (00:39:27).

The real significance of this scene, especially as it relates to Jack's responses to Tyler in this dialogue, slowly becomes clear as the text unfolds. And what sets up this significance is a crucial instance of Cervantine narrativity that Palahniuk develops in the novel but which is made brilliantly explicit in the film. The turning point that occurs in Cervantes's text (though not the plot) as *Don Quixote* transitions from chapter 8 to chapter 9 of part 1 is the precise moment when Cervantes introduces Cide Hamete Benengeli to the world, a character many see as important a literary creation as Don Quixote himself. In the final paragraph of chapter 8, with Don Quixote in the midst of a fight with the Basque rider, the narrator—who functions as a kind of compiler of legends and histories about Don Quixote—announces that he cannot tell us how this fight turns out because the "author" he is currently glossing claims to be unable to find any further information on the subject. Thus, the narrator of *Don Quixote*—a narrative presence James Parr calls the text's "supernarrator" (11)—"suspends" the action at this point, leaving the reader with an image of the two combatants frozen in time, as they might appear if someone were to "pause" a DVD. Chapter 9, then, begins with perhaps the most original metaliterary moment in all of Western literature. The narrator relates how one afternoon while wandering around the bazaar of Toledo he just happened to find an Arabic manuscript written by a Muslim historian named Cide Hamete Benengeli whose biography of Don Quixote allows the narrator to finish the episode of the "gallant Basque" (1.9:73), unfreezing the fight at the exact moment where the other historian left off.[7] This manuscript also becomes the primary "historical" source on which the rest of *Don Quixote* is supposedly based. And as if to provide one more example of metaliterariness within an already metaliterary moment, Cervantes's narrator then tells us that Cide Hamete's Arabic manuscript contains an illustration of the fight between Don Quixote and the Basque, and that this illustration coincides almost exactly with the narrator's visual image of Don Quixote and his opponent frozen in time: "In the first note-book there was a realistic picture of Don Quixote's battle with the Basque, with both of them in the positions described in the history" (1.9:75).[8]

Compare this metaliterary moment to the metacinematic one that oc-curs in Fincher's film version of *Fight Club* at the moment when Jack and Tyler initiate their first fight. Just as the two are sparring off in preparation to throw their first punches, the film freezes and then cuts away to a differ-ent scene of Jack and Tyler inside a cinema projection booth. The dialogue that follows is delivered directly to the camera:

Jack: Let me tell you a little bit about Tyler Durden. Tyler was a night person. While the rest of us were sleeping, he worked. He had one part-time job as a projectionist. See, a movie doesn't come all on one big reel; it comes on a few. So, someone has to be there to switch the projectors at the exact moment that [one] reel ends and another begins. If you look for it, you can see these little dots come into the upper right-hand corner of the screen. [Tyler points to the upper right corner of the screen just as a dot appears and disappears.]

Tyler: In the industry we call them "cigarette burns."

Jack: That's the cue for a changeover. [Another dot appears in the upper right-hand corner signaling a changeover that *Fight Club* then immediately performs.] He flips the projectors, the movie keeps right on going, and nobody in the audience has any idea.

Tyler: Why would anyone want this shit job?

Jack: Because it affords him other interesting opportunities.

Tyler: Like splicing single frames of pornography into family films [which Tyler has been doing during this entire line of dialogue].

Jack: So when the snooty cat and the courageous dog with the celeb-rity voices meet for the first time in reel three, that's when you'll catch a flash of Tyler's contribution to the film. [The shot moves from the projection booth into the audience where we see a flash of light streaking across the auditorium, along with the strangely puzzled reaction of those watching the film.] Nobody knows that they saw it, but they did.

Tyler: Nice, big cock.

Jack: Even a hummingbird couldn't catch Tyler at work. (00:32:21)

This metacinematic scene flows into the next scene as Jack continues to tell us about Tyler's other part-time job as a banquet waiter in a luxury hotel. This new scene shows Tyler urinating into a terrine of soup while Jack informs us that Tyler "was *the* guerrilla terrorist of the food service industry" (00:33:49). In both Palahniuk's novel and Fincher's film, these metaliterary and metacinematic moments set up the kind of mischief later propagated upon society by the so-called space monkeys of Project Mayhem before this group turns genuinely destructive. But within the film itself, this extended scene—in which the actors speak directly into the camera and thus establish with the audience the kind of narrator/ narratee confessional relationship central to the picaresque—also sets up an essential metacinematic moment that is crucial to an appreciation of *Fight Club*'s Cervantine logic.

And with this, *Fight Club*'s famous "secret" suddenly becomes insidiously apparent (a secret that I deliberately elide until now): Jack and Tyler Durden are actually one and the same person. Jack is schizophrenic and Tyler is his alter ego, one of (possibly many) split personalities who emerge when this "insomniac" falls asleep. Says Jack on one particular page of the novel (without realizing his own irony): "If you can wake up in a different place. If you can wake up in a different time. Why can't you wake up as a different person?" (157). The final major turning point of the text, then, comes when Jack finally realizes in a moment of Sophoclean anagnorisis— when he suddenly remembers doing all the things Tyler has supposedly been doing—that it is possible to wake up as a different person. Yet, even if this point is not made explicit until quite late in the text, there are numerous clues embedded for the discerning readers of the novel and viewers of the film (and with particular regard to the film, the metacinematic moment I described earlier sets up one of the keys to breaking this code). In the novel, for example, Jack's oft-repeated statement, "I know this because Tyler knows this" is a telling leitmotiv, alerting perceptive readers to the reality of Jack's psychological situation. The same is true for statements such as: "At the hospital, Tyler tells them I fell down. Sometimes, Tyler speaks for me. I did this to myself" (52).[9]

In Fincher's film, however, Tyler Durden does not appear as a genuine character for almost twenty minutes. And when he does appear, it is at the precise moment when Jack says his line about waking up as a different person (which Jim Uhls's screenplay has front-loaded). This moment of Tyler's formal introduction into the film occurs halfway through a montage showing a seemingly endless string of Jack's business trips, on top of which Jack delivers the following voiceover narrative:

You wake up at SeaTac. SFO. LAX. You wake up at O'Hare. Dallas/Fort Worth. BWI. Pacific. Mountain. Central. Lose an hour; gain an hour. This is your life. And it's ending one minute at a time. You wake up at Air Harbor International. If you wake up at a different time, in a different place, could you wake up as a different person? Everywhere I travel: tiny life. Single-serving sugar, single-serving cream, single pat of butter. The microwave cordon bleu hobby kit. Shampoo/conditioner combos, sample-packaged mouthwash, tiny bars of soap. The people I meet on each flight, they're single-serving friends. Between take-off and landing we have our time together, but that's all we get. (00:19:10).

Two important moments occur during this combination of visual montage and audio voiceover. The first occurs, as previously noted, at the moment when Jack says his line about "waking up as a different person." Here, Tyler Durden suddenly passes behind Jack while standing on a moving sidewalk inside one of Jack's anonymous airports. Significantly, as Tyler enters our field of vision the camera pans from Jack to Tyler as a way of deliberately shifting our focus to suggest what is really going on in the film. The second moment is just as significant but is a bit more difficult to spot. At the very end of this montage, Jack is shown sitting on a bed in yet another anonymous hotel room, watching the hotel's in-house television channel. As Jack says his final voiceover line, a commercial for the hotel's restaurant shows Tyler standing among the rest of the hotel's banquet waiters. Given what we ultimately learn about Jack and Tyler's shared identity, this fleeting image of Tyler on the television screen functions as a mirror for Jack (who somehow neither recognizes his own image nor remembers filming this commercial during one of his somnambulistic part-time jobs) and also evokes a significant scene from Stanley Kubrick's 1980 cinematic treatment of Stephen King's novel *The Shining* in which Jack Nicholson's image appears in a (relatively) ancient photograph hanging on the wall behind a hotel bar Nicholson's character has been frequenting throughout the film. And the atemporal duality of both these texts uncannily evokes Carlos Fuentes's 1962 novel *Aura* in which the protagonist finds himself trapped inside the house of an old widow only to discover his own face staring out at him from within her old photographs.

The scene in *Fight Club* that immediately follows this montage is the one in which Jack first meets Tyler on board the aircraft, assuming that he is just another "single-serving friend." But the brief image of Tyler Durden hidden in the television commercial is important because it represents the culmination of a series of images of subliminal Tylers that have been embedded in Fincher's *Fight Club* itself—and hence into our consciousness as viewers—since the beginning. And these images have been embedded in almost the same way that Tyler's single frames of pornography are inserted into the family-friendly movie; which is to say, *Fight Club*'s editors have digitally inserted transitory "flashes" of Tyler Durden into other scenes. But where Tyler's placement of this guerrilla cinematography may be random, the occurrence of *Fight Club*'s subliminal Tylers is not. The first subliminal Tyler occurs just four minutes into the film during a scene in which an exhausted Jack describes (again, through a voiceover) the symptoms of his persistent insomnia while making photocopies at work. Tyler's fleeting image standing next to the copy machine appears briefly just as Jack says, "With insomnia nothing's real. Everything's far away. Everything's a copy of a copy of a copy" (00:03:58). The second subliminal Tyler appears some two minutes later, standing right beside Jack's doctor when the physician suggests that, if Jack wants to really see people in pain, he should visit a testicular cancer support group (00:06:18). The third subliminal Tyler occurs about one minute later, when the testicular cancer support group leader tells the participants to find a partner for what he calls "one-on-ones" (which turns out to be quite a telling turn of phrase in hindsight). Here Tyler pops up standing next to the group leader with his arm around his shoulder (00:07:33). The fourth subliminal Tyler occurs about five minutes after this, when Jack encounters Marla for the very first time (which is one of the many pieces of evidence that suggests that perhaps Marla is also one of Jack's split personalities). In this fourth appearance, the film superimposes a fleeting image of Tyler on top of Marla just as Jack watches her walk down a dark sidewalk (00:12:35).

What each of these subliminal images implies is that Tyler is an integral part of Jack's symptom long before he makes his explicit appearance. They represent links in a chain of ongoing clues that alert the astute reader/viewer to the true nature of Jack and Tyler's relationship. But there is something else going on here besides just teasing the viewer. Significantly, the fourth subliminal Tyler pops up immediately following the scene in which Jack recognizes Marla as his mirror image: "Her lie reflected my lie" (00:12:12). These inserted flashes of Tyler cannot be understood in isolation. The subliminal Tylers that furtively announce his arrival long before it happens are but "single-serving" signs within an entire system of mirror imagery and reflection that permeates *Fight Club* (particularly Fincher's film) from start to finish. In the cinematic scene where Jack first meets Tyler on the airplane (in which Jack ironically remarks that he and Tyler have the exact same briefcase), Tyler gives Jack a copy of his business card (Figure 6). Close inspection of this card reveals that the central image is of two identical, winged angels (or perhaps devils, since the scroll work suggests they might have tails) staring into each other's eyes across an urn (00:27:44). A vertical line that passes between their profiled faces suggests that each may, in fact, be staring into a mirror at his own reflection. And this reflective imagery is echoed toward the end of the film when Tyler reappears to Jack—as I note earlier, he abandons Jack for a time—just as Jack is on the verge of figuring out who Tyler Durden really is (Figure 7).[10] In this recognition scene, Tyler and Jack sit face-to-face in a hotel room while Tyler carefully explains that the two are actually one and the same (01:54:16). Or is it, that the one-and-the-same is actually two? Given their discursive mirroring, can we even distinguish between these two questions?

Figure 6: Tyler Durden's business card—which contains an image of two figures staring at each other as if each were looking into a mirror—suggests Tyler's true identity as Jack's alter ego. (*Fight Club*, 20th Century Fox, 1999)

In his essay "Symbolic Exchange and Death," Jean Baudrillard argues that "duality" is the central organizing structure of all "singular" systems:

> In all domains, diapoly is the highest stage of monopoly. It is not political will that breaks the monopoly of the market [...]; it is the fact that every unitary system, if it wants to survive, has to evolve a *binary* system of *regulation*. [...] From the tiniest disjunctive unities (the question/answer particle) to the macroscopic level of systems of alternation that preside over the economy, politics, and global coexistence, the matrix does not vary: it is always 0/1, the binary scansion that affirms itself as the metastable or homoeostatic form of contemporary systems. [...] Why does the World Trade Center in New York City have *two* towers? (146; original emphasis)

Plus and minus, 0 and 1, on and off, angels and devils, Jack and Tyler; each member of each of these pairings depends on the other for its very existence. To paraphrase Palahniuk, "individually, they are nothing" (134). So it is for Rinconete and Cortadillo or Scipio and Berganza. Each without the other is discursively impossible. Yet, can we say that these pairings are actually stable? Baudrillard seems to think so (or at least thought so before 9/11), but Palahniuk's novel and Fincher's film suggest (each in its own way) that this entire binary system is not only volatile but actually prone to collapse; which is to say, duopoly may be the highest stage of monopoly, but entropy is still the governing principle.

In this Cervantine reading of *Fight Club* I have essentially been arguing that the relationship between Jack and Tyler is analogous to the rela-

Figure 7: In a scene that mirrors Tyler's business card, Tyler and Jack sit face-to-face in a hotel room as Jack realizes that the two are actually one and the same person. (*Fight Club*, 20th Century Fox, 1999)

tionship between Rinconete and Cortadillo and Scipio and Berganza because of the way each of these bifurcated rogues engages in a picaresque dialogue with the other. With Jack and Tyler, however, this "dialogue" has consisted of a violent conversation of bare-knuckle blows (sometimes delivered just for the fun of it; sometimes delivered as part of a strategic plan; sometimes delivered because of a genuine disagreement between the two). And once we come to realize that Jack and Tyler are the same person, Tyler's initial question to Jack ("How much can you know about yourself if you've never been in a fight?") takes on new meaning. The often-violent picaresque dialogue of *Fight Club* is really a voyage of self-discovery. But, then, is this not also true of the narratives constructed by Lazarillo, Pablos, and Guzmán? Moreover, the central struggle in *Fight Club* is not simply for physical control of the body Jack and Tyler share but for authorial control of the autobiography they cohabit. Jack cannot narrate an action Tyler does not perform, and Tyler cannot perform an action Jack does not narrate. And in this light the importance of the final scene of Fincher's film comes into view (which, of course, brings us back full circle to the opening scene).

Having engaged in an extremely violent confrontation, in which Tyler has thrown Jack down a flight of stairs after Jack discovers Tyler's plot to blow up several major office towers, Jack regains consciousness only to find himself sitting in a chair on one of the upper floors of a skyscraper with Tyler holding a gun in his mouth. Once Tyler removes the gun from Jack's mouth, the two deliver a short exchange of self-referential dialogue in which Jack notes that the film has returned to its opening shot and Tyler accuses Jack of shamelessly indulging in "flashback humor" (02:09:49). Tyler then directs Jack's attention toward the imminent collapse of the various buildings on view outside the windows, whereupon Jack is startled to see Marla on the street below—despite his having sent her away to safety—in the menacing custody of several of Tyler's "space monkeys." Recognizing the immediate volatility of a situation he has unwittingly created, Jack attempts to talk Tyler out of his explosive plans:

Jack: I'm begging you. Please don't do this.
Tyler: "I" am not doing this, "we" are doing this. This is what we want.
Jack: No, I don't want this.
Tyler: Right. Except "you" is meaningless now. We have to forget about you.
Jack: Jesus. Your voice in my head.
Tyler: Your voice in mine.
Jack: You're a fucking hallucination. Why can't I get rid of you?
Tyler: You need me.
Jack: No, I don't. I really don't anymore.
Tyler: Hey, you created me. I didn't create some loser alter ego to make myself feel better. Take some responsibility.
Jack: I do. I am responsible for all of it and I accept that. So please, I am begging you, please call this off.
Tyler: Have I ever let us down? How far have you come because of me? [Pause.] I will bring us through this. As always, I will carry you kicking and screaming, and in the end you will thank me.
Jack: I am grateful to you, for everything that you've done for me. But this is too much. I don't want this.
Tyler: What do you want? You want to go back to the shit job? To the fucking condo world watching sitcoms? Fuck it! I won't do it! (02:10:34)

Unable to reason with Tyler, Jack slowly comes to the realization that, given Tyler's unequivocal defiance, his only hope is to solve the problem himself:

Jack: [To himself] I can figure this out. I can figure this out. This isn't even real. You're not real. The gun isn't . . . the gun isn't in your hand. The gun is in my hand.
Tyler: [Discovering that the gun is now in Jack's hand] Hey, good for you. It doesn't change a thing. [Suddenly seeing that Jack has decided to point the gun at his own chin] Why do you want to put a gun to your head?
Jack: Not *my* head, Tyler, *our* head.
Tyler: Interesting. Where are you going with this IKEA boy? [Jack cocks the gun.] Hey. It's you and me. Friends.

Figure 8: After coming to the realization that he cannot defeat Tyler by fighting against him, Jack turns the gun on himself in a final attempt to kill off his alter ego. (*Fight Club*, 20th Century Fox, 1999)

Jack: Tyler, I want you to really listen to me.
Tyler: Okay.
Jack: My eyes are open. (02:12:00)

As Jack says his final line (which clearly echoes sentiments expressed by both Lazarillo and Pablos during their own moments of epiphany), he puts the gun into his own mouth and pulls the trigger. Jack falls back into his chair, blood running down his neck from a gaping wound in the side of his face, while the camera shows an enormous exit wound in the back of Tyler's head (Figure 8). Smoke comes out of Tyler's mouth as he says his final line, "What's that smell?" after which he falls to the floor and then disappears. Marla arrives shortly thereafter, furious that Jack/Tyler has brought her back once again into the situation. But her anger turns to sympathy when she sees Jack's bleeding face. The two experience a moment of romantic reconciliation just as a series of explosions outside the large window behind them cause the collapse of several office buildings, the last two of which—although existing as part of the Fox Studios complex in the Century City section of Los Angeles—bear an unsettling resemblance for post-9/11 viewers to the "twin towers" of the World Trade Center in New York City.[11]

In Palahniuk's penultimate chapter this scene actually takes place in Jack's bedroom, in which one telling item is missing: "The mirror is gone" (202). Jack's evocation of the mirror at this point in the narrative is significant because its noted absence functions as an ironic reference to the very present Tyler Durden who stands opposite Jack. More importantly, however, this reflective evocation underlines the central Cervantine mo-

tif at play within the text. In *Don Quixote* the climax of part 2 revolves
around Don Quixote's two-fold confrontation with his own mirror image
in the guise of Sansón Carrasco, the Bachelor of Salamanca. We first meet
Sansón in chapter 3 of part 2 when he comes to Don Quixote's house to
inform him of his newfound fame as the subject of a recently published
book entitled *The Ingenious Hidalgo Don Quixote de la Mancha* (as Cervantes's first part was actually titled). When Don Quixote's friends and
family cannot dissuade the mad knight from sallying forth a third time,
Sansón offers to bring Don Quixote back home on the theory that by de-
feating the old man in "battle" he can force Don Quixote to come to his
senses. Accordingly, the first of what turn out to be two encounters between Sansón and Don Quixote occurs in chapters 12 through 15 when
Sansón fights as the "Knight of the Mirrors" (2.14:575).[12] The second encounter occurs near the end of part 2 when Sansón returns in the guise
of the "Knight of the White Moon" (2.64:926), another clearly reflective
symbol. During the first of these two jousts, Don Quixote quite unexpectedly defeats Sansón. During the second joust (which the Bachelor seems to
undertake more as a personal vendetta than as an attempt to bring Don
Quixote back home) Sansón defeats Don Quixote. And this unexpected
defeat shocks Don Quixote so deeply that he abandons his assumed persona and soon dies, not as the chivalric "Knight of the Lions" (2.17:597)[13]
but as the saintly "Alonso Quixano the Good" (2.74:978).[14]

As it turns out, *Fight Club* uncannily mirrors this twofold confrontation. Both the novel and the film come down to a final scene in which Jack
and Tyler, who look "more and more like identical twins" (114) engage in
their ultimate fight. And when we consider that the previous two hundred
pages or the previous two hours of film footage have consisted of nothing
but flashbacks, this final scene is really all there is: it is the present tense of
the narration. (But then, again, so are the narratives of Lazarillo, Pablos,
and Guzmán.) What happens in this final confrontation is that Jack-the-
Narrator understands that the only way to take charge of his narrative is
to annihilate Tyler-the-Character. We have seen something like this before
in Miguel de Unamuno's *Mist* (*Niebla*). But whereas Unamuno vanquishes
his impertinent character, Augusto Pérez, by killing him off directly, Jack
can obliterate Tyler only by turning the gun on himself.[15] This is a unique
narratological twist. But it is indicative of what actually happens in almost
all picaresque novels (at least figuratively) starting with *Lazarillo*. To reconcile himself with society, not only must the picaresque narrator establish
a temporal distance between his current self and his former self but he
must obliterate that former self entirely, which is, arguably, the ultimate
project of the picaresque novel. By narrating the events of a life now abandoned—especially because that narration often includes meta-commentary
on why such a life was morally repugnant in the first place—the picaresque
narrator announces to the world that his previous life is now over, that it is

complete, that his former self is actually dead. The picaresque novel can be read as an obituary—or, better yet, as an elaborate suicide note—in which the narrator essentially says to the narratee: "I am no longer the rogue I once was. Through this act of narration I not only announce the death of my former self, I perform that death." (Again, it is no mere coincidence that John Lydon does not write under the nom de plume "Johnny Rotten" or that he both begins and ends his autobiography with a discussion of the demise of the Sex Pistols.)

This act of "narrative suicide" is precisely what happens in Robert Louis Stevenson's *Strange Case of Dr Jekyll and Mr Hyde*, another text in which duality and narrative control feature prominently (and one that clearly informs both Palahniuk's novel and Fincher's film).[16] Stevenson's text narrates the tale of a stereotypically Romantic "mad scientist" whose pharmacological experimentation with what he calls the "profound duplicity of life" goes badly awry (55). Mr. Hyde, like Victor Frankenstein's monster before him, wreaks havoc on those unsuspecting and unfortunate individuals who happen to cross his path, ultimately bringing about the downfall of his creator. And while this tale is largely told through the voice of an omniscient third-person narrator whose focus is primarily on the character of Mr. Utterson, its final chapter consists of a first-person confession profoundly indebted to the Spanish picaresque. "Henry Jekyll's Full Statement of the Case" (55), like *Lazarillo*, passes itself off as a written document intended to be read not by the real author's ultimately exterior readers but by an internal fictitious narratee—in this case Mr. Utterson—to whom the first-person narrator directs his text. And as with *Lazarillo*, *Guzmán*, and *The Swindler*, this final autobiographical chapter begins with the very birth of the narrator himself and justifies an entire life that unfolds from this point of departure up through to the moment of the confession's composition.

The turning point of *Jekyll and Hyde*'s autobiographical confession comes when its narrator finally realizes that he must put aside the identity he has established as his self-narrated protagonist in favor of a morally superior one: "I chose the better part [and] preferred the elderly and discontented doctor, [bidding] a resolute farewell to the liberty, the comparative youth, the light step, leaping pulses and secret pleasures, that I had enjoyed in the disguise of Hyde" (63); "I resolved in my future conduct to redeem the past, and I can say with honesty that my resolve was fruitful of some good" (65). Still, as Jekyll himself notes, the curse of what he calls the "duality of purpose" cannot be so easily removed simply by seeking to repress the alter ego that constitutes one's former self. Thus, like *Fight Club*, "Henry Jekyll's Full Statement of the Case" is as much about narrative control as it is about duality, and its climax—again, like *Fight Club*—comes when the narrator finally realizes that he and his self-recollected protagonist can no longer share the same text:

> The hatred of Hyde for Jekyll, was of a different order. His terror of the
> gallows drove him continually to commit temporary suicide, and return
> to his subordinate station of a part instead of a person [...]. But his love
> of life is wonderful; I go further: I, who sicken and freeze at the mere
> thought of him, when I recall the abjection and passion of this attach-
> ment, and when I know how he fears my power to cut him off by suicide,
> I find it in my heart to pity him. (69)

The great difference in Stevenson's text, however, is that Mr. Hyde actually
wins the battle; Dr. Jekyll is forced by Hyde's persistent and overwhelming presence to announce in his first-person confession not the death of his
alter ego but the death of the narrator himself: "Will Hyde die upon the
scaffold? or will he find the courage to release himself at the last moment?
God knows; I am careless; *this is my true hour of death*, and what is to
follow concerns another than myself. Here then, as I lay down the pen and
proceed to seal up my confession, I bring the life of that unhappy Henry
Jekyll to an end" (70; my emphasis).

The problem with *Fight Club*, however, is that Jack somehow manages to survive his own suicide, thus unwittingly deconstructing Ginés de
Pasamonte's argument that an autobiography cannot outlast the life span
of its narrator: "Of course, when I pulled the trigger, I died" (206). In part
1, chapter 22 of *Don Quixote*, Ginés—the most violent member of a chain
gang of convicts liberated by the mad knight—brags about his status as the
picaresque author of *The Life of Ginés de Pasamonte*, a work he claims is
superior even to *Lazarillo de Tormes*. And when asked if he has finished
writing this autobiography, Ginés shrewdly replies: "How can I have finished it [...] if my life hasn't finished yet?" (1.22:182).[17] In contrast, *Fight
Club*'s last chapter consists of Jack's description of heaven. Yet, as it turns
out, "heaven" unexpectedly resembles a mental institution; while God, sitting on his divine throne, bears all the hallmarks of a staff psychiatrist.
The novel's final scene consists of a conversation between Jack and one of
heaven's many angels, who quietly leans over to him and says, "We miss
you Mr. Durden. [...] Everything's going according to the plan. [...] We're
going to break up civilization so we can make something better out of the
world. [...] We look forward to getting you back" (208). This exchange,
with its promise of an imminent resurrection, merely reinscribes Jack into
another dualistic existence. He both is and is not dead. He both is and is
not Tyler Durden. Because successful Hollywood movies are in constant
need of happy endings, Fincher's film ultimately forces Jack to reconcile
with Marla, a discursive resolution that clearly implies that the two will
live happily ever after. Jack simply slips from one binary relationship to
another: as Tyler drops dead and disappears, Marla immediately steps in
to fill the gap left behind by Jack's now-defunct alter ego. (But, again, as I
have noted, Marla may very well be one of Jack's split personalities herself,

in which case the symptom merely continues into the hypothetical sequel.) Perhaps Baudrillard is right after all; perhaps the system must always reconfigure itself binarily. Palahniuk and Fincher are certainly trying to have it both ways.

This does not explain, however, what happens in "Rinconete and Cortadillo" and "The Dogs' Colloquy." Having intuited the binary and schizophrenic logic inherent in the picaresque, Cervantes—it seems—has also grasped its fundamental limitation: that a mirror image and its inverse reflection cancel each other out (in much the same way that matter and antimatter annihilate each other). What Cervantes understands is that all balanced equations equal zero (if not now, then sometime down the road). Thus, what he does is simply keep his *pícaros* off balance. In "Rinconete and Cortadillo" he does this first by refusing to give them pride of place within the narrative, by which I mean he tells their stories through a third-person narrator who allows them to narrate their own autobiographies only when he (or she) sees fit. Moreover, once the two boys arrive at Monipodio's patio, they very quickly cease to function as the protagonists they once were, despite what their prominence within the story's title might suggest. At that point, "Rinconete and Cortadillo" really becomes the story of characters like Cariharta, Maniferro, and Gananciosa. As protagonists, Rinconete and Cortadillo, though far from annihilated, are greatly reduced to being just two more characters among many. Cervantes's strategy in "The Dogs' Colloquy" is even more audacious. In the first place, where Palahniuk suggests two explanations for Jack's function as a narrator (that is, his confession is either a heavenly missive or the ramblings of a raving lunatic), Cervantes suggests three possible explanations for Scipio and Berganza's narrative capacities: (1) these dogs can talk thanks to some kind of unexplained divine providence; (2) they can talk because they are actually the human offspring of a witch whose twin babies were transformed into puppies by another witch, and who are now in the process of becoming human again because the conditions of the original curse have largely been fulfilled; or (3) they can talk because they exist as nothing more than the figment of a sick man's feverish delusions.[18] By not giving his reader a simple "either/or" choice, Cervantes ensures that even if two of these explanations somehow cancel each other out, a third will remain to carry the day. Where most picaresque narratives attempt to create some kind of narrative closure (like that produced by the structural circularity of *Rotten* and *The Long Hard Road Out of Hell*), Cervantes denies us this sense of completion by deliberately refusing to end his dogs' colloquy. Berganza finishes his picaresque narration just as the sun comes up; Scipio promises to relate his own picaresque autobiography the following night (provided that his magical capacity for speech remains intact). This marks the formal end of the story, even as it sets up a narrative sequence that never materializes. So long as the sun of that day never sets, Scipio's autobiography remains an immanent possibility. So long as night never falls, there is no chance that Scipio's narrative will annihilate that of his reflective counterpart. It is no wonder that Ginés de Pasamonte flatly refuses to finish his own picaresque autobiography. Like Cervantes, he knows that any genuine ending can mean only one thing. And he's having too much wicked fun as the book's protagonist to let his other half wipe him out with a narrative confession. Unlike the now-deceased Tyler Durden (or is it the now-deceased Jack and the now-committed Tyler Durden?), Ginés knows the value of asymmetry in forestalling death.

Chapter 4

John Lasseter's *Toy Story*
as Postmodern *Don Quixote*

Since its publication nearly four centuries ago, Miguel de Cervantes's *Don Quixote* has given rise to numerous imitators, ranging from the unauthorized 1614 "Alonso Fernández de Avellaneda" sequel to the early 1990s television cartoon *Don Coyote and Sancho Panda*, while his famous knight-errant has become a well-recognized archetype within the Western tradition. Indeed, the title character's effluence is so complete that he shares with only a limited number of literary protagonists (among them Oedipus and Faust) the high honor of engendering an English adjective. That we can speak of a "quixotic" endeavor—that the expression "tilting at windmills" is as immediately meaningful to contemporary readers as the various ballad verses Cervantes inserted into his own novel were for readers of his day—demonstrates how thoroughly "Don Quixote" has become an indispensable sign within our cultural lexicon. Sancho Panza's suggestion that Cervantes's masterpiece (along with its characters) is "so well-thumbed and well-perused and well-known by all kinds of people that as soon as they see a skinny nag pass by they say: 'Look, there goes Rocinante'" (2.3:507) is as true today as it was four hundred years ago, except that today Sancho's spindly master (literary cousin of Ichabod Crane) and not his master's hack is likely to generate this kind of reaction on the horseless streets of the twenty-first century.[1]

Don Quixote's widespread renown has occurred for a variety of reasons, not the least of which is that almost immediately upon its publication Cervantes's novel was translated into numerous languages. A recent panel of contemporary authors—including Salman Rushdie, Nadine Gordimer, Carlos Fuentes, V. S. Naipaul, Wole Soyinka, Nawal El Saadawi, and Norman Mailer—voted *Don Quixote* the "best book of all time" (Chrisafis). This claim may or may not be empirically verifiable, but it does demonstrate the impact Cervantes has had on world literature; which is to say, even those who cannot identify Cervantes as the author of *Don Quixote* know enough about the novel's protagonist to achieve some level of what E. D. Hirsch calls "cultural literacy" on the topic (1). Many people—even those who readily admit to never having read *Don Quixote*—can say something about the windmills episode. Likewise, others understand the phrase "the impossible dream" even when they have only a vague awareness of its provenance. If Cervantes can truly be said to have written one of the most influential books in Western literature, he has received an enormous amount of recent help (at least within the Anglo-American context of the Unites States and Canada) from Dale Wasserman, Joe Darion and Mitch Leigh, whose 1965 Broadway musical—and subsequent 1972 film—*Man of La Mancha* has been the primary vehicle for making Cervantes's discourse part of the cultural memory of contemporary English-speakers.

Consider its impact on Terry Gilliam (to name just one prominent example). During an interview with Salman Rushdie conducted at the twenty-ninth annual Telluride Film Festival in connection with a screening of Keith Fulton and Louis Pepe's *Lost in La Mancha* (which documents the stunning collapse of Gilliam's visionary cinematic adaptation of *Don Quixote*), Rushdie asks Gilliam about his interest in Cervantes's novel. After a brief digression in which the two discuss (somewhat sardonically) the naming of *Don Quixote* as "the greatest work of art of all time," Gilliam states that, while he had never actually read the novel until the early 1990s (when he claims to have started thinking about making *The Man Who Killed Don Quixote*), "the story has always been basic to [his] view of the world" (Gilliam). Indeed, Gilliam's entire body of cinematic work has a kind of Cervantine quality about it, from his own parodic treatment of the medieval romances of chivalry in *Monty Python and the Holy Grail* to his recapitulation of the Quixote myth in *The Fisher King* to his exploration of madness, illusion, and reality in *Twelve Monkeys*. And "like most people," Gilliam admits, his acquisition of this Cervantine worldview came about largely through *Man of La Mancha*, and specifically through Peter O'Toole's performance of "The Impossible Dream (The Quest)."

Among the more recent works to borrow from this Cervantine worldview are the commercially successful and (at the time of their release) technically innovative Walt Disney/Pixar films *Toy Story* (1995) and *Toy Story 2* (1999), where the literary genre providing the context for the central character's delusions is not that of the medieval romances of chivalry but rather the movies, television shows, and video games of twentieth-century juvenile science fiction. The central conceit of these films—both of which were written, produced, and directed by John Lasseter, co-founder of Pixar Animation Studios—is the well-worn notion that inanimate objects, particularly toys, come to life when humans are not looking at them and that these occasionally animate figures carry on an existence independent of their functional relationship to the human world. (In this regard, Lasseter's *Toy Story* films hearken back, at least thematically, to such precursors as E. T. A. Hoffman's *Nutcracker* and Glen MacDonough's *Babes in Toyland*.) *Toy Story* focuses primarily on the character of Buzz Lightyear (Tim Allen), a high-tech action figure—the "star" gift of Andy's birthday party—who unexpectedly enters the world of "Andy's bedroom" and in doing so upsets the delicate balance of power the other toys have established. Particularly annoyed by Buzz's sudden arrival on the scene is Woody (Tom Hanks), a low-tech cowboy doll who worries not only that Buzz will challenge his authority as the de facto "manager" of the entire bedroom staff but that this shiny newcomer will replace him as Andy's "favorite toy." In typical Disney fashion, Woody imprudently engineers Buzz's expulsion from the bedroom only to discover too late the value of true friendship. This recognition leads to a search and rescue mission though which Andy's entire menagerie of playthings work together to save Buzz from a fate worse than death—becoming a "lost toy"—and the film achieves its requisite happy ending when all the toys have finally been re-united and reconciled.

Toy Story 2, which focuses primarily on Woody, is a somewhat darker film that deepens its exploration of death by suggesting that becoming a "lost toy" is less of an existential concern than becoming an "unloved" one. In this narrative, an unethical toy dealer named Al (Wayne Knight) steals Woody in order to sell him to a Japanese toy museum where Woody is promised eternal fame as part of an exhibit of vintage toys, but only in exchange for forever losing contact with Andy. This offer creates a real dilemma for Woody. Having already been supplanted by Buzz as Andy's favorite toy, Woody now has a chance, through Al's act of thievery, to resume his position of centrality, even if only inside a glass box high on a pedestal. When Woody ultimately decides to try to escape, however, pre-ferring to return to be with his friends in Andy's bedroom, his escape is sabotaged by another doll whose own entry into the toy museum depends on Woody's centrality within the collection. As with the first film, *Toy Story 2* culminates with a rescue mission in which Buzz and the rest of Andy's toys save Woody just seconds before his airplane takes off for Ja-pan. And again, this predictably happy ending suggests that friendship is the most important and ultimately enduring value.

As with Gilliam's films, Lasseter's *Toy Story* and *Toy Story 2* have ab-sorbed much of the discourse of *Don Quixote*, particularly through *Man of La Mancha*. This does not mean, however, that they should be mis-taken for mere flattering imitations of Cervantes's imaginative creations (as was, say, the short-lived character "Donkey Hote" in the long-running PBS children's program *Mister Rogers' Neighborhood*). As "emulations" that approach an almost Bloomian "misprision" (Bloom, *Anxiety*, 14), rather than "renditions" that simply attempt to recapitulate a precursor, *Toy Story* and its sequel have their own thematic agendas, their own dis-tinct narrative structures, and their own particular webs of intertextu-ality. Eric Bateman, for instance, describes the first film as "The Wild, Wild West meets Brave New World, two places that, it turns out, are more similar than they appear" and notes that Buzz's introduction into Andy's bedroom evokes a familiar western trope: "The most dependable motif of the western is the arrival of a stranger, whose function is to disrupt the established order" (83). This western motif plays itself out in the first installment as *Toy Story*'s two protagonists tussle, argue, and eventually come to blows in a running battle for supremacy. Woody's attempt to knock Buzz behind a desk (where he will presumably be lost forever) demonstrates the kind of childish impulses we might expect to find in a child's toy while reenacting what Richard Slotkin calls the western's penchant for "regeneration through violence." Still, whether deliberately or through some kind of latent cultural intuition, Lasseter's films engage Cervantes's masterpiece in an intertextual dialogue, thus supplying contemporary viewers with a compelling postmodern reading of the best known of all the texts of the Spanish baroque.[2]

The most obvious way in which the first of the two films integrates the discourse of the novel is through character transference. Don Quixote has "morphed" (to use the terminology of children's television programs like the *Mighty Morphin' Power Rangers*) into Buzz Lightyear, a science fiction toy who refuses to accept his status as such and insists—all evidence to the contrary—that he is a genuine "space ranger." As in *Don Quixote*, Buzz constantly (perhaps deliberately) misreads reality in an attempt to play this self-assigned role. Sancho Panza has become the rustic (although admittedly very thin) Woody, who serves as a foil for Buzz, and who, throughout the film, suffers hardship and physical abuse because of his acquaintance with this deluded newcomer. Less prominently, Rocinante, Don Quixote's hack, has become Buzz's wounded spaceship that, like Cervantes's dual-natured "basinelmet" (1.44:418),[3] also doubles as the torn carton in which he was packaged; Clavileño, the "flying" hobbyhorse, has become a radio-controlled race car that carries Buzz and Woody on a very real flight at the end of the story; and the evil enchanter, Frestón, who incessantly pursues Don Quixote and Sancho, has become the mean-spirited next-door neighbor, Sid, a seemingly omnipotent figure whose greatest thrill is to torment any toys he can get his hands on. Finally, in place of *Don Quixote*'s supporting cast of characters who spend much of the novel trying to cure the self-appointed knight-errant of his mania, *Toy Story* provides us with a menagerie of toys who spend much of the first film trying to rescue Buzz.

This thematic metamorphosis of character is complemented by a similar "morphing" of plot. Like Don Quixote, whose genealogy is deliberately ambiguous, Buzz has no real history before the narrative of the film begins; he wakes up ex nihilo from his shelf-life "hypersleep" just as suddenly as Alonso Quixano apparently "awakens" to his new identity as a knight-errant in the opening chapter. Thus, when Buzz arrives on the scene he introduces himself to the other toys by citing the text from the side of his spaceship/carton. In this way, the advertising copy functions for Buzz much the same way *Amadís de Gaula* functions for Don Quixote; it becomes a written document on which to found his identity in the absence of any genuine personal history: "As a member of the elite Universe Protection Unit of the SPACE RANGER corps, I protect the galaxy from the threat of invasion from the Evil Emperor Zurg* [*sic*], sworn enemy of the Galactic Alliance" (*Toy Story*, 00:16:54). Yet because this advertising copy, like *Amadís*, describes a reality that never existed (which is to say, it creates a world rather than represents one), it demonstrates the kind of circular epistemology invoked by Jean Baudrillard in his essay "Simulacra and Simulations": "The whole system becomes weightless; it is no longer anything but a gigantic simulacrum: not unreal, but a simulacrum, never again exchanging for what is real, but exchanging in itself, in an uninterrupted circuit without reference or circumference" (173). The other toys, who have a firm grasp on the economic realities of their own late-capitalistic existence, do not know quite what to make of Buzz's declaration. Mr. Potato Head replies: "Oh really? I'm from Playskool," while a green dinosaur adds: "And I'm from Mattel. Well, I'm not really from Mattel; I'm actually from a smaller company that was purchased in a leveraged buyout" (*Toy Story*, 00:17:07). In this way, Buzz's new companions (like the numerous level-headed people who surround Don Quixote and who often berate his rather loose interpretation of reality) remain extremely skeptical of his farfetched claims; nevertheless, like Don Quixote's, Buzz's vision of self—based as it is on the chimera of a simulacrum—remains impervious to this exterior skepticism. As Álvaro Ramírez says of Don Quixote in his own Baudrillardian analysis of Cervantes's novel, but which is equally apropos of Buzz, "he enters the realm of simulation and the unbound sign, where signification rules" (86).

Meanwhile, Woody suspiciously plays along with Buzz during a substantial portion of the film, believing that he has merely assumed this persona as a way of gaining an unfair advantage over the other toys. When it later becomes obvious, however, that Buzz is indeed seriously deluded, his suspicion turns to sheer exasperation. After a brief skirmish at a local gas station, when the two suddenly find themselves as "lost toys" (after Andy's mother has driven away and left them stranded in the parking lot), Buzz's greatest concern (in stark contrast to Woody) is not for himself but for his supposed role as defender of the galaxy: "Because of you the security of this entire Universe is in jeopardy!" Woody cannot take much more of this space-speak and furiously shouts: "You are a toy! [...] You aren't the real Buzz Lightyear; you're an action figure! [...] You are a child's plaything!" To which Buzz merely replies: "You are a sad, strange little man, and you have my pity. Farewell" (*Toy Story*, 00:32:15). From this point on, the film adopts the basic structure of the quest narrative (inherent in Cervantes's own parodic treatment of the romances of chivalry) as Buzz attempts to find a "spaceship" that will take him back to his "home planet," while

Woody (like Sancho before him, who quickly learns to manipulate his master's fantasies) attempts to find a way to transport Buzz back to Andy's bedroom using Buzz's delusions to his own utilitarian ends.

This thematic intertextuality, however, is not the only nexus between Cervantes's novel and Lasseter's films. *Toy Story* also evokes much of the novel's baroque milieu. For instance, the film subtly suggests the book's pastoral elements (if only inadvertently) by providing Woody with a girl-friend in the form of Little Bo Peep (Annie Potts), a character who is constantly escorted by an entourage of happy little sheep, and who glides through her environment wearing petticoats, a pink hoop skirt, and a frilly bonnet. Like most of the pastoral figures in *Don Quixote*, however, *Toy Story*'s Bo Peep in no way resembles an actual shepherdess. In fact, because she is nothing but the iconographic representation of a pastoral literary character, plucked from the pages of a children's nursery rhyme and dropped unexpectedly into Andy's bedroom, where she soon falls in love with—and very actively pursues—yet another literary/cinematic stereotype (Woody, after all, is no more a working cowhand than she is a working shepherdess), *Toy Story*'s sexually liberated Bo Peep is a close analogue, if not a kindred spirit, to Cervantes's Marcela, whose elegant speech in defense of her sexual and intellectual independence is considered by many critics to be a startlingly modern moment in the text: "I was born free, and to live free I chose the solitude of the countryside" (1.14:109).[4]

Interestingly, Little Bo Peep was not Lasseter's first choice of ingénue. *Toy Story*'s original screenplay called for Woody's love interest to be played by Barbie, a much more sexually charged icon of American culture. But, because the Mattel Corporation is famously protective of its "Barbie" brand, jealously controlling her image whether this means shutting down "unauthorized" Barbie fan sites on the Internet or filing lawsuits against serious artists whose work uses Barbie in "unflattering" ways, Mattel initially refused to allow Lasseter to use its flagship doll. When sales of Hasbro's Mr. Potato Head increased exponentially following the film's release in 1995, however, Mattel suddenly discovered the postmodern power of product placement. Hence, by 1999 when *Toy Story 2* was released, Barbie's corporate owners were all too happy to let her make an extended cameo appearance. Ironically, however, even this legal change of heart has a kind of Cervantine quality about it. Don Quixote frequently makes reference to an extra-textual "sage" who, he says, can manipulate his history at will, changing the course of events and transforming objects from one thing into another. Barbie's preproduction "metamorphosis" from platinum blond into bonneted shepherdess essentially reinscribes *Don Quixote*'s "sage" into the margins of Lasseter's cinematic text. Viewers who are aware of the legal negotiations that took place during the initial stages of *Toy Story*'s creation cannot help but "read" Lasseter's slightly sultry

Little Bo Peep as a kind of reified Barbie, transformed beyond (legal) recognition by a crew of corporate enchanters.

More obvious than this pastoral element, however, is the incorporation of the picaresque into Lasseter's suburban world. As a figure of *Don Quixote*'s omnipresent enchanter, Frestón, Sid is a malevolent force who first torments Buzz and then winds up nearly destroying him. Noting Sid's penchant for turning toys into "speechless mutants," Bill Brown astutely associates him with the evil protagonist of *The Island of Doctor Moreau* (963). But Sid also doubles as a kind of Ginés de Pasamonte, a sociopath whose violence toward society remains completely unexplained, if not wholly unexplainable. As I note in the previous chapter, Ginés is first introduced into the text as a violent convict and part-time picaresque author. Having been freed by Don Quixote (who unshackles the convicts out of a misplaced sense of duty to those whose liberty has been taken from them by force), Ginés repays the kindness first by attacking his liberator and then later by returning under cover of night to steal Sancho's donkey literally out from under him. In this regard, there is some significance, I think, in the name "Sid," which is one of the many (perhaps unintentional, perhaps deliberate) puns in the *Toy Story* films. Sid is a particularly "vicious" little boy whose familiar name, spiked haircut, ubiquitous sneer, and black T-shirt (adorned only with a rather frightening icon of a human skull) inevitably suggest his association with Sid Vicious and thus with one of the most infamous of all postmodern *pícaros*.

Sid's bedroom, which contrasts starkly with the clean, warm, and friendly atmosphere of Andy's, is an extremely dark and sordid place and resembles many of the interior spaces depicted in Fernando de Rojas's *Celestina* or Francisco de Quevedo's *Swindler*. Furthermore, this bedroom is cluttered with the remnants of dozens of mutilated toys. Roberto González Echevarría reminds us of the importance of the grotesque in baroque art by underlining the prominence of deformed "monsters" in Calderón de la Barca's theater and of hunchbacks and dwarfs in Diego Velázquez's paintings (81–113). Tellingly, the mutilated toys confined in Sid's upstairs bedroom (itself, reminiscent of Segismundo's prison tower because Buzz finds himself trapped there) have been reassembled into a number of monstrous, hybrid reconfigurations: a convertible car with arms and legs instead of wheels; a frog with wheels instead of hind legs; a fishing rod equipped with a pair of Barbie Doll legs attached to its reel, making it look something like a decapitated ostrich; and finally a figure that defies typological classification, one whose bottom half consists of the legless torso of a weight-lifter doll whose hefty arms provide locomotion, whose upper half is the torso of a smaller male doll, and whose head is that of a giant insect. Moreover, these pathetic monsters, like Luis de Góngora's seventeenth-century Polyphemus, represent misunderstood figures and are not the "cannibals"

Buzz and Woody initially make them out to be. In fact, when Buzz finds himself severely wounded toward the end of the first film, these all-too-baroque monsters put him back together and then prove instrumental in helping the two heroes escape from Sid's house. Like so many Renaissance and baroque adventurers before them—as Frank Lestringant makes clear in documenting the tendency of early modern Europeans to imagine whole races of dog-headed anthropophagi in the New World (15–22)—Buzz and Woody completely misread the alien reality they find outside their immediate and insular geography.

In many ways, Sid's bedroom exists as a kind of baroque microcosm unto itself. It typifies what José Antonio Maravall calls an early seventeenth-century "consciousness of crisis" that sees "the world as a *confused labyrinth*" (*Culture*, 153; original emphasis). In place of the Renaissance (or even modernist) *locus amoenus* exemplified by Andy's idyllic and well-ordered bedroom, Sid's room is that chaotic space in which Maravall's baroque themes of madness, bewilderment, disharmony, instability, mutability, and disillusionment play themselves out in a grotesque spectacle (*Culture*, 149–72).

> The gruesomeness, violence, and cruelty so evident in baroque art were rooted in that pessimistic conception of the human being and of the world and which they, in turn, reinforced. [...] The real violence was probably no greater, no more harsh in the seventeenth century than in prior epochs, but consciousness of violence was more acute, as was acceptance of it, which came to inspire an aesthetics of cruelty. (Maravall, *Culture*, 162)

But whereas this seventeenth-century aesthetics of cruelty writes itself upon the body of the human being, Lasseter's postmodern version inscribes itself upon a simulacrum, as Baudrillard demonstrates:

> If there is a species which is more maltreated than children, then it must be their toys, which they handle in an incredibly off-hand manner [...]. Toys are thus the end point in that long chain in which all the conditions of despotic high-handedness are in play which enchain beings one to another, from one species to another—from cruel divinities to their sacrificial victims, from masters to slaves, from adults to children, and from children to their objects. This is actually the only strong symbolic chain, the one through which a victim of the whim of a superior power passes it on to an inferior species, the whole process ending with someone taking it out on a powerless simulacrum, like a toy [...]. (225)

And no inhabitant of Sid's labyrinthine bedroom is more cruelly written upon than a mutant toy the screenplay calls "Babyface."

Of all the various Cervantine characters figured in *Toy Story* one seems conspicuously absent: Don Quixote's idealized ladylove, Dulcinea del Toboso. This apparent omission is undoubtedly due to the fact that, while the code of chivalry, informed as it is by the tradition of courtly love, insists that each knight have a lady to whom he can commend himself, the code of science fiction does not include such provisos for space rangers. In fact, protagonists of science fiction tend to conform to two very different schools of thought on amorous behavior. On the one hand, there are the swashbuckling philanderers, embodied by such figures as Captain James T. Kirk (William Shatner)—much more Don Juan than Don Quixote—from the original *Star Trek* television series. On the other hand, there are the very aloof, very disinterested professional astronauts, embodied by such figures as Captain Jean-Luc Picard (Patrick Stewart) of *Star Trek: The Next Generation*. Buzz is decidedly an example of this latter type. For, while we certainly catch a glimpse of Woody blushing from the amorous advances of Little Bo Peep, at no time during either film is there any hint that an "inappropriate" thought ever crosses Buzz's mind.

Nevertheless, the specter of Dulcinea figures prominently in *Toy Story*. Like the Aldonza of *Man of La Mancha*, who first appears as one of Cervantes's co-prisoners in the Spanish dungeon, Dulcinea has become Babyface, the queen of the mutant toys imprisoned in Sid's bedroom. Early in the original novel, when Don Quixote encounters the Jewish merchants on the highway and demands that they acknowledge Dulcinea as the most beautiful maiden in the whole world, one of them, while asking to see some tangible proof of her beauty, makes the following assertion:

> Indeed I believe we are already so far inclined in her favour that, even if her portrait shows that one of her eyes has gone skew-whiff and that sulphur and cinnabar ooze out of the other one, we will, just to please you, say in her favour whatever you want us to say. (1.4:46)[5]

This grotesque picture of Dulcinea is echoed in a later chapter when Don Quixote once again imagines a beautiful damsel in the rather disfigured person of Maritornes, who is described as

> an Asturian lass with broad jowls, a flat-backed head, a pug nose, blind in one eye and not very sound in the other. It's true that the loveliness of her body offset her other shortcomings: she didn't measure five feet from her head to her toes, and her shoulders, with something of a hump on them, made her look down at the ground more than she liked. (1.16:122)[6]

Toy Story uncannily combines these two descriptions and imagines a very crablike Dulcinea/Maritornes whose distorted body consists of eight erector-set legs (the front two equipped with pincers) commanded by an enormous

Figure 9: *Toy Story*'s "Babyface" uncannily reflects the sordid descriptions of Dulcinea and Maritornes in Cervantes's *Don Quixote*. (*Toy Story*, Walt Disney/Pixar, 1995)

doll's head whose hair has been cropped to stubble. The right eye of this head is missing, while the remaining left eye stares glassily forward. At one point, as the "camera" passes by her face, we are allowed a glimpse through the empty eye socket into the hollowness of the head cavity, where we can detect several holes at the back of the skull where some of the missing hair plugs were once inserted (Figure 9). It is a wonderfully horrific phantasm this cyberpunk portrayal of what J. M. Cohen's translation of *Don Quixote* calls (in another context) "Dulcinea Enchanted" (Cohen, 525), and one I think Cervantes probably would have greatly appreciated.

These thematic and aesthetic borrowings certainly tie the film to the novel, but the most important way in which *Toy Story* engages *Don Quixote* in an intertextual dialogue is through the development of a particularly postmodern reading of the central figure's identity crisis. In the novel, the psychological climax of this crisis occurs late in the second part when Don Quixote is defeated in battle by his mirror image (as I note in Chapter 3) in the person of Sansón Carrasco disguised first as the Knight of the Mirrors and then the Knight of the White Moon. In the film, Buzz's disillusionment also occurs through a confrontation with his reflection, although here the mirror has appropriately become a television screen, while the image reflected is that of the mechanically reproduced plastic commodity of late twentieth-century childhood. Having escaped from Sid's picaresque bedroom, Buzz inadvertently wanders into another room in which

Figure 10: Confronting his own mirror image on a television screen, Buzz Lightyear discovers in horror that he is not unique in any way, much less a genuine "space ranger." (*Toy Story*, Walt Disney/Pixar, 1995)

a television happens to be featuring a commercial for the Buzz Lightyear action figure. He stares in utter disbelief at the frightening spectacle of a little boy playing enthusiastically with a doll identical to him in every way. And as the voice of the announcer describes the toy's lasers, sound effects, and other gadgets, Buzz takes a self-inventory and finds that he too has each of these features. He even notices for the first time the words "Made in Taiwan" stamped indelibly in his left arm, thus confirming a consumerist genesis no less mundane than that of his plastic comrades-in-arms. The commercial ends with the "camera" pulling back from a tight focus on a single Buzz Lightyear doll to reveal an entire store filled with thousands of Buzz Lightyears, each one identical to the others (Figure 10).

If Don Quixote's dementia stems, in part, from his inability to bear the weight of his own ordinariness in an all too unjust world, then Buzz's imbalance here is multiplied a million times over, since he is virtually indistinguishable from every other Buzz Lightyear doll ever fabricated in this hostile universe. In a way, Don Quixote's anxiety toward the false Avellaneda "Don Quixote" prefigures Buzz's dilemma, except that Buzz must contend not with just one imposter but with an entire legion. More crucial yet, he has been "decentered" by the experience. For, among these rivals he cannot be certain—as can Don Quixote in Cervantes's second part—that he is any more "authorized" than another, being a product of the same overseas factory that produced the thousands of Buzz Lightyears featured on the screen. Where Don Quixote spends much of the second part contending to all who will listen that his "other" remains nothing less than the libelous fabrication of a plagiarist too cowardly to use his real name (i.e., Avellaneda), Buzz stands speechless in the face of an ever-multiplying army of clones.

The most damning aspect of this television confrontation with his mass-marketed (over-the-)counterparts, then, is that during the commercial the screen prominently flashes the words "Not a flying toy," a disclaimer that calls into question what has been the single most important defining element for Buzz's sense of self-worth. In Buzz's first meeting with the other toys, he insists that among his other marvelous capabilities he can fly, and he deploys an impressive set of wings to prove it. When Woody refuses to accept this aeronautical claim and initiates a childish "can-can't-can-can't" debate, Buzz dives from the top of the bedpost, bounces off a rubber ball, and surfs down a Hotwheels track (doing a loop-de-loop in the process), from which he is catapulted toward the ceiling, where he hitches a ride on a mechanical airplane, and then lands back on the bed with a definitive "Can!" To which Woody replies: "That wasn't flying; that was falling with style" (*Toy Story*, 00:19:20). After seeing the television commercial, then, and in a moment of supreme existential angst, Buzz leaves the room determined to prove the advertisement wrong—just as earlier he proved Woody wrong—by flying out of the house to safety.

This scene greatly multiplies the discursive intertextualities existing between several later Cervantine imitations. Randy Newman's soundtrack, for instance, boldly misreads Leigh and Darion's famous song "The Impossible Dream (The Quest)." Where *Man of La Mancha* exhorts its knight-errant "To reach the unreachable star, / Though you know it's impossibly high, / To live with your heart striving upward / To a far, unattainable sky!" (Wasserman, 82), Lasseter's film, voicing Buzz's fears that his desire to sail "out among the stars" is perhaps a "dream that ended too soon," urges its Space Ranger on to his own quixotic heights by proclaiming, "If I believe I can fly, why I'd fly!" (*Toy Story*, 00:47:44). Even so, as Buzz leaps from the top of a stairwell toward an open window—his version of tilting at windmills—we see on his face the realization of what could be called his "non-flying toyness," and he falls some thirty feet, smashing onto a hardwood floor and losing an arm in the process. Battered and disillusioned, he gives up on life, as the song underscores this moment for us by poignantly lamenting, "clearly, I will go sailing no more" (*Toy Story*, 00:48:08).

Because *Toy Story* is a film expressly distributed by the Walt Disney Company, it cannot allow Buzz to die the same poignant death as Don Quixote. First, without a happy ending the movie could never have been marketed to its intended audience. Second, unlike Cervantes at the end of the second part of *Don Quixote*, Lasseter—who can count on contemporary international copyright laws far stricter than those of seventeenth-century Spain—undoubtedly wanted to leave open the very real possibility of a sequel. Thus, while Sancho is unable to persuade Don Quixote to live long enough to pursue other sallies, Woody does succeed in shaking Buzz out of his existential quandary by convincing him of the rather postmodern notion that his uniqueness lies not in his abilities (or lack thereof) but in his functional relationship to Andy. Buzz is special not because he flies but because he has a specific "use value" in that he brings hours of pleasure to a singular little boy much in need of friendship. What Baudrillard argues regarding the function of the consumerist subject within a capitalist economy is equally apropos of *Toy Story*'s consumerist objects, because the latter exist as quasi-subjects in their own right inseparably bound up with the subjectivity of the former:

> Utility, needs, use value: none of these ever come to grips with the finality of subjects who face their ambivalent object relations, or with symbolic exchange between subjects. Rather, it describes the relation of individuals to themselves conceived in economic terms—better still, the relation of the subject to the economic system. Far from the individual expressing his or her needs in the economic system, it is the economic system that induces the individual function and the parallel functionality of objects and needs. The individual is an ideological structure, a historical form correlative with the commodity form (exchange value), and the object form (use value). (69–70)

In other words, Buzz, the central protagonist of *Toy Story*, in no way exists as an autonomous subject (or autonomous object, for that matter), differentiated from all other Buzz Lightyears by some inherent set of material or ethereal qualities; rather, he exists purely as a sign whose meaning is determined by the specific "reader" who responds to him. Indeed, the only reason this particular Buzz Lightyear matters at all outside the (con)text of Andy's bedroom is that he happens to be the one articulated for us by this particular Disney/Pixar film; which is to say, every other Buzz Lightyear posited in the television commercial could just as easily become a different central protagonist within a discrete narrative, provided that there also existed a distinct text/reader relationship to give him meaning.

Toy Story 2 later follows up on this idea in two significant ways. First, the film begins with a narrative sequence that places Buzz somewhere in outer space where he successfully destroys a whole host of evil robots only to find himself staring down the Evil Emperor Zurg, who quite unexpectedly blows away Buzz's upper torso, leaving behind nothing but his smoldering legs. The shock of this violent demise is immediately dissipated, however, when it is revealed that this entire sequence was merely part of a "Buzz Lightyear" video game whose current player (Andy's plastic dinosaur, Rex) has been beaten by the game. When Rex (Wallace Shawn) laments this failure, Buzz—by which I mean the central protagonist of the *Toy Story* films—attempts to console him with a phrase that clearly underlines the radical fungibility of the Buzz Lightyear identity: "You're a better Buzz than I am" (*Toy Story 2*, 00:04:35). Second, and more importantly, *Toy Story 2* explores the Cervantine narrativity inherent in this multiplicity of Buzz Lightyears by playfully reinscribing the conflict between the two Don Quixotes in Cervantes's second part of the novel.[7] Here the film pits the "real" Buzz Lightyear against a "false" doppelgänger who has managed to escape from his factory-sealed box and has "contaminated" Lasseter's text by conflating his own narrative line with that of the sequel. While the "real" Buzz, no longer deluded about his identity as a toy, focuses his energies on the plot at hand (rescuing Woody from Al's clutches), the "false" Buzz ignorantly and blithely wanders in and out of the various narrative sequences—often being mistaken for the "genuine" article—until at long last he disappears into the margins of the text to pursue his own individual "toy story," a narrative that exists as a self-conscious parody of George Lucas's first *Star Wars* trilogy combined with any one of several 1950s "family" sitcoms such as *Father Knows Best*. The culmination of this clash of Buzz Lightyears in *Toy Story 2* occurs when both figures—after engaging in a physical altercation that readers of the second part of *Don Quixote* can only wish Cervantes had been sufficiently brash enough to fictionalize—stand together facing a bewildered cast of toys who cannot seem to differentiate between them. At this moment the "real" Buzz proves his identity to the others by demonstrating his functional relationship to Andy. For, what separates "our" Buzz (to use a particularly Cervantine turn of phrase) from the other one is the presence of Andy's name inscribed in indelible ink on the bottom of his foot. This "sign" marks him as the only Buzz Lightyear that currently matters; this possessive "writing" authenticates his centrality within *Toy Story 2*.

Returning to the first film, *Toy Story* suggests a number of ways in which Buzz might deal with his sudden self-awareness as a plastic toy, his sudden recognition that he is nothing but "use value." On the one hand, like Nora, from Henrik Ibsen's 1879 play *A Doll's House*, where the central character decides to leave her husband rather than continue to suffer the indignity of being his "doll-wife" in the "playroom" that has constituted their home (170), Buzz could simply refuse to participate any further in a functional relationship that denies him his individuality. After all, he has been separated from Andy for some time and must exert an enormous effort to reunite himself with his adolescent owner. Although he may not exist as the genuine "space ranger" he thought himself to be, he could nonetheless go off in search of a fulfilling existence as an "action figure" independent of someone else's overdetermining will. Like Don Quixote, he could leave behind the banal world of bedrooms and birthday parties and sally forth with the deliberate purpose of coming to the aid of wronged toys like those tormented by Sid. The fact that he is not a genuine "space ranger" does not prevent him from moving forward as a champion for justice in the Universe. Such a course of action, in which "Buzz-the-child's-plaything" simply declined to cooperate with "Andy-the-child," would provide a kind of social critique of Don Quixote's function as a "toy" for the Duke and Duchess, suggesting that Cervantes's knight-errant perhaps should not have allowed himself to be manipulated by the oligarchy for its mere amusement. But it would also be a shrewd cinematic performance of the kind of symbolic revolution Baudrillard implicitly calls for in his critique of consumerist society.[8]

On the other hand, like Augusto Pérez from Miguel de Unamuno's 1914 novel *Mist*, however, where the central protagonist confronts the author in his study and, in one of the most original metaliterary moments of Western literature (which anticipates by some six years Luigi Pirandello's masterpiece *Six Characters in Search of an Author* [although in an obviously inverted way]), tries to assert his own free will within the context of the narrative, Buzz could break the hard and fast rule of toydom and simply show himself to Andy as the truly animate being he is, demanding his autonomy in the process. *Toy Story* suggests just this possibility by having the menagerie of toys confront Sid in the same manner to frighten him out of his malicious behavior toward them. But this would represent a rather perilous tactic for Buzz, since Andy could respond to him in much the same way the metafictional Unamuno responds to Augusto Pérez: by destroying the action figure rather than allowing it to lead an existence independent of his overarching narrative desires. Such an ending, in which his own annihilation forced Buzz to finally accept his status as a toy, would provide a philosophical figure of Don Quixote's own final reconciliation with God, where Don Quixote—despite his valiant attempt throughout the novel to construct an identity separate from the one bestowed on him by the Divine "authorial" will—dies accepting his rightful place as Alonso Quixano within the great chain of being.

Of course, the studio executives at the Walt Disney Company would not for a moment have allowed Pixar Animation Studios to produce a film that followed either of these philosophically unsettling narrative paths. Thus, *Toy Story* instead prefers to return to one of the central themes of Cervantes's baroque novel: that true nobility lies not in the success of an endeavor but in the mere daring to do. This much more appealing approach (at least as far as Disney's juvenile target audience is concerned) has become prominent in the twentieth and twenty-first centuries, again due in no small part to Unamuno, whose study *The Life of Don Quixote and Sancho* distills this "quixotism" into the following benediction:

Bravo, my Lord Don Quixote, bravo! The law was not made for you, nor for us, your believers; our statutes are our own wills. You spoke truly; you had enough courage to cudgel any four hundred troopers who got in your way, or at least you had enough courage to try it, and the value of an act lies in the intention. (*Our Lord Don Quixote*, 149)[9]

And in pursuing this theme to the end, *Toy Story* shows itself to be a genuine follower of *Man of La Mancha*, whose own author, Wasserman, cites Unamuno in the prologue to the published edition of the play: "If there was a guiding precept for the whole endeavor it lay in a quotation I found long ago [...]: 'Only he who attempts the absurd is capable of achieving the impossible'" (ix). And what could be more absurd (or seemingly impossible) than for two toys to orchestrate a mass escape from a well-guarded house in an attempt to catch up with a speeding moving van that is transporting their owner's belongings from one side of town to the other? Yet, this is precisely the course of action Buzz and Woody undertake, and it is their valor in the face of this quixotic enterprise that cements their friendship, just as surely as Don Quixote and Sancho's relationship is forged on the plains of La Mancha.

Toy Story's narrative climax, then, occurs during this final confrontation with the impossible. After Buzz and Woody have finally escaped from Sid's house, they find that their only available mode of transportation is a radio-controlled race car. This little car valiantly attempts to keep up with the moving van, but just when it appears that they will succeed—when the two are within arm's reach of the other toys' out-stretched hands—the car's tiny batteries die, and the van disappears over the horizon, leaving all three stranded in the middle of an unknown street. Once again Buzz and Woody face an uncertain future as "lost toys" and once again they seem to lose the meager faith they have rekindled. Remembering, however, the rocket that Sid had taped to Buzz's back with the intention of blowing him to pieces, Woody manages to ignite the fuse, and all three shoot high into the air on a flight that Don Quixote, Sancho, and Clavileño (the "flying" hobbyhorse of Cervantes's second part) could only imagine. During this flight, Buzz locates the van and launches the race car into its open bay door just as Woody points out that their newfound source of propulsion will shortly explode, thus destroying them both. At this point Buzz regains some of his lost Unamunian "quixotism," but not all, as we shall see. Insisting that, whatever else may happen, he will not agree to such a mundane defeat, Buzz deploys his wings—miraculously jettisoning the rocket in the process—and begins a final descent into the back seat of Andy's car, which is traveling just ahead of the moving van. When Woody, who by this time has been infected by some of Buzz's quixotic contagion, exclaims: "Buzz, you're flying!" Buzz exhibits symptoms of his own "sanchification" by repeating Woody's earlier statement: "This isn't flying; this is falling with style" (*Toy Story*, 01:14:17).

The film appears to come full circle with this recapitulation, and yet this cyclical structure quickly spins out of control. Harold Bloom points out in *The Western Canon* that before Alonso Quixano the Good can die literally Don Quixote must die metaphorically (139–40). So too, the Buzz Lightyear who returns to Andy's bedroom is not the same Buzz Lightyear who left it early in the story. Like Cervantes's knight-errant, he has been tempered by his journey, and his return is far less triumphant than his initial arrival. He no longer dreams impossible dreams; he no longer sails out among the stars. Unlike Don Quixote, however, Buzz must suffer this metaphoric demise without ever acquiring the benefits a very literal death bestows on Alonso Quixano. And in this way, *Toy Story* again shows itself to be informed by a postmodern discourse that steadfastly resists transcendence. In place of Cervantes's closing authorial comments, which attempt to delimit the significance of both the novel and its central character, *Toy Story* leaves its viewers with an open-ended epilogue in which the reunited toys sheepishly discover that Andy has received a new puppy for Christmas. This indeterminate ending does little more than defer the film's meaning into a series of sequels yet to be made. Thus, *Toy Story* "decenters" Buzz one final time, because just as he has displaced Woody as Andy's "favorite toy" in this particular rendition (and we must assume that Woody has earlier displaced someone or something else), so too the new puppy will displace Buzz in the posited version that must surely follow. And this puppy, in turn, will almost certainly be displaced by some future gift. And so, and so on, and so on. *Toy Story*, in stark contrast to *Don Quixote*, virtually erases its hero from the text, for somewhere out there in the unending chain of implied sequels, Buzz will simply fade away entirely like so many other mislaid childhood relics: unremembered, unremarked, and unaccounted for. In short, there will be no Sansón Carrasco to declare for posterity, "He granted death no victory, / Not even when in death's last throes" (2.74:981), no lingering "specular other" to write his epitaph.[10]

Nevertheless, the final shot of these two toys standing precariously, as it were, on the edge of a mise-en-abîme provides the very point of departure for the actual sequel that follows. *Toy Story 2* is, in essence, a study of the ontological problem posited by this indeterminate epilogue. But instead of centering on the new puppy—as the first film suggests it might—the sequel reconfigures its Cervantine mirror by refocusing our attention on Woody, who now discovers his own "literary" identity as the star of a 1950s television puppet show called *Woody's Roundup* (clearly modeled on *Howdy Doody*). And like Don Quixote in Cervantes's second part, who becomes self-aware of his importance as a literary figure through contact

Figure 11: Coming face-to-face with his own mirror image, Woody discovers—much like Don Quixote in Cervantes's own sequel—that he is the protagonist of a previous narrative called *Woody's Roundup*. (*Toy Story 2*, Walt Disney/Pixar, 1999)

with several new characters who have previously read his "story," Woody suddenly finds himself surrounded by a new group of toys—a horse named Bullseye, a cowgirl named Jessie (Joan Cusack), and a prospector named Stinky Pete (Kelsey Grammer)—who restore for him a "history" he did not even know existed.[11] Having been stolen from Andy's front yard by the unscrupulous owner of Al's Toy Barn (who is attempting to amass a complete *Woody's Roundup* set), Woody confronts his own mirror image on a whole array of theme merchandise related to his show (Figure 11). These include a breakfast cereal called "Cowboy Crunchies," a record player, a lunch box, a guitar, a yo-yo, a piggy bank, a set of plastic dinnerware, a larger-than-life cardboard cutout, the January 12, 1957, cover of *Life* magazine, and, finally, episode after episode of *Woody's Roundup* archived on videotape. (Ironically, we learn that *Woody's Roundup* was cancelled shortly after the launch of Sputnik because the "use value" of cowboy toys declined sharply as consumer interest in "space toys" increased.)

Significantly, Woody's voyage of self-discovery in *Toy Story 2* is a kind of allegory; that is, his itinerary exists as an uncanny reading of the second most important conflict in Cervantes's sequel. The original enchanter who robs Don Quixote of his triumphs in part 1 is largely exchanged in part 2 for a pseudonymous literary pirate guilty of much more than just stealing his glory. The malevolent cipher that haunts the second half of *Don Quixote* is not Frestón but Avellaneda, who, with his own pre-emptive sequel, has surreptitiously "purloined" Cervantes's famous protagonist. Likewise, the villain of *Toy Story 2* is not the mean-spirited Sid but Al. As is often noted, the verb "to plagiarize" has its etymological roots in notions of "kidnapping." But our modern conception of the verb "to kidnap"— whereby we assume that the "victim" has been taken against his or her will—masks the original semantic value of the metaphor. The *Oxford English Dictionary* states that the term "plagiary" initially referred to "one who abducts the child or slave *of another*" (my emphasis). In other words, the original "victim" of the crime was not the captive but the person from whose possession the captive had been unfairly wrested. Thus, it is truly significant that both sequels—*Don Quixote II* and *Toy Story 2*—involve the "abduction" (in one form or another) of the hero himself, a hero who expressly belongs to someone else. And in this way, Andy (although he is never actually aware of Woody's disappearance) becomes a figure for Cervantes who must contend with an unknown nemesis over "ownership" of the main protagonist. Likewise, Woody (by thwarting Al's plans) becomes a figure for Don Quixote, who, in defending his own honor, also champions the proprietary rights of his "owner."

Unlike Don Quixote, however, who personally stands to gain nothing from Avellaneda's literary affront, Woody's abduction in *Toy Story 2* actually offers him a tempting alternative to the unhappy fate suggested by the previous film's epilogue. Here, he finds that he must make a crucial choice. On the one hand, he can attain "immortality" in the museum, where he is promised a never-ending stream of eager admirers; on the other hand, he can return to Andy's bedroom, where, although he may enjoy a few years of happy companionship, he will surely be displaced and forgotten as the young boy matures into adulthood. The dangers of this existential dilemma are made manifest by the presence of Jessie, who woefully recounts the circumstance of her own final displacement. As her young owner, Emily, inevitably outgrew her, Jessie was gradually moved from the core of the bedroom to the periphery, until at long last she was simply put in a box and given away as a charitable donation. (And, as a matter of fact, Woody's abduction actually occurs when he attempts to rescue an older toy that had been consigned to a yard sale by Andy's mother.) Having literally been "decentered" and tossed out (later to be acquired by Al), Jessie has spent the rest of her existence locked in a dark box—in a kind of toy limbo—awaiting the day when Al could obtain the elusive "Woody" figure who would complete the set and thus make possible their collective passage into toy heaven.

Jessie's story essentially recapitulates the trope at the center of Margery Williams's well-known children's book, *The Velveteen Rabbit; or, How Toys Become Real*, in which a much-loved stuffed animal is thrown away by its owner's nanny because it is said to be contaminated with scarlet fever germs. Discarded and left in a trash heap, the little toy becomes so overwhelmed with sadness that a real tear falls from its eye, and from this real tear emerges a fairy who turns the little velveteen toy into a real animal. And Williams's book merely recapitulates Carlo Collodi's *Adventures of Pinocchio*, in which—at the behest of his publisher—a fairy also appears at the end of the story to convert the famous marionette into a "real boy." In both stories, transcendence from a presumed lower state of being to a presumed higher one requires a supernatural intervention, and in both stories, "ascension" into the "heavenly" state of "reality" necessarily substitutes for achieving "immortality."

Being a postmodern text, *Toy Story 2* eschews the transcendence inherent in Collodi's and Williams's works. As Woody soon realizes, the tantalizing offer of "immortality" in the Japanese toy museum comes at a heavy price. Although life as part of the museum's permanent collection holds out the possibility that he will never have to suffer the humiliation of being forgotten or displaced, it augurs at the same time a very lonely existence within the confines of an ascetic glass case in which he will forever be denied all physical contact. And in this, *Toy Story 2* posits a very postmodern ontology, for what Woody comes to understand is that "being," as Martin Heidegger argues, necessarily means "being-in-the-world" (*Concept of Time*, 7E). In short, to accept the seductive transcendence offered him by the toy museum means that he must give up the very thing that defines him: the act of being played-with. Once he enters that space, he will no longer be able to say (to paraphrase René Descartes), "I am a toy [therefore I am]."

Thus, in order to bestow on Woody the transcendence necessary for him to pass into the timeless realm of the museum, the dishonest toy dealer must first sever all contingencies that tie him to a material reality: Al must obliterate all traces of Woody's "being-in-the-world." Woody must become as "unblemished" as Stinky Pete, who supposedly remains in mint condition within his factory-sealed box. For this reason, it is supremely important that Woody pass through a restoration process in which he is "redeemed" of the "original sin" of having been played with. This redemptive refurbishment is effectuated though a kind of priestly specialist who meticulously mends the slashes in Woody's cloth body, removes years of grime from his surfaces, and finally gives him a fresh coat of paint. This is a cathartic purification that culminates—significantly—in the removal of Andy's name from the bottom of Woody's foot, an act of "erasure" that deliberately forecloses his ability to authenticate his unique centrality within any specific "toy story." In being literally "unmarked," he becomes a sign untethered to reality; again, he becomes what Baudrillard calls "hyperreal" (175).[12]

For this same reason, Woody's ultimate decision to forgo "immortality" is underscored by his literal reinscription of Andy's mark of ownership: he deliberately rewrites Andy's name on the bottom of his foot.

In essence, what Woody does by restoring this definitive "sign" of possessive interdependence is to reconfirm Cervantes's closing comments in *Don Quixote*, which he places in the mouth of Cide Hamete's pen: "For me alone was Don Quixote born, and I for him; it was for him to act, for me to write; we two are as one" (2.74:981).[13] Yet Cervantes's statements in this regard are part of his deliberate attempt to bury his protagonist once and for all: "leave Don Quixote's weary mouldering bones at rest in his tomb" (2.74:981).[14] Thus, Woody's recognition that his authentic existence as a toy necessarily means "being-in-Andy's-bedroom" is also a self-acknowledgment that his potential disappearance from that space is an inescapable eventuality. In short, Woody's rejection of life in the museum epitomizes Heidegger's ontological statement, "*sum moribundus* ['I am in dying'], *moribundus* not as someone gravely ill or wounded, but insofar as I am, I am *moribundus*" (*History*, 317; original brackets). Woody's deliberate self-reinscription of Andy's name on his foot is an affirmative declaration: "Only in dying can I to some extent say absolutely, 'I am.'" (*History*, 318). Again, as Ginés de Pasamonte would say, "How can I have finished [my picaresque autobiography] if my life hasn't finished yet?" (1.22:182).[15] Nevertheless, *Toy Story 2*, like its predecessor, denies its heroes this "absolute" declaration by steadfastly refusing to cast them in anything approaching a scene of sublime moribundity. For, where Cervantes deposits Don Quixote firmly in the tomb, *Toy Story 2* simply abandons Buzz and Woody to their uncertain fate within Andy's bedroom, an (ironically) atemporal space where—like Samuel Beckett's Estragon and Vladimir—they sit endlessly awaiting a sequel that will never be made, forever anticipating an epitaph that will never be written.

Chapter 5

Salman Rushdie,

Author of the Captive's Tale

On the night of February 13, 1989, five months after the publication of *The Satanic Verses*, the Ayatollah Khomeini issued a *fatwa* sentencing Salman Rushdie to death. This *fatwa* initiated what Daniel Pipes calls an international "diplomatic crisis" between Iran and the West (especially Great Britain) as Western secular notions of freedom of speech came into direct conflict with Islamic Sharia laws against blasphemy, heresy, and apostasy (30). In an attempt to diffuse the growing international crisis, members of the Iranian government backpedaled slightly by suggesting that if Rushdie were to repent he might be forgiven (29). Nevertheless, Khomeini insisted that his *fatwa* was irrevocable and vigorously reiterated his call for Muslims everywhere to execute the death sentence as quickly as possible. When he died just four months later, as Pipes eloquently notes, the *fatwa* became permanent, something "no mortal now has the power to invalidate" (204). And even though the intervening years have officially diminished the enthusiasm with which Rushdie's assassination is seemingly desired, the permanence of the *fatwa* remains theoretically true as long as there are those who continue to revere the irrevocable words of the Ayatollah Khomeini. In fact, over the past several years one Iranian group or another has often marked the anniversary of the *fatwa* (or other such notable world event) with a staunch reaffirmation of its continuing juridical force.[1]

Within twenty-four hours of Khomeini's edict, Rushdie had gone into hiding under British government protection, and for the next several years surfaced only occasionally, and then always in danger of being ambushed by some unknown assailant. During one of his brief, surreptitious excursions into the outside world—in a speech he delivered at Columbia University on December 12, 1991, entitled "One Thousand Days in a Balloon"—Rushdie attempted to widen the context of what amounted to his virtual "house arrest" by tying his plight to that of other "Western hostages" (i.e., the various U.S. and European businessmen held captive in Lebanon, Iran, and Iraq at the time), all of whom had also become pawns in a geopolitical conflict that went well beyond the publication of his controversial novel (*Imaginary Homelands*, 430). He described his situation as a version of the well-known "balloon debate" (in which people trapped in a sinking balloon must decide whom to throw overboard) and plaintively noted that all of his "fellow-travellers" had been quietly redeemed one by one (through various diplomatic channels), leaving him all alone in the still-sinking balloon (430–39).

Cervantes scholars will hear in this tale of geopolitical conflict—of hostages taken and redeemed, of incarcerated writers—echoes of Miguel de Cervantes's experience as a captive over four hundred years ago. In September 1575—only a few years after his active participation in the Battle of Lepanto (1571), in which he permanently lost the use of his left hand—Cervantes and his brother Rodrigo set sail from Italy on their way back to Spain. Carrying with him letters of recommendation from Juan de Austria and the Duke of Sessa, Cervantes hoped to arrive in Madrid and obtain some kind of high government post in the Spanish court. Instead, the ship on which they traveled became separated from the rest of the fleet and was captured by Turkish pirates who then sold the two brothers into slavery in Algiers. Under these circumstances, the letters of recommendation Cervantes carried became a clear liability because his Algerian captors assumed that he and his brother must be much more important than they actually were and hence increased the required ransom to a level nearly impossible for members of their socioeconomic status to amass. Cervantes's family managed to raise enough money to ransom Rodrigo in the summer of 1577, but Cervantes—who made numerous unsuccessful attempts to escape—remained in captivity until September 1580, almost five years to the day from the moment of his capture.

Cervantes's biography in this regard is so well known—thanks in large measure to the fact that he made it a recurring theme of so many of his works, especially the autobiographical segment of *Don Quixote* commonly known as "The Captive's Tale"—that it can only have struck even a well-read nonspecialist like Rushdie as somehow familiar. Thus, it is perhaps not coincidental during this period of imposed confinement, when Rushdie began to identify not just with his contemporary "fellow-travellers" but perhaps with those of previous centuries as well (most notably Cervantes), that he wrote and published his 1995 novel *The Moor's Last Sigh*, a work whose principle leitmotiv is the notion of captivity and that is profoundly indebted to *Don Quixote*.

Even a cursory reading of Rushdie's novels reveals his inclination toward Cervantine prose, especially his affinity for carefully crafted narrators. Whether mere third-person raconteurs or first-person storytellers intimately connected to the narrative, these narrators typically drift in and out of the text, freezing the action, commenting on its construction, or debating its verisimilitude. Rushdie has long engaged Cervantes in a kind of intertextual conversation across the centuries, and much of his fiction can be read—at least in this regard—as an ongoing homage to the inventor of the modern novel. For instance, the narrator of *The Ground Beneath Her Feet*, Rai, is a photographer who recounts the events surrounding the lives of the rock stars Ormus Cama and Vina Apsara. This biography—of which Rai, too, is an important part—also documents much of this rock history on film, and in so doing provides the world (though not the reader) with a series of visual texts that both support Rai's verbal narrative and stand outside it. Moreover, like Don Quixote, whose deliberate change of identity marks his own professional aspirations, Rai abandons his real name, Umeed Merchant, to adopt the nom de plume by which he is known throughout the novel:

> I began to use the workname "Rai" when I was taken on by the famous Nebuchadnezzar Agency. Pseudonyms, stage names, worknames: for writers, for actors, for spies, these are useful masks, hiding or altering one's true identity. But when I began to call myself *Rai*, prince, it felt like removing a disguise, because I was letting the world in on my most cherished secret [...]. It [Rai] also meant desire: a man's personal incli- nation, the direction he chose to go in; and will, the force of a man's character. (18)

At other times, Rai sounds remarkably like the narrator during the first part of *Don Quixote* who, as I note in Chapter 3, freezes the combat between Don Quixote and the Basque rider—blaming this occurrence on the unnamed "author" who apparently lacked documentary evidence to conclude the battle—and then introduces Cide Hamete as the solution to the narrative impasse. This solution, in turn, because of the inherent un- reliability the narrator attributes to Cide Hamete, provides the narrator with an opportunity to engage in a lengthy commentary on the nature of "truth" and "lies" in historiography: "If there is any objection to be made about the truthfulness of this history, it can only be that its author was an Arab, and it's a well-known feature of Arabs that they're all liars" (1.9:76).[2] Upon concluding this diatribe, in which he insists that "histori- ans should and must be precise, truthful and unprejudiced (1.9:76),[3] Cer- vantes's narrator picks up the story where he left off, essentially unfreezing the frame and allowing the narrative to continue. For his part, Rai—a man for whom freezing moments in time is a professional perk—indulges in a similar digression when he leaves Ormus Cama suspended in a Man- hattan high-rise apartment in order to comment on his own narrative by comparing it to that of another transcultural "Moor" (one famously con- nected to *Don Quixote*):

> What hope can I, a mere journeyman shutterbug, a harvester of quotid- ian images from the abundance of what is, have of literary respectabil- ity? Like Lucius Apuleius of Madaura, a Moroccan colonial of Greek

ancestry aspiring to the ranks of the Latin colossi of Rome, I should (belatedly) excuse my (post)colonial clumsinesses and hope that you are not put off by the oddness of my tale. Just as Apuleius did not fully "Romanize" his language and style, thinking it better to find an idiolect that permitted him to express himself in the fashion of his Greek ancestors, so also I . . . but look here, there is an important difference between myself and the author of *The Transformations of Lucius*, better known as *The Golden Ass*. Yes, you will say, there is the small matter of talent, and you'll hear no argument from me on that score; but I'm driving at something else: viz., that while Apuleius happily admits to the fictionality of his fiction, I continue to insist that what I tell you is true. In his work he makes an easy separation between the realms of fancy and of fact; in my own poor effort, I am trying to set down the true-life account of the life of a man who saw, long before the rest of us, the artificiality of such a separation. (388)

And at the end of this disquisition on the infinite mutability of reality, Rai returns to Ormus, whose "double vision" mirrors that of Don Quixote in that it allows him to see at one and the same time the world as it exists and an alternative reality that threatens to undo the first (not to mention allowing him to see a phantasmagorical Dulcinea figure who appears out of nowhere to have sex with him).[4]

Likewise, Saleem Sinai, the autobiographical narrator of *Midnight's Children*, perceptively glosses the initial chapter of *Don Quixote* (and, by extension, *Lazarillo de Tormes*) in his own opening paragraph, demonstrating the inherent conflict between Cervantes's narrative ambiguity and the picaresque's meticulous attention to biographical and geographical detail:

> I was born in the city of Bombay . . . once upon a time. No, that won't do, there's no getting away from the date: I was born in Doctor Narlikar's Nursing Home on August 15th, 1947. And the time? The time matters, too. Well then: at night. No, it's important to be more . . . On the stroke of midnight, as a matter of fact. Clock-hands joined palms in respectful greeting as I came. Oh, spell it out, spell it out: at the precise instant of India's arrival at independence, I tumbled forth into the world. (3)[5]

Where Cervantes's narrator invokes and then immediately undermines the opening lines of *Lazarillo* by deliberately refusing to provide anything but the most sketchy of details surrounding Don Quixote's biography, Saleem Sinai inscribes himself well within *Lazarillo*'s picaresque narrative tradition by telling us exactly when and where he was born. And yet, the Cervantine ambiguity that haunts Sinai's meandering discourse is unmistakable. Indeed, while not explicitly mentioning Cide Hamete by name, Rushdie freely admits to having created Saleem Sinai as something of a deliberately "unreliable narrator" (*Imaginary Homelands*, 22).

Thus, *The Moor's Last Sigh*, a novel peppered with numerous Cervantine allusions, represents the apex (at least so far) of Rushdie's narratological engagement with Spain's most influential author. And as with *Midnight's Children* and *The Ground Beneath Her Feet*, the most obvious Cervantine component of this text, again, is its narrator. If Rushdie can be said to have been writing versions of *Don Quixote* all along, this fact is made explicit through the deliberate creation of Moraes Zogoiby (a.k.a. "Moor"), an Indian "cross-breed" from Bombay (the offspring of a Christian mother and a Jewish father) who composes his narrative while being held prisoner in the fictional Spanish town of "Benengeli" (a place not coincidentally situated between the villages of "Erasmo" and "Avellaneda").[6]

More than one critic has commented on the obvious kinship between "Moor" and Cide Hamete. Paul A. Cantor, for instance, examines the ways in which Rushdie incorporates the history of medieval Spain into his text as a way of "rethinking" the cultural multiplicity of contemporary India. He begins by highlighting the literary ties between Cide Hamete and Moraes Zogoiby and notes that *Don Quixote* is a "precursor" to *The Moor's Last Sigh* (323). From this point of departure Cantor traces what he calls the "Islamic expansionism" of the seventh through the fourteenth centuries, which resulted in the establishment of "al-Andalus" on the Iberian Peninsula and produced an India that was "always already invaded" long before the arrival of either the Portuguese or the British (326–27). He discusses the *Reconquista* and comments on the co-existence of Christians, Jews, and Muslims in medieval Iberia, while explaining the significance of the work's title for readers perhaps unaware of the events surrounding the fall of Granada on January 2, 1492, when the last "Moorish monarch" of the Iberian Peninsula, (commonly known as Boabdil, but supposedly called "al-zogoybi" ["the unfortunate"] by his Muslim subjects), surrendered the keys to his beloved Alhambra to the "Catholic Kings" (*los Reyes Católicos*), Ferdinand and Isabella, with a notoriously heavy sigh. Cantor argues that Rushdie's incorporation of this segment of Spanish history into his novel "places him squarely in the camp of the contemporary ideology of multiculturalism [through which he] condemns efforts to impose a uniform culture on a nation and celebrates instead cultural hybridity" (325). Later, however, he problematizes this assertion by exploring Rushdie's contrastive vision of a contemporary multicultural Spain dominated by foreign tourists and multinational corporations like Gucci and Hermès, a commercial multiculturalism that in turn is opposed in places like India by an increasingly vociferant religious fundamentalism: "I began by arguing that Rushdie offers multiculturalism as the antidote to religious conflict, but now I am saying that Rushdie views religious conflict as marking the inevitable limit to the success of cultural hybridity" (336).

Stephen Henighan also examines the connection between Hispanic culture and Rushdie's novel. But unlike Cantor, Henighan does not focus so much on historical and political questions as he does on the literary intertextualities between Rushdie's work and that of other writers, specifically the novelists of the Latin American "boom."[7] Thus, while Henighan evokes Cervantes's work in his title ("Coming to Benengeli"), and while he cites *Don Quixote* in his conclusion, he is much more interested in exploring the influence of such figures as Mario Vargas Llosa, Gabriel García Márquez, Carlos Fuentes, and (particularly) Juan Rulfo on Rushdie's work. He does not seem interested in teasing out the multiple Cervantine allusions that pervade the text. In this way, then, Henighan traces Rushdie's growing intellectual engagement with Latin American fiction, and through a close comparative analysis he documents Rushdie's literary debt in *Midnight's Children* and *The Moor's Last Sigh* to such works as *One Hundred Years of Solitude*, *The Death of Artemio Cruz*, and *Terra Nostra* (55–64).

"Coming to Benengeli" culminates, as its title implies, with a close reading of part 4 of *The Moor's Last Sigh* (also entitled "The Moor's Last Sigh") in which Moraes travels to Benengeli on a quest to recover his lost heritage: several paintings by his famous mother, the renowned artist Aurora Zogoiby, which have been stolen from the Indian national gallery and clandestinely imported into Spain by Vasco Miranda, another famous artist (and former family friend) who now lives in a kitschy re-creation of the Alhambra. Henighan persuasively argues that this journey to Benengeli, in which Moraes encounters a number of phantasmagorical figures before ultimately dying, is modeled on Juan Preciado's journey to Comala in Rulfo's *Pedro Páramo*, in which the protagonist also goes in search of his past and also dies in the process. Henighan ends his analysis by noting the several references Rushdie also makes to *Don Quixote* (especially with regard to Cide Hamete) and argues that through these allusions Rushdie "pushes his engagement with the Hispanic tradition back to its foundations" (71).[8] In short, Henighan argues that Rushdie's early work, which demonstrated a kind of "Third World solidarity" with the Latin American boom writers, "has blossomed [in *The Moor's Last Sigh*] into his most extended incursion into the Hispanic tradition, following the tensions embedded in Spanish American society back to the rifts plaguing the society of the medieval and Renaissance Spain that conquered most of America, then appropriating salient elements of this society to elaborate a symbolic system rich enough to nourish his commentary on the suppression of multiplicity" (71).

Thus, while both Cantor and Henighan acknowledge Rushdie's Cervantine borrowings, their interest in Cide Hamete's ghostly presence in the text remains limited to his function as a figure of the cultural, linguistic, and religious hybridity of medieval Spain. For them, Moraes represents the key to an allegory that is both the point of departure and the point of arrival for Rushdie's exploration of the realities of postcolonial India, what Cantor calls "the full complexity of the problem of multicultural-ism" (336). In essence, both view Rushdie's Cervantine allusions in *The Moor's Last Sigh* within the global context of colonial repression and postcolonial resistance in which the "history" that matters most is that of the Da Gama/Zogoiby dynasty, whose "family" history—like that of the Buendías and Macondo in *One Hundred Years of Solitude*—is insepara-ble from that of India itself. And because of the family's origins "beneath [Boabdil's] roof, and then between his sheets" (82), Moraes's narration of this tale—along with his return to Granada at the end—bring the dynastic history and the colonial history to a full-circle conclusion.

Yet, despite Cantor's and Henighan's appreciable insights into Rush-die's intellectual engagement with Spain and Latin America, their broad, historical approaches do not represent the only way of reading the Cer-vantine intertextualities embedded in *The Moor's Last Sigh*. Moraes's autobiographical narration, which he writes while being held prisoner in Benengeli, can be read at the same time on a much more intimate level. That is, woven into the fabric of the interrelated dynastic history of the Da Gama/Zogoiby families and the colonial and postcolonial histories of the Iberian Peninsula and the Indian subcontinent is an exploration of a much more personal—although no less global—tale, which reinscribes Rush-die's experience as a "captive writer" in the late twentieth century within a fictional context Cervantes himself might also have found familiar. In other words, like "The Captive's Tale," the novel occupies—and, indeed, constitutes—an intermediate discursive space, what Rushdie has called a "middle ground" (*Midnight's Children*, 6), where the larger histories (po-litical and literary) of Spain and India intersect with the personal histories (again, political and literary) of Cervantes and Rushdie. In this regard, *The Moor's Last Sigh* is a brilliant performance of textual hybridity itself, a discursive example of Homi Bhabha's "in-betweenness" (127).

While various critics have noted the relationship between "Moor" and "Cide Hamete," no one has noted Moraes Zogoiby's clear resemblance to both Don Quixote and Cervantes. Early in the novel, when Moraes's narrative briefly flashes forward to the actual moment of textual creation (as opposed to the more common moments of memorial reconstruction), Rushdie allows us a fleeting glimpse of this explicitly Cervantine narrator who contemplates his own withering physiognomy:

The mirrors of Benengeli reflect an exhausted gent with hair as white, as thin, as serpentine as his great-grandmother Epifania's long-gone chevelure. His gaunt face, and in his elongated body no more than a memory of an old, slow grace of movement. The aquiline profile is now merely beaky, and the womanly full lips have thinned, like the dwindling corona of hair. [...] Chicken-necked and pigeon-chested, this bony, dusty old-timer still manages an admirable erectness of bearing [...]; but if you could see him, and had to guess his age, you'd say he was fit for rocking-chairs, soft food and rolled trousers, you'd put him out to pasture like an old horse, or—if by chance you were not in India—you might pack him off to a retirement home. Seventy-two years old, you'd say, with a deformed right hand like a club. (145–46)

Spotting Don Quixote in this description is fairly easy, as is catching the brief, secondary appearance of Rocinante in the horse put out to pasture (Figure 12). But linking this passage with Don Quixote's creator is fraught with a bit more difficulty. First, such a linkage necessarily implies an autobiographical connection between Moraes and Rushdie similar to that between Ruy Pérez de Viedma (the "Captive" of *Don Quixote*) and Cervantes. Rushdie, however, rejected this kind of linkage during an interview in which he insisted, "[Moor] ain't me" just as "Bellow is not Herzog" ("*The Moor's Last Sigh*: Charlie Rose," 206). To this objection one might respond by noting that Cervantes insisted to the end that *Don Quixote* was nothing more than a burlesque of the chivalric novel, a claim most readers over the past four hundred years have found somewhat untenable. Likewise, while Bellow may not be Herzog, Ruy Pérez de Viedma both is and is not Cervantes; he too is a "half-and-halfer" (*Midnight's Children*, 13) by occupying Bhabha's space in-between. Second, however, and setting aside Rushdie's authorial disclaimers, while Moraes's deformed right hand is—to say the least—highly suggestive of Cervantes's famous disability, the fact remains that Moraes's debilitation is a birth defect rather than a war wound and—moreover—is conspicuously located on the wrong side of his body. To this caveat one need only point out that in a rhetorical move highly reminiscent of Diego Velázquez—and Rushdie mentions the sight lines of *Las Meninas* at least once in the text (246)—what he has described is a mirror image, so that what we actually see as we look at Moraes's reflection through his eyes is a quixotic figure with an apparently lame left hand, thus making Moraes an inverted, baroque reflection of "el manco de Lepanto" ("the one-handed [hero] of Lepanto"), as he is commonly known throughout the Spanish-speaking world. (And we should not forget that Rushdie includes Cervantes among his list of literary "parents" [*Imaginary Homelands*, 21]).

Now, while there is ample circumstantial evidence to see a bit of Rushdie in Moraes, there is no reason to insist that this is purely a one-to-one correspondence; Rushdie is far too fine a writer to have created such a ham-handed self-allusion. As a matter of fact, in the previously cited interview, in response to a question about his authorial presence in the text,

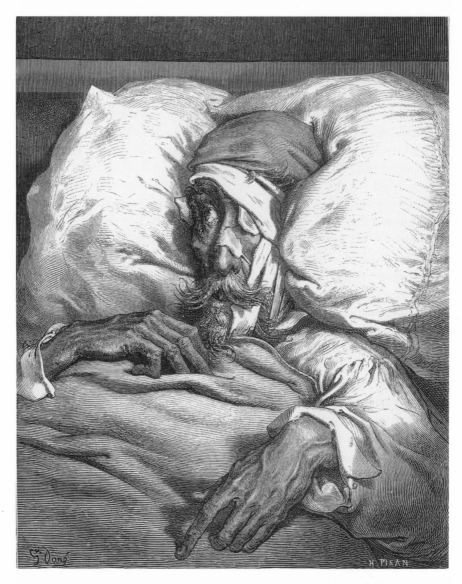

Figure 12: Salman Rushdie's Cervantine description of Moraes Zogoiby in *The Moor's Last Sigh* is profoundly indebted to visual representations of Don Quixote like those created by Gustave Doré.

Rushdie indicated that he actually felt a much greater personal affinity toward Moraes's mother, Aurora, since "the kind of painter she is is a little bit the kind of writer I would like to be" ("Charlie Rose," 206–7). Appropriately, then, painting becomes a metaphor for narrative throughout the text, and Moraes's several lengthy commentaries on art—especially his mother's work—can be taken as a kind of extended *ars poetica* of the novel itself, similar to remarks made by the canon at the end of part 1 of *Don*

Quixote, whose commentaries on the chivalric novel can be read as an *ars poetica* of the very text in which he makes these comments (1.47:441–42).

Significantly, Aurora's career begins precisely during a moment of captivity. Having been locked in her bedroom for a week by her father (as a punishment for pilfering a number of household items), Aurora uses the period of her "house arrest" as the "true moment of her coming-of-age" and fills the walls of her room with images that depict the ancient and modern history of India, creating a sweeping collage that "pullulated with figures, human and animal, real and imaginary" (58–59). This narrative tendency—the very essence of Rushdie's novel—with its proclivity for what Moraes calls a "thousand-and-one anecdotes" in which "history, family, politics, and fantasy jostled each other like the great crowds at V.T. or Churchgate Stations" (102; 203–4), will mark Aurora's work throughout her career, even as her artistic technique becomes more and more abstract. And nowhere is this tendency toward anecdote and abstraction better represented than in the series of so-called Moor paintings—begun in 1957 and culminating with her "last, unfinished, unsigned masterpiece, *The Moor's Last Sigh*" (218)—in which she creates a pastiche (based on Boabdil's famous capitulation) that chronicles at once the contemporary history of India and that of her immediate family (203–4). And as with Rushdie's novel, these paintings—Moraes explains—are an "attempt to create a romantic myth of the plural, hybrid nation" in which Aurora "was using Arab Spain to re-imagine India" (227).

For as "trans-historical" as this series of paintings might be, however, these works exhibit a distinct autobiographical quality as well, since Moraes provides his mother with both a physical and a metaphorical model for Boabdil:

> As the Moor pictures moved further down this fabulist road, it became plain that I barely needed to pose for my mother any more; but she wanted me there, she said she needed me, she called me her *lucky talis-moor*. And I was happy to be there, because the story unfolding on her canvases seemed more like my autobiography than the real story of my life. (227)

And as the paintings become more and more intimately biographical, they become more and more fragmented:

> *The Moor was an abstract figure now, a pattern of black and white diamonds covering him from head to foot. The mother, Ayxa, was black; and the lover, Chimène, was brilliant white. [...] He was black and white. He was the living proof of the possibility of the union of opposites. But Ayxa the Black pulled one way, and Chimène the White, the*

other. They began to tear him in half. Black diamonds, white diamonds fell from the gash, like teardrops. (259; original italics)

In light of the many references to "Mother India" that occur throughout the novel, it is not difficult to read this family romance—in which a possessive mother and a (frankly) dangerous beloved fight over the affections of a protagonist who is literally torn apart by the conflict—as an allegory of Rushdie's sense of East/West alienation, a conflict he characterized in his "Balloon" speech as "the warring halves of the world, which were also the warring halves of [his] soul" (*Imaginary Homelands*, 435). This psychological interpretation becomes even more meaningful when we remember, as Timothy Weiss notes, that the name "Aurora" alludes to a Roman goddess, while the name "Uma Sarasvati" (Moraes's lover) derives from two distinct Hindu goddesses (paragraphs 23–24). Moreover, Uma has been transformed by Aurora in the painting mentioned earlier into a kind of postmodern pastiche that erases any clear boundaries between Indian, Spanish, French, and American cultures: "Uma, fictionalised, Hispanicised, as this 'Chimène', Uma incorporating aspects of Sophia Loren in *El Cid*, pinched from the story of Rodrigo de Vivar and introduced without explanation into the hybrid universe of the Moor" (247). Still, I am less interested here with the ways in which Rushdie's psychological autobiography seeps into the book than I am with what this particular passage says about his narrative technique. The same proclivities toward abstraction and fragmentation that Moor sees in his mother's paintings are just as evident in Rushdie's text. And when viewed through the prism of this *ars poetica*, Rushdie's Cervantine intertextualities take on an important significance. For, scattered throughout the text are shards of various Cervantine allusions (often tied to those of other authors) that, when scooped up and reassembled, create a patterned exploration of the interplay between captivity and narrativity, and more importantly, between madness and reading.

One of the more notable aspects of Rushdie's work is his prolific use of playful and complex word games, especially bilingual puns. In this respect, *The Moor's Last Sigh* does not differ from his other works. Rushdie justifies this punning in his explanation of the memorable nickname of Lambajan Chandiwala, the Da Gama/Zogoiby clan's one-legged household servant: "In those days many more people would have understood the inter-lingual joke: lamba, long; jan, sounds like John, chandi, silver. Long John Silverfellow" (126). And in fact, Rushdie uses the nicknames of the four Zogoiby children as an extended set-up to a punch line that he seems to insert solely for the pleasure of telling it. Shortly after the birth of their first daughter, Christina, Moraes's parents shorten her name to simply "Ina"; likewise his next sister, Inamorata, becomes "Minnie"; and his third sister, Philomina, becomes "Mynah." Thus, when Moraes, the youngest and only male in the family, comes along, acquiring his own nickname, the pun is complete: "Ina, Minnie, Mynah, and at last Moor. That's me: the end of the line" (142–43). (This is a sophisticated pun in its own right, since "Moor" represents both the "end" of the poetic line and the genetic "end" of his family line, since he dies without an heir.)

In similar fashion, Rushdie peppers his text with a variety of off-handed Cervantine puns and allusions that serve as grace notes to the work's more prominent themes. This trend is revealed almost immediately, for instance, when Moraes characterizes his family narrative as "the story of our comings-together, tearings-apart, our rises, falls, our *tilto-ings up and down*" (12; original emphasis). Shortly thereafter, he obliquely evokes Cervantes's exemplary novel "The Glass Graduate" in a passage that reads: " 'So Abie,' [Flora Zogoiby] said slowly, not looking directly at him in case she found she could see through him, which would prove that she had finally cracked into little pieces" (109).[9] Monipodio, the head of a Sevillian crime syndicate in "Rinconete and Cortadillo" (and whose name is almost an "inter-lingual" joke by itself) also makes an extended appearance in the guise of the peg-legged Lambajan Chandiwala, a.k.a. Long John Silverfellow, the "private pirate" (126) whom Moraes refers to as his "Beloved monopod guardian" (126).[10]

These linguistic and narrative grace notes serve two functions within the text. First, they ornament the principal themes of the work: captivity and narrativity. Second, Rushdie's seemingly throw-away allusions also serve as narrative signposts, alerting the reader to the more substantive pathways he has constructed within the book. These pathways trace the distribution of the various Cervantine fragments he has scattered throughout. In this regard, there are, in fact, two distinct "Don Quixote" lines within the text—one "positive" and one "negative"—that form an "arabesque" subexploration of the relationship between reading and madness. (Not coincidentally, when Moraes finally arrives in Benengeli, one of the first things he sees is a sign hanging above the door to a school that reads "*Lectura-locura*" [386].)

On the one hand, for instance, Moraes's family seems to have a deep streak of "quixotism" running through its genealogy, and this "quixotism" manifests itself as an idealism that stems in large part from too much reading. For instance, Rushdie ties Francisco da Gama, Moraes's maternal great-grandfather, to Cervantes's now archetypal protagonist (just as he tied Moraes to Cervantes's now archetypal narrator) when he describes him as "hero material from the day he was born, destined for questions and quests, as ill-at-ease with domesticity as Quixote" (17). Francisco's wanderlust and idealism combine to lead him out into the greater world on a mission to fund orphanages and free health clinics, build schools and research institutes, and even sponsor such humanistic endeavors as an annual contest of oral storytellers. His political activism, however, eventually lands him in prison (again, the question of captivity), where he is transformed under the enormous pressure into a total quixotic buffoon: "Nobody ever worked out where, in what reject-goods discount-store of the mind, Great-Grandfather Francisco got hold of the scientific theory that turned him from emerging hero into national laughing-stock" (19–20). From his prison cell he writes and publishes a convoluted paper entitled "*Towards a Provisional Theory of the Transformational Fields of Conscience*," in which he proposes the existence of global networks of "spiritual energy" that are "nothing less than the repositories of the memory—both practical and moral—of the human species" (20). This quest for unification contrasts markedly with Francisco's previous attitudes on global culture. Earlier in his life he had attempted to separate his colonial hybrid world (at least architecturally) by constructing separate "East" and "West" houses (with all that those adjectives imply) on a single piece of property and then alternatively inhabiting each edifice during brief intervals. Now imprisoned, he seeks to unify all of humanity through his writing. The man who once considered himself a "disciple of Bertrand Russell" (17) has now apparently read too much "Theosophy" and has taken too seriously the Mahatma Gandhi's "insistence on the oneness of all India's widely differing millions" (20). The only "oneness" he manages to provoke with his treatise, however, is a negative reaction so universal that he eventually sinks "into introversion and despondency" (22) before finally swimming out to sea to his death during a rainstorm.

Francisco passes this innocuous and ineffective "quixotism" onto his sons, Camoens and Aires, who fiercely oppose each other in the debates on history, empire, and nationalism on the Indian subcontinent. Camoens literally follows in his father's footsteps when he breaks into the "West" house's library and begins to voraciously "devour the books" (24). Yet, as with his father before him, this "Western education" eventually leads to a quixotic activism that also leads to his own disillusionment and downfall. He embraces Marxism and attempts to build a genuine alliance between India and the Soviet Union. But when a visiting troupe of "Lenin-thesps" (29)—that is, Lenin impersonators who tour the world re-enacting the greatness of the Russian Revolution in a type of socialist "auto-sacramental"—prove to be every bit as racist as the British, Camoens is deeply disillusioned and becomes instead a staunch Nationalist; ironically, though, one with a "fierce love of English literature" (32) and an "equally fierce determination that the British *imperium* must end" (33). In a way, Camoens—whose nationalism attempts to nullify the colonial invasion so elegantly extolled by his namesake, the author of *Os Lusíadas*—can be read here as a figure of the "third world" as that Cold War term was originally understood before it achieved its postcolonial significance as an adjective describing the subaltern peoples of developing countries: Camoens remains defiantly "non-aligned" with either the capi-

talist "first world" or the socialist "second world," and his personal disillusionment functions in the text as a symbol of the collective frustration of
the postcolonial world within such a rigidly binary international system.

Aires da Gama, for his part, avoids activism entirely and retreats instead into a kind of cocoon of nineteenth-century Anglophilia. Thus, when
independence comes to India, when he is forced to give up "his secret fantasy that the Europeans might one day return to the Malabar Coast," he
takes to wearing spats and a monocle and enters into a reclusive retirement
in which he devotes himself to a complete reading of the English canon,
"consoling himself with the best of the old world for the distasteful muta-
bilities of history" (199). It is not difficult to detect in this rhetorical flour-
ish the ghost of Matthew Arnold, who functions as a kind of Amadís de
Gaula for this new Don Quixote clad in both the armour and the philosophy of a bygone age. But Aires's twentieth-century escape into an idealized
nineteenth-century past turns out to be as impossible as Alonso Quixano's
epochal retreat and as frustrated as Camoens's political "non-alignment"
with the bipolarities of the twentieth century.

Camoens and Aires represent fairly harmless quixotic figures; they
are clearly eccentric but not dangerous. They are reflected, however, in
Rushdie's Cervantine mirror by two darkly negatively characters. The
first of these is Raman Fielding (a.k.a. Mainduck), the overtly Hitlerian
"failed artist" and dictatorial politico who rises to power by invoking
an Indian golden age, "when good Hindu men and women could roam
free" (299). (Compare this to Don Quixote's own nostalgia for the golden
age [1.11:84–85].) Fielding is a politically active Quixote figure. Unlike
Camoens, however, he exists as a kind of study in the negative power of
unbridled idealism, especially when this is reduced to an opportunistic
fanaticism. Fielding ultimately realizes the very dangerous potential that
always lies just below the surface of Don Quixote's own guileless desire
to restore a long-lost golden age. For, despite his many virtues, Don Quixote is at base a single-minded, quasi-religious fanatic (as the episode with
the Jewish silk merchants makes clear [1.4:45–47]) whose often belligerent
aims are limited only by his advanced age and by the fact that, once in
the company of Sancho, the priest, the barber, Dorotea, and the others,
he is surrounded by people who tend to exert a calming influence.[11] Fielding, however, is much younger and much stronger, and he is accompanied
by no such cadre of wise counselors. Except during a brief period when
Moraes plays thuglike Sancho to Fielding's violent Quixote, Fielding surrounds himself with like-minded fanatics.[12] And the only thing that ultimately prevents his success (or so we think) is that his Sancho eventually
turns on him. If, as Rushdie has said, the novel is a critique of the dangers
of religious fundamentalism in a pluralistic society, then Fielding is the
maximum symbol of this danger in the world ("Charlie Rose," 202–3).

The second, and probably most important dangerously quixotic, figure of the novel is Vasco Miranda, a self-invented "madman" (165)—and, again, frustrated artist—who provides the mirror image to Aires da Gama. For, where Aires retreats from the realities of postcolonial India into the imaginative "British" universe of his father's colonial library, Vasco greets Indian independence with an equally "literary" reaction. At the stroke of midnight on April 15, 1947, he rises and delivers the following accusatory toast at a party thrown by Aurora Zogoiby, a toast that drips of Cervantine and quixotic irony:

> "What are you all so pleased about?" he shouted, swaying. "This isn't your night. [...] Don't you get it? Bunch of English-medium misfits, the lot of you. Minority group members. Square peg freaks. *You don't belong here.* Country's as alien to you as if you were what's-the-word *lunatics. Moon-men.* You read the wrong books, get on the wrong side in every argument, think the wrong thoughts." (165–66; original italics)

Declaring himself henceforth "Portuguese" (167)—both because he is from the state of Goa and despite that fact—Vasco eventually makes his way back to the Iberian Peninsula and retreats not into an Anglocentric library but into a labyrinthine simulacrum of the mighty Alhambra in which he attempts to recreate "the fabulous multiple culture of ancient al-Andalus" (398). And as he grows ever more imbalanced, he abandons even this new "Portuguese" identity—like Aires, who forsakes all vestiges of his Indian self, assuming instead the costume of a proper English gentleman—and begins to dress up like "an old-time Sultan" (398), wearing "baggy pantaloons and embroidered waistcoat, worn open over a ballooning collarless shirt" (410). He even enjoys a kind of "dulcinated" harem in the form of the so-called Larios sisters, Renegada and Felicitas, whose surname Moraes speculates might actually be "Lorenço" or "del Toboso" (417), and who turn out, in the end, to be lovers rather than siblings.[13]

For Rushdie, colonialism is viewed as a kind of madness; or at least it seems to spawn madmen. First, there is Uma, Moraes's darkly sinister lover (the "Chimène" of Aurora's "Moor paintings"), who becomes a kind of enchanter figure—quietly executing an ultimately failed plan to alienate Moraes from his family and then kill him—but who also shares Don Quixote's shattered sense of self, which she eventually passes on to Moraes. She is described as a kind of shape-shifter capable of taking on "radically different personae in the company of different people," whose "highly inventive commitment to the infinite malleability of the real [and] modernistically provisional sense of truth" may have actually deprived her of "a clear sense of an 'authentic' identity that was independent of these performances" (266, 272). And when Moraes realizes too late the consequences of her machinations, when he finally admits to himself that he had been bewitched by a "pure malevolence" that had destroyed his life, he describes his state of mind in terms that would apply quite well to Don Quixote: "To give up one's own picture of the world and become wholly dependent on someone else's—was not that as good a description as any of the process of, literally, *going out of* one's mind? In which case—to use Aurora's contrast—I was the mad one. And lovely Uma: the bad" (267–68; original emphasis).

Thus, in the "Little Alhambra" the various narrative skeins of the novel—its running puns, its leitmotivs, its splintered allegories—all converge. Vasco Miranda's "Mooristan" is the place where "worlds collide" (408): East and West, past and present, fact and fiction. It is the site where the novel's primary themes of captivity and narrativity come to fruition, as Moraes notes when he ties himself to the world's most famous captive storyteller: "[Vasco Miranda] had made a Scheherazade of me. As long as my tale held his interest he would let me live" (421). In fact, dressed up here as "The Great Turk," Vasco functions as a double parody that once again connects Rushdie with Cervantes. On the one hand, he can be read as a mocking symbol of the Ayatollah Khomeini, a kind of megalomaniacal "sultan" who had effectively imprisoned Rushdie (ironically, to punish him for his stories rather than impel a command performance) as part of a colossal plan to re-establish a long-lost world. On the other hand, Vasco can be seen here as a kind of postmodern "renegade" (in this case, a "Portuguese" pilgrim who renounces his Christian identity in order to transform himself into a medieval Iberian Muslim, if only as a hollow cultural sign). He can be read as a burlesque echo perhaps of Arnaute Mami, the renegade captain (of Greek origin) who captured Cervantes in 1575 and who thus inspired, however indirectly, "The Captive's Tale."

But the Little Alhambra is also the place where one reality overlays another: Benengeli is also what Moraes calls "Palimpstine" (409). And thus, it is here that Rushdie's Cervantine allusions not only converge but actually expand to envelop and include another famously Cervantine writer, Jorge Luis Borges. Moraes Zogoiby is not the only prisoner held captive in the Little Alhambra. Vasco Miranda has also taken a "second hostage" (419) in the person of a Japanese-born art restorer named Aoi Uë whom he has forcibly enlisted to liberate from its "long imprisonment" (420) *The Moor's Last Sigh*, Aurora's original masterpiece that now lies hidden beneath Vasco Miranda's own painted version of this same historical scene, which, not coincidentally, also bears the title *The Moor's Last Sigh*.

In many ways, Aoi mirrors another important character from Cervantes's "Captive's Tale": Zoraida, the Muslim woman who facilitates Ruy Pérez de Viedma's escape from the bagnios of Algeria and who accompanies him to Spain, where she insists on being called "María" because, like so many other Muslim characters in early modern Spanish literature, she yearns to convert to Christianity (1.37:353). María Antonia Garcés calls Zoraida an ambiguous sign that "fluctuates between history and fiction, between the Spanish and the Arab cultures, between the Castilian and the Arabic languages, between the socio-economic language of power and the unspoken language of desire" (69). She is entirely right in this regard, and her astute reading of Zoraida's "indeterminacy" points to Aoi's importance as a co-captive within *The Moor's Last Sigh*. Aoi's east Asian origins and her violent demise are significant, and not just because she can be read perhaps as a figure of the real-life Japanese translator of *The Satanic Verses* who was killed in 1991 by militants enforcing the *fatwa*. Moraes speculates in his narration—which Aoi pointedly reads even as it is being written—that "in another life, down a fork in the road" (428) the "story in which she was so unfairly trapped" (427) might have turned out differently. One can discern in this phrasing the discursive echoes of Borges's "The Garden of Forking Paths," in which East also fatally meets West and in which imperial struggles and family histories play a significant role.

Rushdie's allusion to this story is important through the notion of palimpsests. "The Garden of Forking Paths" is nothing if not the story of multiple realities—multiple narratives—overwriting each other in a kind of mise-en-abîme. *The Moor's Last Sigh*, then, functions as a kind of "performance" of Borges's implied forking narratives. It contains multiple "Moors" and multiple "Moor's last sighs." The "Moors" include Boabdil (the historical figure), Boabdil (the protagonist of Aurora's painting), Boabdil (the protagonist of Vasco Miranda's painting), Cide Hamete, Clayton Moore (the actor who originally played the Lone Ranger on television and whom Moraes invokes in a shrewd West/East parody of the Cowboys-and-Indians discourse of American westerns [413]), Mrs. Moore from E. M. Forster's novel *A Passage to India* (a character who, at the very least, hovers over Rushdie's text ever so obliquely through the lingering echoes associated with the name Fielding), and finally, Moraes Zogoiby himself. The "Moor's last sighs" include Rushdie's novel as a whole, his final section of the same title, Boabdil's historical lament, the "¡Ay de mi Alhama!" ballad this lament inspired (a text absent for most readers, though inevitably present for those familiar with the Hispanic literary tradition), Aurora's painting based on this story, Vasco Miranda's own artistic rendering painted over Aurora's earlier work, and finally, Moraes's tale itself, a narration literally uttered with his dying breath. And this final "Moor's last sigh"—that is, Moraes's blood-stained manuscript that begins and ends in Benengeli, and in which at least three characters read along as their own histories are recounted—folds back on itself in such a way as to create the kind of Cervantine circularity García Márquez constructs at the end of *One Hundred Years of Solitude* and Borges provocatively posits in "The Garden of Forking Paths":

> I recalled, too, the night in the middle of *The Thousand and One Nights* when Queen Scheherezade, through a magical mistake on the part of her

copyist, started to tell the story of *The Thousand and One Nights*, with the risk of again arriving at the night upon which she will relate it, and thus on to infinity. (97)[14]

Yet Rushdie is no distracted copyist. Nothing would be better, of course, for Scheherazade—at least from her own perspective—than to be trapped in an infinite narrative loop that forever deferred the threat of imminent death. For, although she does eventually escape the fate suffered by her own "fellow-travellers," this escape is by no means assured until the very end when the Sultan abrogates his own imposed death sentence. Likewise, nothing could be better for Moraes Zogoiby—a narrator genetically cursed by an accelerated aging that threatens to kill him long before his time—than to exist within a circular (and hence temporally infinite) narrative in which his own subjectivity is mirrored through a series of other "moors," all of whom exist simultaneously both inside and outside a narrative loop that is itself part of an interlocking mise-en-abîme in which one "Moor's last sigh" reflects another and another and another. And for this reason it is significant that, although Moraes claims to sit down and write the end of his story (an ending that more or less appears as the novel's first chapter), the text denies us both this very ending and Moraes's imminent demise. Instead, the final two pages of the book exist as a kind of oral epilogue—Moraes's literal "last sigh" uttered to the four winds—in which his death is (Borges-like) ultimately deferred: *"I'll lay me down upon this graven stone, lay my head beneath these letters R I P, and close my eyes, according to our family's old practice of falling asleep in times of trouble, and hope to awaken, renewed and joyful, into a better time"* (433–34; original emphasis). And while Moraes slumbers, waiting for a better fork in the temporal path, he is content to let his tale replay itself over and over again in a verbatim loop, somewhat like an old 8-track tape.

"The Garden of Forking Paths" is not the only Borges text, however, that profoundly informs Rushdie's novel, especially with regard to *Don Quixote* and the question of palimpsests. Borges wrote (or, at least, proposed) his own version of Cervantes's novel in "Pierre Menard, Author of the Quixote." This hypothetical text, which functions as a kind of "hall of mirrors" also related to *Las Meninas* (Del Río, 462–63), explores the ultimate narrative palimpsest, recreating Cervantes's novel "word for word and line for line" (Borges, "Pierre Menard, Author," 49).[15] Yet, Pierre Menard's *Don Quixote* is an incomplete text, since it consists merely of three "isolated" segments: the ninth and thirty-eighth chapters of part 1 and a fragment of the twenty-second chapter (Borges's narrator does not stipulate from which part). Part 1, chapter 9, includes the moment in the text where Cervantes introduces Cide Hamete to the world; chapter 38 consists of Don Quixote's disquisition on the relative merits of arms and letters, a segment that functions as a prologue to "The Captive's Tale"; and the enigmatic chapter 22 is either the chapter in part 1 where we first meet Ginés de Pasamonte (yet another captive narrator who manages to escape from his own constrictive autobiography in order to reappear later on, down another narrative path) or the chapter in part 2 where Don Quixote descends into Montesinos's cave and falls asleep only to have his vision of a corrupted ideal partially confirmed for him a short time later by Ginés de Pasamonte in his new role as Maese Pedro, the puppeteer.

That Pierre Menard would succeed in recreating these 3 chapters (out of the 126 written by Cervantes) is curious, and a number of scholars have attempted to explain this particular collection of episodes.[16] Whatever nexus may exist in Pierre Menard's (or Borges's) imagination, however, Rushdie has clearly intuited a new interrelationship between these narrative fragments. Indeed, *The Moor's Last Sigh* can be read as a version of *Don Quixote*. But Rushdie's novel is not a reconstruction of Cervantes's *Don Quixote*; rather, it is a rewriting of Pierre Menard's *Don Quixote* in which Cervantes, Cide Hamete, Don Quixote, Ruy Pérez de Viedma, and Ginés de Pasamonte all merge into a single captive narrator who falls asleep at the end, hoping to reappear in a better story the second time around; hoping in fact—even if this second tale turns out to be a verbatim palimpsest of the first—that it will at least be, as Borges says, "infinitely richer" ("Pierre Menard, Author," 52).[17] But where Pierre Menard's text exists as an abbreviated palimpsest, erasing 123 other Cervantine chapters, Rushdie's is a supplemental one that connects Pierre Menard's 3 chapters together by filling in the gaps between them. And the center of this new text—like Pierre Menard's—is a debate about arms and letters, which Rushdie allegorizes by making it at once both literal and symbolic.

As previously noted, Moraes's deformed right hand inversely mirrors Cervantes's left one. The irony of this deformity, as Moraes points out, is that he remains nonetheless "right-handed," which means that he must learn to do everything (including and especially write) with his still functional left hand, despite the difficulties involved in such an endeavor: "It was as hard for me to learn to write with my left [hand] as it would be for any righty in the world. When I was ten, and looked twenty, my handwriting was no better than a toddler's early scrawls. This, too, I overcame." (153). But along the way, Moraes discovers that his clublike right hand is not entirely useless either, and he learns to use his very potent (indeed, lethal) arm in the boxing ring, becoming a formidable opponent. Thus, for a narrator whose tale ultimately forces him to become a writer, this "handicap" is doubly significant: Moraes is the literal embodiment of "arms" on the one hand and "letters" on the other. And the debate between the two occurs within the third of Rushdie's four structural divisions—tellingly entitled "Bombay Central"—and plays itself out in two decisive moments.

At the end of part 2, Moraes is arrested on what amounts to trumped-up murder charges (after Uma has accidentally poisoned herself in trying to kill him), and he spends much of the first chapter of "Bombay Central" locked in solitary confinement within a roach-infested jail cell so horrific that it evokes Dante, Kafka, and Orwell simultaneously. Yet, he does not languish there for long before unexpectedly finding himself "raised from the dead" (294) by Raman Fielding, who offers him his freedom in exchange for his services as a henchman. And as with Vasco Miranda's later nonchoice of either writing or dying, Fielding also makes him choose between his left hand (the lettered one) and his right hand (the armed one). For a protagonist who describes his deformity with yet another pun ("life had dealt me a bad hand" [153]), the decision imposed on him by Fielding carries a profound rhetorical resonance: Fielding literally forces Moraes's hand: "My zombie, my hammer: are you for us or against us, will you be righteous or will you be lefteous?" (295). Given no real choice, Moraes initially follows Don Quixote's advice and chooses the soldier's life. He becomes the "righteous" enforcer of Fielding's fanatical vision; he becomes Fielding's "right-hand-man." But even the manual labor associated with this nefarious vocation provides an outlet for Moraes's writerly tendencies: "Did I not tell you with what difficulty I had learned left-handedness, how unnaturally it came to me? Very well: but now I could be right-handed at last, in my new life of action I could remove my doughty hammer from my pocket and set it free to write the story of my life" (305).

Over the course of part 3, however, Moraes comes to regret this defense of arms—what he calls his "pulverising Hammer period" (364)—because it forces him to undergo a kind of Fieldingesque metamorphosis that essentially transforms him from Sancho into Sansón Carrasco.[18] Moraes becomes a mirror image of his crazed employer: "So I had become a murdering fanatic, too" (365). And this realization leads him—Carrasco-like—into a decisive final battle with Fielding. Yet, when he confronts his reflective enemy, on the pretense of delivering a secret message, and determined to take his life, despite all of Fielding's elaborate precautions, circumstance (or better yet, Fielding) again forces Moraes's hand one last time:

> The green frog-phone stared up at me from his desk. God, I hated that phone. I bent towards Mainduck; who flung out his left hand, at high speed, caught me by the hair at the nape of my neck, and jammed my mouth into the left side of his head. Off-balance for a moment, I realised with some horror that my right hand, my only weapon, could no longer reach the target. But as I fell against the edge of the desk, my left hand— that same left hand which I had had to force myself, all my life, and against my nature, to learn how to use—collided, by chance, with the telephone.
>
> "The message is from my mother," I whispered, and smashed the green frog into his face. He made no sound. His fingers released my hair, but the frog-phone kept wanting to kiss him, so I kissed him with it, as

hard as I could, then harder, and harder still, until the plastic splintered and the instrument began to come apart in my hand. (367)

Moraes does in fact succeed in killing Fielding here, and thus at first glance it would seem he has maintained a violent defense of arms. But just as his right hand earlier allowed him to "write the story of his life," the particular way in which he annihilates his enemy is significant, especially at the level of metaphor. Moraes's act of resistance is ultimately a "lefteous" act, one performed with his "writing" hand and accomplished—as he himself notes—through the use of a "telecommunicative" weapon (368). In the end, what triumphs over Fielding's superior physical strength is precisely Moraes's lettered hand, the same lettered hand with which he will soon write the manuscript that will eventually save his life. And this crucial act of "lefteous" resistance brings me back to my own point of departure.

I began this chapter by noting that Rushdie wrote *The Moor's Last Sigh* during a period of forced confinement, and I have suggested throughout that the work exhibits more than just a passing nod both to Cervantes's own captivity and to *Don Quixote*. Tradition has long held that *Don Quixote* is the product of one of its author's several incarcerations, as Borges notes in a poem "spoken" by Cervantes: "Cruel stars as well as benevolent stars / presided over the night of my genesis; / to the latter I owe the prison cell / in which I first dreamed *Don Quixote*" (my translation).[19] But no matter how rightly scholars may insist that we should not take Cervantes's (or Borges's) claims literally (Murillo, "Introducción," 1:24), the reality of the supposed prison genesis of *Don Quixote* matters very little in a world of ever proliferating intertextualities, as Rushdie's narrators in both *Midnight's Children* and *The Ground Beneath Her Feet* point out: "Sometimes legends make reality, and become more useful than the facts" (*Midnight's Children*, 47); "If the facts don't fit the legend, print the legend" (*Ground Beneath Her Feet*, 300).[20] Yet, despite what the title of this chapter might imply, I have not argued that *The Moor's Last Sigh* exists as a kind of "version" of Ruy Pérez de Viedma's autobiographical account of Cervantes's Algerian captivity, or that the events presented in the text have any direct relationship to Rushdie's biography. Still, I would not go as far as Rushdie does in disclaiming any connection between the text's narrator and its author. Bellow and Herzog notwithstanding, one can argue that at a certain level Moraes is, in fact, Rushdie, and that this connection is established in the metaphoric debate over arms and letters he has woven into the text.

Commenting on Pierre Menard's twentieth-century reinscription of this debate, in which Don Quixote still decides in favor of arms, Borges's narrator claims astonishment. Cervantes's preference for arms, he says, is easily explained since he was an old soldier. But the fact that Pierre Menard's Don Quixote—whose "author" was a contemporary of Bertrand

Russell—would choose arms over letters is incomprehensible, unless we allow for the fact that Pierre Menard had the peculiar habit of propagating in print ideas completely opposite to those he actually held ("Pierre Menard, Author," 52).[21] Be that as it may, we cannot—I think—attribute the same ironic detachment to Salman Rushdie, who at the very moment of composing his Cervantine palimpsest was a virtual prisoner of the Iranian government. For Rushdie, solitary traveler in a sinking balloon, "Lone Ranger" surrounded by hostile "Indians," the only weapon available to him was his pen. Accordingly, what he did with his several years of precarious solitude was publish a series of texts—*Haroun and the Sea of Stories* (1990), *East, West: Stories* (1994), and finally *The Moor's Last Sigh* (1995)—that on the one hand explore the most complex geopolitical issues of the late twentieth century, while on the other hand defend—above all— the importance of fiction in the world. For, as Rushdie vehemently argued in his "Balloon" speech, "those who do not have power over the story that dominates their lives, power to retell it, rethink it, deconstruct it, joke about it, and change it as times change, truly are powerless, because they cannot think new thoughts" (*Imaginary Homelands*, 432).

In Dale Wasserman's *Man of La Mancha* the central character—a composite Cervantes/Don Quixote—finds himself in a prison in which he must defend his art while awaiting a decision on his freedom. Between 1989 and 1999 (roughly) Salman Rushdie found himself in an uncomfortably similar situation. But where the Cervantes/Don Quixote of *Man of La Mancha* defends himself by advocating the Romantic notion that the "impossible dream" is what matters most, Rushdie focuses on something much more basic. Responding to one critic who had said that the Western concept of free speech was a "non-starter," Rushdie insists that free speech is "the whole ball game" (*Imaginary Homelands*, 439). "*Suspiro ergo sum*," Moraes tells us (53; original italics). But he adds to this ontological declaration—alluding to the well-known song, "As Time Goes By"—that a sigh is not just a sigh: "We inhale the world and breathe out meaning. While we can. While we can" (54).

Stephen Baker notes that "grasping the present as history, *The Moor's Last Sigh* accepts the contingency of imaginative expression, while simultaneously refusing to accept that such contingency relegates art to the status of trivial textual playfulness" (53). Glossing Jacques Derrida, Chris McNab reads this passage as an ethical commentary on the paradox between our collective, shared existence and the solitude of our lonely mortality: "Death is that which is irrevocably our own. No-one can die for us, even in the act of sacrifice, for our unique moment of death forever remains a matter of non-substitution" (137). He is right, of course, but Moraes's declaration reveals something more, as Borges himself recognized in "The Secret Miracle" (a story in which God suspends time in order to give its protagonist, Jaromir Hladík, a prisoner executed by the Nazis, the opportunity to finish an important manuscript).[22] Being a writer necessarily implies "breathing out meaning" even when facing an imminent death, even when the author will probably be the sole reader. Thus, threatened by the Ayatollah Khomeini's *fatwa* and hidden deep inside the basket of his solitary balloon, Rushdie "breathed out" *The Moor's Last Sigh*, a deeply personal manifesto that insists, above all, that "free speech is life itself" (*Imaginary Homelands*, 439). It is a defiant, lettered manifesto that powerfully demonstrates that the voice of an author—any author—matters in the world, even if—by unfortunate happenstance—his or her words represent a "last sigh" before dying.

Chapter 6

Terry Gilliam's Apocryphal *Brazil*; or, Blame It on Dulcinea

As 1984 drew to a close, Terry Gilliam was finishing up production on a new film. Gilliam had originally intended to release this film under the title *1984½* as a homage to George Orwell's 1948 novel *Nineteen Eighty-Four* and Federico Fellini's 1963 film *8½*. As it turned out, however, *1984½* did not appear in American theaters until late December 1985, and by then it bore a completely new and seemingly unrelated title: *Brazil*. Two factors contributed to this double change. First, during the production process Gilliam discovered that Michael Radford was already working on his own version of *Nineteen Eighty-Four* for Virgin Films, which he too planned to release around the same time.[1] Given this unexpected coincidence, Gilliam could hardly persist in using his own Fellini-esque title, despite *Brazil*'s clear originality. Second, and more importantly, Gilliam also found himself in a power struggle with Sidney Sheinberg, head of Universal Studios, over the final cut of *Brazil*. Sheinberg believed that Gilliam's preferred ending (which had appeared in the final cut of the U.K. version released a few months earlier) was far too pessimistic for U.S. audiences. Sheinberg insisted that Gilliam conclude *Brazil* on a much more upbeat note. In response to these studio demands that he "radically rethink" his film (Mathews, 11), Gilliam dug in his heels and launched a counteroffensive that quickly turned into what Jack Mathews has called "the battle of *Brazil*." When the smoke finally cleared, Gilliam had won the war, but by then it was nearly 1986.

Despite its change of title (and the fact that its release missed the year 1984 by an entire calendar year), *Brazil*'s intertextuality with *Nineteen Eighty-Four* remains unmistakable. *Brazil* encompasses a main plot and two principal subplots. *Brazil*'s main plot is essentially a love story revolving around Sam Lowry (Jonathan Pryce) and Jill Layton (Kim Greist). Sam works as a petty bureaucrat in the "Information Retrieval" department of an unnamed totalitarian state's Ministry of Information. As part of his official duties Sam undertakes the task of correcting (at least bureaucratically) a paperwork error that has resulted in the accidental arrest and death by torture of a relatively insignificant cobbler. This man's personal tragedy arises when a dead fly ("beetle" in the screenplay) accidentally falls into the workings of a teletype machine, creating a typographic error that changes the name of a suspected terrorist, Archibald Tuttle, to Archibald Buttle. Jill, Buttle's upstairs neighbor, attempts to extract from the Ministry of Information some kind of justice for his widow and orphaned children, only to be accused of being a terrorist herself. Within this main Orwellian plotline Sam and Jill eventually fall in love and form an alliance against the Ministry of Information.[2]

The first of *Brazil*'s two principal subplots revolves around the subversive activities of Archibald "Harry" Tuttle (Robert De Niro). Tuttle is depicted as a renegade heating and air conditioning repairman who swoops into people's apartments like some kind of superhero and repairs their climate control systems without the proper governmental authorization (hence, his designation as a terrorist). Over the course of the film, Tuttle comes to Sam's rescue on three crucial occasions. Alongside this first subplot, there is a second subplot within which Sam experiences a series of dreams in which he imagines himself as a winged knight-in-shining-armor (Figure 13). Within these sequences, a quixotic "Dream Sam" fights a variety of monsters, dwarfs, and colossal samurai warriors as he essentially struggles to rescue an ethereally beautiful "Dream Jill" who has been kidnapped by what the screenplay calls the "Forces of Darkness" (Mathews, 252).

Brazil's three interrelated plotlines all converge when Sam hacks his way into the Ministry of Information's mainframe computer to delete Jill's file—essentially declaring her "dead" within the government's system of records—as a way of keeping her from being arrested as a terrorist. Following this action, he returns to Jill, who has been hiding in his mother's secluded penthouse apartment, and the two spend what his now-rescued damsel-in-distress coyly calls a night of "necrophilia." Immediately the next morning, however, storm troopers invade the apartment and place Sam under arrest. While in custody he learns that Jill has been killed escaping arrest, and the film ends with Sam sitting in a torture chair, begging for his life. Yet, at the precise moment when *Brazil*'s chief Orwellian inquisitor, Sam's friend Jack Lint, comes in to begin the torture session, a squad of commandos led by Harry Tuttle storms the Ministry of Information to rescue Sam. Sam and Tuttle run into the chaos of the streets, where Sam is picked up by Jill, who drives him off into the countryside so that the two can live "happily ever after."

But, of course, this is not how *Brazil* actually ends.[3] Just as the film establishes its final "high shot of SAM and JILL's valley hideaway" (Mathews, 336), the camera pulls back to reveal that Sam is still sitting catatonically in the torture chair inside the Ministry of Information. "He's got away from us Jack," Mr. Helpmann remarks; to which Jack replies (in *Brazil*'s final line of dialogue): "Afraid you're right, Mr. Helpmann. . . . He's gone" (Mathews, 338). The entire last thirteen minutes of the film—comprising

Figure 13: Unable to bear the banality of life, Sam Lowry (Jonathan Pryce) dreams of being a winged knight in shining armor who comes to the rescue of his idealized damsel-in-distress. (*Brazil*, Universal, 1985)

the commando raid on the Ministry, Sam's escape with Tuttle, and his happily-ever-after moment with Jill—have consisted of one long, highly elaborate false ending. And while Linda Ruth Williams calls this ending "one of the bleakest in 1980s cinema" (158)—which is why the executives at Universal Studios so desperately wanted to re-edit it—it is also one of the most Cervantine (and not just because it finds its antihero essentially lying on his deathbed).

Because of its genesis as an homage to *Nineteen Eighty-Four*, critics have naturally read *Brazil* through an Orwellian lens. Comparing the omnipresent television screens in Gilliam's film (which supply a constant stream of escapist entertainment) to those in *Nineteen Eighty-Four* (which relentlessly spy on all the inhabitants of Oceania), Katrina G. Boyd notes that Gilliam "shifts the emphasis from overt control to the subtler method of fulfilling the desire for distraction" (35). In this, she rightly identifies more than just a superficial distinction between Gilliam's and Orwell's dystopian worlds, a distinction that revolves around the interplay of reality and fantasy. Orwell's Winston Smith is essentially a man trapped inside an oppressive fantasy of someone else's making, contrived by the "Party" ostensibly to create a utopian paradise of total equality but so "unreal" that it requires the ever-vigilant attention of bureaucrats like Winston to constantly smooth over the cracks that inevitably develop in its facade. Winston's greatest desire, then, is to escape from this ubiquitous illusion. "Reality," for him, is defined as that which is not controlled by the Party apparatus; which is why the seemingly untouchable mathematical equation $2 + 2 = 4$ is so crucial to him. Gilliam's Sam Lowry, in contrast, is a man trapped in an all too mundane reality in which bureaucratic vigilance is its own pitiable reward. Conversely, then, Sam's greatest desire (along with that of most of his fellow functionaries) is to simply escape into a fantasy world where existence is, if not more meaningful, then at least more interesting than it is in "real" life. Hence, where Winston's escape is a physical act that forces him to take refuge in the supposed "safe house" outside the control of Big Brother's watchful eye, Sam's escape is a mental act though which he takes refuge in either the collective experience of popular radio songs (like the one from which the film takes its title) and televised movies (like *Casablanca* and the Marx Brothers' *Horse Feathers*) or the individual experience of his personal dreams of flying through the stratosphere. And this is what makes the similar, yet quite different, endings of *Nineteen Eighty-Four* and *Brazil* so important. Where Winston and Sam are both tortured beyond their breaking points, Winston's mental surrender to Big Brother represents his ultimate defeat, while Sam's abrupt slide into madness represents his ultimate escape from what Salman Rushdie calls *Brazil*'s "shackles of actuality" (*Imaginary Homelands*, 121). As Richard Rogers astutely notes, "it is not *in* his dreams but *with his dreams* that Sam actually does defeat the bureaucracy" (40; original emphasis); which is why Dream Jill is such a crucial figure within the text and why her first appearance on screen wrapped in a shimmering veil—what Williams calls an "ethereal gauze" (166)—evokes Sandro Botticelli's *Birth of Venus* (Figure 14). Jill is not just Sam's dream girl; she is love itself.

Several critics have commented on Jill's dual existence as both real and ideal. Eckart Voigts-Virchow argues that "Gilliam disavows Lowry's dreams as corrupted escapist images from the very beginning by making his 'dream girl' Jill a blurred and idealised feminine long-haired vision beckoning Lowry to kiss him [*sic*] in a secondary dream world, while portraying her as a short-cropped, masculine, independent woman in the primary discourse" (280). Williams bases her entire theory of gender performance within the text on this real/ideal dichotomy. Concomitantly, several critics have also commented on Sam's dual existence alongside Jill as both the timid bureaucrat of the film's "real world" and the brave and handsome knight-in-shining-armor of the dream sequences. In this regard, the notion that the film's representation of Dream Sam derives from either Arthurian or Carolingian romance is a recurring theme of *Brazil* criticism; which is not out of place since Gilliam's first major film was *Monty Python and the Holy Grail*. As Robert Stam rightly notes, "*Don Quixote* was the *Monty Python* of its time" (57).

What is surprising, however, is that no one seems to have commented on the relationship between Real Sam and Dream Sam on the one hand and Real Jill and Dream Jill on the other; which is to say, from the perspective of Cervantes scholars, Sam and Jill's most important precursors are not Winston Smith and Julia (despite the alliterative similarities between the female names), but Don Quixote and his idealized ladylove, Dulcinea

Figure 14: Sam's dream image of Jill (Kim Greist) mirrors both Don Quixote's creation of his idealized Dulcinea del Toboso and Sandro Botticelli's well-known painting *The Birth of Venus*. (*Brazil*, Universal, 1985)

del Toboso. In short, Jonathan Pryce's performance as both "lowly" bureaucrat—the name Sam *Low*ry, like Arthur Miller's Willy *Low*man, is linguistically significant—and self-imagined "lofty" knight-errant is not only a thematic recapitulation of Peter O'Toole's performance in *Man of La Mancha* but a performance of the very idea that "to dream the impossible dream" is what "inspires a man to move forward" (Gilliam, "Salman Rushdie and Terry Gilliam"). As the film so forcefully points out, Sam has no interest in professional promotion until it becomes clear that moving up the company ladder is the only way to save Jill. Likewise, Kim Greist's performance as both earthy Real Jill and ethereal Dream Jill mirrors perfectly the Aldonza/Dulcinea dichotomy established by Dale Wasserman and the Maritornes/Dulcinea bifurcation created by Miguel de Cervantes.[4]

Like Sam Lowry, Don Quixote also lives a double life. His "real" identity is that of a poor, elderly hidalgo named Alonso Quixano whose mundane existence seems so pointless that he invents a new persona for himself to give his life meaning. Taking his cues from the (too) many chivalric novels he has read, most notably among them *Amadís de Gaula*, he digs up his ancestors' ancient and decrepit armor, rechristens himself Don Quixote de la Mancha, rechristens his horse "Rocinante" in order to make a new steed out of an old hack, and embarks on a quest to right wrongs, rescue damsels, and in general make the world a better place, all to the greater honor of his lady, Dulcinea del Toboso, an idealized damsel he models on Amadís's ladylove, Oriana. Dulcinea also leads a double life, even if she, like Jill, is unaware of this fact. Her "real" identity is that of a local peasant girl named Aldonza Lorenzo. In what is clearly Cervantes's commentary on the literary tradition of courtly love, Don Quixote has long admired this peasant girl from afar, and thus when he embarks on his wholesale re-creation of his own persona he undertakes to remake Aldonza as well. Throughout Cervantes's novel, "Dulcinea" is to Don Quixote what Laura is to Petrarch, what Beatrice is to Dante, and what Oriana is to Amadís: she is his inspiration, his reason for living, his platonic ideal.

Cervantes introduces Dulcinea to the reader of *Don Quixote* as a kind of idealized absent presence. She forms part of an ironic prologue that includes a eulogistic sonnet to her written by Oriana herself. And although we are aware from the very first chapter that Aldonza Lorenzo's transformation from peasant girl into aristocratic damsel is a deliberate construct of Don Quixote's imagination, her constancy as an ideal object goes largely unchallenged for the first twenty-five chapters. We see Dulcinea through Don Quixote's eyes as the "fairest of the fair" (1.4:45).[5] It is not until much later, when the knight-errant sends Sancho to Dulcinea's "castle" to deliver a letter, that we get a very different glimpse of Aldonza Lorenzo:

> "I know her well," said Sancho, "and let me tell you she pitches a bar as far as the strongest lad in all the village. Good God, she's a lusty lass all right, hale and hearty, strong as an ox, and any knight errant who has her as his lady now or in the future can count on her to pull him out of the mire! The little baggage, what muscles she's got on her, and what a voice! Let me tell you she climbed up one day to the top of the church belfry to call to some lads of hers who were in a fallow field of her father's, and even though they were a good couple of miles off they could hear her just as if they'd been standing at the foot of the tower. And the best thing about her is she isn't at all priggish, she's a real courtly lass, enjoys a joke with everyone and turns everything into a good laugh. (1.25:214–15)[6]

Compare this startling juxtaposition of the ideal and the real with the way *Brazil* first presents Jill. As with *Don Quixote*, *Brazil* introduces us to Jill as a kind of absent presence within the confines of what can only be considered the film's prologue. The film opens with a point-of-view shot taken from above a "skyscape" of sunlit clouds as the song "Brazil" plays over the top of this transcendent imagery. We later realize in retrospect, when Sam's first full dream sequence occurs, that the point-of-view to which we have been privy in this prologue is that of "Dream Sam," and that the absent object of his searching gaze is "Dream Jill." In this regard, Gilliam's opening scene gives us a bird's eye view of what Arthur Efron might call *Brazil*'s "Dulcineated" world (15), a view that comes to a very abrupt end when Gilliam cuts away to a scene of a nighttime terrorist explosion on an urban sidewalk. Immediately following this scene, the title "*Brazil*" appears in neon lettering and the plot begins to unfold. There is a

Figure 15: Like Cervantes's Aldonza Lorenzo (the real woman behind Don Quixote's Dulcinea), Gilliam's real Jill is a decidedly less than archetypal embodiment of feminine beauty. (*Brazil*, Universal, 1985)

clear temporal doubling in this prologue between "dream" time and "real" time. Because the film takes place at Christmas, while the idealized point-of-view shot encompasses what is apparently a summer afternoon sky, the caption "8:49 P.M. [...] Somewhere in the 20th century" can be applied only to the nighttime terrorist bombing that intrudes on this bucolic vision. The "skyscape" must belong to a different plane of reality.

Shortly thereafter—much sooner, in fact, than in *Don Quixote*—we are presented with an "objective" view of Jill as she really exists. Following a scene in which we see the Rube Goldberg machinery of the Ministry of Information spit out the typo that will cause the arrest of Buttle instead of Tuttle, *Brazil* takes us into the heart of Jill's working-class apartment, where we see her taking a bath (Figure 15). In stark contrast to the idealized Jill posited by Gilliam's prologue, this Jill—like the Aldonza Lorenzo of Sancho's churlish description—is all too real and more than just a little bit manly. With her hair cropped short and her right hand wrapped in some kind of cloth bandage that makes her look like a boxer or a biker wearing some kind of fingerless glove, she sits in viscid water, smoking a cigarette and laughing coarsely at a Marx Brothers movie on her television. And like Aldonza before her (not to mention Beatrice and Laura before Aldonza), Jill is not only ignorant of Sam's existence; she is completely unaware that he has transformed her into the idealized object of his desire.

In fact, if viewed in splendid isolation, each upon the heels of the other, the first four dream sequences of *Brazil* can easily be read as a kind of *Don Quixote* in miniature. Sam's first full dream sequence, like the first chapter of *Don Quixote*, sets up the various relationships that will play out over the course of the narrative. This first dream (which occurs roughly ten minutes into the film) shows Sam flying above the clouds in a suit of armor equipped with giant wings. In this incarnation, he functions as a kind of Don Quixote/Icarus: a man who feels so imprisoned by his present circumstances that a single, self-fashioned identity is apparently insufficient to provide for his escape. The second dream sequence (which occurs roughly twenty-four minutes into the film) follows up on the first by reinscribing the basic events of Cervantes's famous windmills episode, in which Don Quixote attacks what he thinks are "giants," only to be thrown from his horse by the wings of these mechanized adversaries. Here, Gilliam returns us to images of Dream Sam flying high above a pastoral landscape toward a floating Dream Jill, but his path is abruptly obstructed by several giant monoliths that violently shoot up out of the earth toward the sky, knocking him so far off his flight path that he disappears from our view.

Mathews indicates that Gilliam originally intended this succession of rising monoliths to "form an instant metropolis" whose dark streets would form a labyrinth (197). The final version of this scene dispenses with this complex vision, but the recognizable traces of this invasive cityscape still constitute a metaphor for the way in which—at least according to baroque "pastoral" theory—a nefarious urbanity always encroaches on the Arcadian values of the countryside.[7] Many critics have read *Don Quixote*'s windmills as symbols of the dehumanizing nature of technology, essentially arguing that Cervantes anticipates by several hundred years the social criticism of authors like Elmer Rice, whose play *The Adding Machine* launched a similar attack on the industrial culture of the early twentieth-century. Cory Reed, however, sees Don Quixote's "confrontations with machinery and with the burgeoning empiricist thought of his age" as a metaphor for the "brave new world of social and scientific change" made possible by Copernicus, humanism, "the development of mechanics," and "the advent of the modern nation-state" (168–69).

The third and fourth dream scenes are actually a single sequence divided into two parts, each separated by two rather brief scenes within the primary narrative. In the first half of this sequence, Dream Jill no longer floats freely in the ether. She has been captured by little grotesque hooded figures who have imprisoned her in a cage that floats high above the ground and that is tethered to the earth by giant ropes held tightly by these "Forces of Darkness." Seizing his moment of opportunity, Dream Sam swoops down upon these hooded figures and unsheathes his sword in anticipation of his attack. At this point the dream sequence cuts away. When it reemerges following an interruption by the primary narrative, Dream Sam no longer confronts the Forces of Darkness by themselves. Instead, he suddenly finds himself face-to-face with a giant samurai warrior in full body armor who jealously guards the caged Dream Jill.

This episode conflates and reinscribes two very important components of *Don Quixote*. First, it rearticulates the central dilemma Don Quixote must face within his own narrative: Dulcinea's transformation by the evil enchanters who pursue Don Quixote over the course of the novel.[8] *Brazil*'s samurai warrior can magically disappear and reappear to avoid being wounded by Dream Sam's sword and thus evokes at one and the same time Frestón—chief among the enchanters who relentlessly pursue Don Quixote—and "Tim the Enchanter" from *Monty Python and the Holy Grail*. But this giant samurai warrior can also be read as a figure of Cervantes's Knight of the Mirrors. Thus, when Dream Sam cuts the ropes that tether Dream Jill to the ground, he realizes Don Quixote's greatest desire in the novel, which is to release Dulcinea from her "enchantment." Likewise, when he fights and kills the samurai warrior, he rearticulates Don Quixote's greatest success, which is to defeat his own mirror image. This dream sequence—which ends with Dream Sam removing the samurai mask only to discover in horror his own face—evokes both Luke Skywalker's vision of finding his own face beneath Darth Vader's mask and Don Quixote's shock to discover the face of Sansón Carrasco lurking beneath the visor of the Knight of the Mirrors (a last-minute transformation he attributes to Frestón).

Yet, Dream Sam's apparent discovery of his own face beneath the samurai mask is markedly different from Luke Skywalker's discovery of his own face (which foreshadows the dangers of his possible surrender to the dark side of the force) and Don Quixote's discovery of the face of the Bachelor (who has merely dressed up as the Knight of the Mirrors in just another ruse designed to help return the hidalgo to his sanity), because the face Gilliam exposes in *Brazil* is not Dream Sam but Real Sam (Figure 16). This distinction is crucial. As a mirroring of the two previous literary moments, this particular version of the trope can be read as a commentary on both texts. What *Brazil* essentially suggests, on the one hand, is that when Luke Skywalker looks into the mirror of Darth Vader's mask, the face he sees only seems to be his own. Although it is an apparently exact reflection of his own face, the very exactness of the reflection highlights the fact that appearances can deceive. The Luke beneath the mask is not real; he is simply a projection of the real Luke's fears. With Don Quixote, on the other hand, when Cervantes's protagonist looks into the face reflected by the Knight of the Mirrors, he sees what he thinks is someone else. But just as the face hidden beneath his opponent's visor is apparently not that of his supposed antagonist, the real face beneath his own visor is not that of Don Quixote but rather that of Alonso Quixano. Because "Don Quixote" is the mental projection of Alonso Quixano, the face he indeed discovers turns out—in a significant way—to be his own: Sansón Carrasco's is also the self-invented face of a regular man pretending to be a knight-errant. As Gilliam's well-recognized pun lays bare ("samurai = Sam-or-I"), the ultimate battle in each of these scenes revolves around the identity of the dreamer, which is attached to circumstances well beyond the confines of the dream itself. And it is hardly coincidental that the acronym for the Ministry of Information where Sam-or-I works is M.O.I: *moi*, "me" in French. In each instance, the dreamer is his own worst enemy.

For these reasons it is impossible to read *Brazil*'s various dream sequences in what I previously called a "splendid isolation." The events depicted whenever Sam falls into his dream world are clearly provoked by real-world incidents.[9] At the same time, many of *Brazil*'s real-world scenes play themselves out against the backdrop of Sam's dream-world adventures such that the Cervantine discourse of the dream sequences also spills over into the Orwellian narrative of Gilliam's dystopia. One such Cervantine-inflected real-world scene shows Sam driving to Buttle's house, where he plans to deliver a crucial refund check that he hopes will settle the Buttle/Tuttle fiasco once and for all. Riding along in a tiny Messerschmitt (a comically inadequate vehicle that offers us a rather Gilliamesque idea of what Rocinante might look like if he were a "horseless carriage"), Sam seems to pass through an alley of nuclear reactor towers, each cheerfully painted sky blue and adorned with fluffy little white clouds. Suddenly, a giant head ominously appears above these nuclear "windmills," and as the camera pulls back, we realize that this landscape is actually a model, and that the "giant" is not some kind of enchanter seeking to do Sam bodily harm but rather a curious old man simply looking into the model's glass case. It is a very clever sight gag, but it seems somewhat arbitrary unless understood within the Cervantine context of *Brazil*'s dream-world monoliths and subsequent samurai warrior: at this point in the narrative, Sam has embarked on a quixotic quest to re-right the world. The sight gag with the nuclear reactors functions as a kind of foreshadowing that sets up his ultimate defeat against a bureaucracy metaphorically embodied in a Sam-or-I enchanter.

All of this explains the samurai as a figure of an enemy bureaucracy that turns out to be Sam himself, but it still does not quite explain the other major component of the dream sequences: Dream Jill's imprisonment.[10] An explanation of this metaphor requires an analysis of the other major Cervantine allusion embedded in the third dream sequence—Dulcinea's enchantment—and, in particular, the way in which this trope has also spilled over into *Brazil*'s real-world narrative. In Cervantes's novel Dulcinea's enchantment occurs early in part 2 when Sancho promises to take Don Quixote to Dulcinea's castle (something he clearly cannot do). Believing that his master (who has several times mistaken inns for castles and windmills for giants) will simply accept any woman he might indicate as Dulcinea, Sancho merely points to three peasant girls riding along the road to El Toboso and declares them to be Dulcinea and her retinue. Much to Sancho's surprise, Don Quixote, for once, sees nothing but plain reality: " 'All I can see, Sancho,' said Don Quixote, 'is three peasant girls on three

Figure 16: Like Don Quixote, who is shocked to find the face of his friend Sansón Carrasco beneath the visor worn by the Knight of the Mirrors, Sam discovers in horror his own face underneath the mask of the Samurai ("Sam-or-I") warrior. (*Brazil*, Universal, 1985)

donkeys'" (2.10:547).[11] When Sancho insists that these rustic women are the aristocratic ladies he has declared them to be, Don Quixote decides that enchanters must have transformed Dulcinea so that she does not appear to him as she really is. Faced with this corrupted reflection of his own ideal (note that for him the ideal is the real), he spends the rest of the novel attempting to find a way to "disenchant" Dulcinea.

Brazil reinscribes this enchantment not only in the dream sequences but within the real-world narrative as well, and it does so in a particularly Cervantine way. For the first ninety minutes of the film, Jill's status as Sam's ideal remains largely intact. With the exception of a couple of very minor moments, he sees her exclusively within two domains: in his dreams and reflected (projected) in various mirrors and monitors. He never comes into contact with the real Jill. All this changes, however, when Sam and Jill unexpectedly rescue each other from the storm troopers who are trying to arrest them inside the Ministry of Information. Sam escorts Jill out of the building, after which the two end up inside her truck, where Sam begs her to make a quick getaway (Figure 17). At first, Jill is furious at this strange functionary who has (perhaps) accosted her. She finally acquiesces, however, just long enough to remove them from the immediate danger of the approaching storm troopers. But when Sam starts to confess that she is the girl of his dreams, she decides he is crazy ("Christ, you're paranoid. You've got no sense of reality," she later tells him) and literally kicks him out of her fast-moving truck.[12] Sam manages to hang onto the grill of the truck; he and Jill eventually come to a provisional understanding; and the two continue on their journey to pick up a package Jill has waiting for her at the power plant.

Figure 17: In his first real meeting with the girl of his dreams, Sam confesses his love to Jill, who responds by telling him that he has no sense of reality before literally kicking him out of her fast-moving cargo truck. (*Brazil*, Universal, 1985)

There are many points of superficial contact between this scene and the one in *Don Quixote*. In the first place, Real Jill (like Cervantes's peasant girl before her) is nothing like the Dream Jill Sam has conjured up. Where Dream Jill conforms closely to Botticelli's Renaissance notions of beauty, Real Jill bears almost no resemblance to this ideal. Moreover, like Cervantes's Aldonza Lorenzo, Real Jill works for a living in what is traditionally viewed as a "manly" occupation—hauling industrial freight—and is a woman whose rather "butch" mannerisms are more in character with an American teamster than with the Roman goddess of love. Moreover, when Sam finally encounters his dream girl driving a rugged truck (itself a Cervantine reflection of the "enchanted" Dulcinea's rustic donkey), his first genuine encounter with Jill can only remind us of Don Quixote's first meeting with "Dulcinea":

> Don Quixote had by now knelt at Sancho's side and was staring with clouded vision and bulging eyes at the woman whom Sancho called queen and lady; and since all he could see there was a peasant girl, and not a very pretty one at that, because she was moon-faced and flat-nosed, he was dumbstruck and didn't dare open his mouth." (2.10:548)[13]

And just as Cervantes's peasant girl cruelly spurns Don Quixote's courtesies—"Get out of the bloody way and let us through, we're in a hurry" (2.10:548)—Jill's first real words to Sam hardly represent the response he hoped to receive: "Get out of my cab. [...] You touched me. Nobody touches me" (Mathews, 292–93).[14]

But this discursive clash between the Real Jill that Sam finally confronts and the Dream Jill he has previously imagined does not lie at the crux of her "enchantment," just as the objective distinction between Aldonza Lorenzo and Dulcinea does not create any psychological dissonance for Don Quixote:

> And so, Sancho, for what I want of Dulcinea del Toboso, she is as good as the most exalted princess in the world. [...] Do you really believe that the Amaryllises, Phyllises, Sylvias, Dianas, Galateas, Alidas and others that fill books, ballads, barbers' shops and theatre stages were real ladies of flesh and blood, and the mistresses of those that praise and have praised them? No, of course not, the poets themselves invent most of them [...]. And so it is enough for me to be convinced that the good Aldonza Lorenzo is beautiful and virtuous [because] for me she is the greatest princess in the world. [...] And to put it in a nutshell, I imagine that everything I say is precisely as I say it is, and I depict her in my imagination as I wish her to be. (1.25:216)[15]

Neither Don Quixote nor Sam is so addled as to be unable to tell the difference between his dreams and reality. Álvaro Ramírez correctly reads this passage as an example of a Baudrillardian simulacrum in which Dulcinea functions as an "unbound sign, a sign without a referent in the 'real world'" (85). But what is more important than the fact that Dulcinea is "clearly an absence" (Ramírez, 85), is the fact that for much of the novel Don Quixote is unable to fill this void even with a simulacrum. What is at stake in Dulcinea's and Dream Jill's respective "enchantments" is less a question of their objective appearances than a question of Don Quixote's and Sam's loss of faith in these idealized women. For Cervantes, this crisis manifests itself in a reversal—a reflective inversion—of the imaginative creed Don Quixote outlines in the previous passage. In other words, everyone else (at least according to Sancho) can see Dulcinea in her "true" form; only Don Quixote is deprived of this pure vision by the "clouds and cataracts" placed over his eyes by the malicious enchanter who pursues him (2.10:549).[16] With Gilliam, Sam's loss of faith stems from the fact that bureaucratic "enchanters" from the Ministry of Information have classified Jill as a "terrorist," making it impossible for Sam to see her—irrespective of her actual embodiment in this scene—through the frosted lens Gilliam has used to film her.[17]

For this reason, what is at stake for Sam and Jill during their first real encounter is "trust" (a word whose etymological roots inextricably link it to the whole notion of "faith"). And although Jill realistically has more reason to distrust Sam than he does to distrust her, the object of their mutual "trust" is the package Jill retrieves from the power plant. Mathews calls this package a "red herring," noting that Gilliam actually joked during production that the package should have actually contained red herrings as a kind of explicit joke (299). But this package represents much more than just a narrative strategy for maintaining our suspense. It remains the central metaphor for Jill's "enchantment" as a terrorist. Sam is asked to take "on faith" that Jill's mysterious package does not contain a bomb. Thus, when an explosion at a shopping mall seems to confirm his worst fears, his loss of "faith" in his Dulcinea is complete. "Are you all right? [he asks, pulling Jill from the rubble.] Well, you don't deserve to be! How could you? What a bloody stupid thing! It was a bomb! A bomb! I knew it, I knew it" (Mathews, 304). When she throws the tattered package at him saying, "There's your bomb, asshole! [...] A bribe for official monkeys like you" (Mathews, 304), he realizes his critical error and determines to do everything possible to protect Jill from the official suspicion of the Ministry of Information. Like Don Quixote before him, Sam spends the rest of the narrative trying to find a way to "disenchant" his dream girl.

And this brings us back to the symbolism of Sam's fourth dream sequence in which he fights and defeats the giant samurai warrior. What Sam comes to realize during his encounter with this bureaucratic "Sam-or-I" from "MOI" is that he is both Jill's problem and her solution. What he understands is that Jill's "enchantment"—like the Buttle/Tuttle issue itself—really amounts to little more than a paperwork dilemma. Thus, Sam's solution for "disenchanting" Jill is to "kill" her, at least as far as the Ministry of Information is concerned. To perform this necessary disenchantment, he hides Jill in his mother's empty apartment while he goes to the Ministry of Information to delete her file. When he returns, Jill emerges wearing a long blond wig and an ethereal dress, as if to mark her "disenchantment" by reassuming her previous incarnation as Venus. Their union ("re-union") culminates in a final dream sequence in which Dream Sam and Dream Jill fly high above the clouds, bathed in golden sunlight. Sam's Dulcinea has been returned to her pristine state and the two live "happily ever after." That is, at least until *Brazil* demolishes this false happy ending with its final scene of Sam's catatonic face.

What are viewers to make of this false ending? Several times during his lengthy narrative, Cervantes deliberately destabilizes his text by calling into question its authenticity. Most of the time, this de-authorization occurs because of *Don Quixote*'s famous narratological structure. As I note in previous chapters, the vast majority of the novel purports to be a "history" written in Arabic by the Muslim historian Cide Hamete Benengeli. This "Arabic" document is then said to be "translated" into Spanish by a bilingual Morisco, after which it is finally summarized by the narrator in the form published as the novel.[18] Even if this elaborate game of "telephone" were not sufficient all by itself to cause readers to question the veracity of the text, Cervantes's narrator goes to great lengths to undermine the integrity of the written "history" he claims to have found in a Toledo bazaar. He points out, again as I note in Chapter 5, that because the "Arab nation" is made up of nothing but liars, Cide Hamete's word as a "historian" cannot be trusted, even if it has managed somehow to escape unscathed the complex process of translation and summary it undergoes. More importantly, there are several segments of the novel that either the narrator or the translator (or even Cide Hamete) suggests should not be taken seriously. Early in the second part, for instance, Cervantes's narrator begins a chapter devoted to a conversation between Sancho and his wife with the following disclaimer:

> As the translator of the history begins this fifth chapter, he says that he considers it to be apocryphal, because Sancho Panza speaks here in a way that is quite different from what could be expected from his dull wits, and makes incisive comments that seem beyond his capabilities; the translator adds, however, that, concerned as he is to do his job properly, he has decided not to leave it untranslated, and so he continues. (2.5:514)[19]

This early "apocryphal" chapter, however, is neither the last nor the most important apocryphal moment in Cervantes's text. Much later, after having encountered Dulcinea in her corrupted form along the road to El Toboso, Don Quixote descends into the famous "Cave of Montesinos" where (according to him, and much to his surprise) not only does he have the privilege of asking Montesinos specific questions about the history of chivalry but also he encounters Dulcinea and her handmaidens (again in their corrupted form) trapped there with other enchanted characters from the chivalric tradition.[20] When Don Quixote again attempts to speak with Dulcinea, she turns her back on him and runs away, perhaps embarrassed to be seen guised in such a shabby demeanor. The high point of this overtly Dantean descent into the underworld comes when one of Dulcinea's maids approaches him to ask to borrow, on her mistress's behalf, six *reales*. As if this request for money were not base enough in and of itself (coming from so high-born a character as his ideal ladylove), Don Quixote is devastated to find that he can give Dulcinea only four *reales*. Not only is he unable to disenchant her, he cannot even provide for her most basic needs. In many ways, this scene marks Don Quixote's lowest psychological point in the novel.

As with the chapter between Sancho and his wife discussed earlier, however, the veracity of this episode is also called into question by Cervantes's text. In the first place, there is a discrepancy with regard to how long Don Quixote actually spends inside the cave. Sancho and those who have waited outside insist that no more than an hour has passed. But Don Quixote claims his descent into the underworld lasted three days. This three-day period is meant to evoke the three days that transpired between Christ's death and resurrection (during which time, in one apocryphal gospel, he descended into Hell). But even in a text where time and space are highly (if accidentally) amorphous, this discrepancy is hard to resolve.[21] Moreover, even Cide Hamete himself seems unable to come to terms with it:

> I cannot bring myself [he says in a supposed margin note glossed by the translator] to believe that everything recorded in this chapter happened to the brave Don Quixote exactly as described, and this is because whereas all the previous adventures have been feasible and credible, I cannot see my way to considering the adventure of this cave to be a true one, for it goes so far beyond what is reasonable. [...] You, wise reader, must make up your own mind, because I should not and cannot do more than this; even though it is believed to be the case that when he was dying he is said to have retracted it all and stated that he had made it up because he thought it tallied well with the adventures that he had read about in his histories. (2.24:648)[22]

And if this "legendary" deathbed retraction—which neither Cide Hamete nor the narrator sees fit to include in the final chapter—were not already enough to obscure matters, Don Quixote is later informed by a fortune-telling ape that "part of what [he] saw or experienced in the said cave was false, and [part] was credible" (2.25:662).[23]

All of this brings us back to *Brazil* and to its own "apocryphal" ending. The film suggests—in part through the notion that Jill was killed "twice" resisting arrest, and in part through the fact that Gilliam's already surreal film takes an even more surrealistic turn—that the false ending begins shortly after Sam has been arrested following his night of "necrophilia" with Jill. Having been processed through the system and admonished to "co-operate" by various people, Sam is strapped into the chair of the torture chamber, at which point Jack Lint (appropriately played by Michael "Nobody expects the Spanish Inquisition!" Palin) enters and begins what he euphemistically calls their "professional relationship" (Mathews, 329). The false ending seems to commence at the precise moment when, as the screenplay indicates, "a shot rings out and blood spurts from a bullet hole in the middle of the forehead of JACK's mask" (Mathews, 329). Here the commandos descend into the torture chamber and events transpire as I describe earlier, leaving Sam sitting there as the credits roll, humming "Brazil" to himself as he imagines himself inside a world that doesn't really exist. If Sam can be said to be a mirror image of Don Quixote, he is an inverse reflection. For, where Cervantes's antihero emerges from his lunacy in the final deathbed chapter, just long enough to disavow the self-invented identity he has spent the entire novel constructing, Sam is a Don Quixote who never regains his sanity. His "death" at the end of *Brazil* is defined as going so far over the edge as to be incapable of coming back. Where Don Quixote seems almost indifferent to the news that Dulcinea has been disenchanted, Sam is so convinced of Jill's disenchantment that he joins her, even if this union occurs nowhere else but in his head.

The problem with this false ending, however, especially because it occurs within a context dependent on the notion of dream sequences, is that one cannot be sure where it begins, as Sheinberg insisted in a meeting that followed *Brazil*'s first test run for a preview audience (Mathews, 74). To borrow a phrase from Mr. Helpmann when he informs Sam of Jill's double-death, *Brazil*'s meaning is ultimately "a bit of a disputed call" (Mathews, 326). Like Cervantes's readers, Gilliam's viewers have no choice but to wrestle with the interpretive ambiguities established by *Brazil*'s false ending. As Barbara Fister correctly notes, "the audience becomes implicated by having to play an active role in examining the reliability of cues" (292). In short, the film invites a number of "apocryphal readings" that are clearly supported by its complex discursive strategies but that—like all apocryphal narratives—will ultimately be open to dispute.

The first of these apocryphal readings involves pushing back the false ending only slightly, to the point at which Sam and Jill awaken on Christmas morning to find themselves staring down the gun barrels of the storm troopers who have come crashing into the apartment to take Sam into custody. Although shifting the commencement of Sam's final dream sequence to this point does not radically alter our view of the total text, it is—logically speaking—a much more appropriate point of transition. Recall that, according to *Brazil*'s traditional false ending, Sam's dream begins some five minutes later while he is sitting in the chair waiting to be tortured.[24] Conversely, if one wishes to read the Christmas morning arrest as the actual point of transition, *Brazil* does provide a clue that the discourse of the film might just have entered a different psychological dimension. As Sam is being dragged from the room, with Jill screaming hysterically at the storm troopers, Gilliam inserts a fade-to-black that he eerily punctuates with the sound of gunfire. Significantly, when this fade-to-black occurs, the storm troopers seem to have no interest in arresting Jill, only in keeping her at bay while they arrest Sam. Within the context of the traditional false ending, this eerie gunfire provides an oblique confirmation that Jill has been killed (for the second time, as Mr. Helpmann later remarks) resisting arrest. However, within the context of the apocryphal reading I am suggesting here, this gunfire is much more ambiguous. For, if everything that happens after the fade-to-black is part of Sam's final dream sequence, then his conversation with Mr. Helpmann is also part of that fantasy; which means that Jill may not be dead after all. Sam becomes a Don Quixote who effectively "dies" at the end (as does Cervantes's antihero). But for all intents and purposes, his Dulcinea has been "disenchanted" (as occurs in *Don Quixote*) by Sam's deletion of her file from the database at the Ministry of Information.

A second apocryphal reading can be teased out of *Brazil*, however, if we push back the final dream sequence some twenty minutes further, to the moment when Sam and Jill are first arrested in the aftermath of the explosion at the shopping mall. This moment too suggests a much stronger point of transition than the one traditionally recognized. Here the storm troopers enter the mall, intent on arresting Jill, whereupon Sam's mind immediately flashes to a vision of the samurai warrior, the one we have already seen holding his Dulcinea hostage. Yet, when Sam is about to engage this samurai warrior in battle, a trooper knocks him on the head with his rifle, and again Gilliam fades to black, suggesting that what follows from this point on (up through the final scene of the film) happens in Sam's mind as he lies there unconscious.

Readers might object, of course, to my attempt to relocate the commencement of *Brazil*'s false ending. But if we do not take this shopping mall fade-to-black to be the beginning of Sam's final dream sequence, then a number of questions arise that the traditional false ending sequence cannot answer. For instance, when Sam wakes up inside the prisoner transport vehicle shortly after being knocked out by the storm troopers, why is he not shackled like everyone else? And why is Jill (as far as we can tell) not among the other prisoners? Furthermore, why do the authorities simply let Sam go back to work? And how does Jill mysteriously—some might say miraculously—show up at Sam's apartment later that evening when she has never been there before? How did she escape from the Ministry of Information? And if she did not escape, why did the Ministry simply release someone who had clearly been listed as a "terrorist"?

If, however, we do take the shopping mall fade-to-black to be the initial moment of Sam's final dream sequence, all these questions naturally disappear into the surreal logic of the dream and a number of other crucial elements fall into place. Chief among these elements is the significance of Sam and Jill's love scene inside his mother's apartment. If we read all this material as if none of it really happened outside of Sam's imagination, the scenes that take place inside the apartment and inside Mr. Helpmann's office on the top floor of the Ministry of Information function as analogues to Don Quixote's experience inside the Cave of Montesinos. These settings exist as spaces apart from the rest of *Brazil*'s world. Thus, when Jill suddenly shows up on Sam's doorstep looking confused and distraught, the two enter into the separate world of the apartment, where they are free to explore their relationship without the intrusions of "reality." And within this separate reality Sam hits upon the idea of "killing" Jill within the Ministry's records as a sure way to "disenchant" her from the accusation of terrorism. Hence, he leaves her there and travels to the Ministry, where he is somehow able to enter Mr. Helpmann's (miraculously vacant) office to hack into the computer and delete her file. And if we willfully read all of this as a dream sequence (which, as Cervantes might say, is at least partially true and partially false), it necessarily means that Sam never actually succeeds in "disenchanting" Jill. In fact, reading this sequence apoc-ryphally suggests that Mr. Helpmann is right when he says Jill was killed twice resisting arrest: the first killing occurred when she and Sam were captured at the shopping mall (which helps explain why she is not in the transport with him); the second killing occurs when Sam hacks into the system (inside his dream world) and deletes her.

If, as I note earlier, Sam's dreams are provoked by real-world events, then his later (perhaps imagined) "conversation" with Mr. Helpmann re-garding Jill's "double-death" can be read as a demonstration that he is un-consciously aware that Jill is actually dead long before he imagines delet-ing her from the system. In other words, the second arrest sequence (that is, the one taken to be the start of the traditional false ending), coming on the heels of Sam's successful deletion of Jill from the system, can be read as a reflection of the shopping mall arrest sequence in which Jill has actu-ally been shot resisting arrest. The second sequence is simply a spectral im-age of the first, conjured up by Sam's imagination once he unconsciously realizes that Jill is in fact dead. But if Sam imagines that it is he who has "killed" Jill (at least one of the two purported times), how should we read the symbolic significance of this particular dream? Does the very idea of "deleting" her itself represent Sam's unconscious recognition that he is somehow responsible for her death (and not just in his dream world but in the real world as well)? A third apocryphal reading suggests this just might be the case.

In many ways, the central character of *Brazil* is not Sam Lowry but Harry Tuttle. For, despite the film's suggestion that the catalyst for all the events that play out in the course of the film is the fly that causes the typo on the bureaucratic form in the initial scene (Gilliam's nod, perhaps, to the "butterfly effect" of chaos theory), Tuttle is actually the key to *Brazil*'s complex causalities. Fly or no fly, without Archibald "Harry" Tuttle, Jack Lint would not have tortured Archibald Buttle to death, mistaking the ro-bust physical condition of the subversive "heating engineer" for that of the feeble "shoe repair operative" (Mathews, 205): "It wasn't my fault Buttle's heart condition didn't show up on Tuttle's file" (Mathews, 285). But how much do we actually know about Harry Tuttle? We see him three times over the course of the film. The first time occurs right after Sam's second dream sequence, when he wakes up to find that his heating system has malfunctioned. Tuttle miraculously appears in Sam's apartment almost immediately after Central Services has refused to respond to Sam's call for service. He bypasses Sam's ducts (an act that will come back to haunt Sam) and then, aided by a cable, flies off Sam's balcony like some kind of superhero. Tuttle's second appearance occurs shortly after Sam and Jill's first arrest, immediately prior to Jill's arrival at Sam's apartment. Spoor and Dowser, the Central Services repairmen, have "requisitioned" Sam's apartment for work that looks more like revenge than "necessary repairs"

(Mathews, 314). Here again, Tuttle helps Sam thwart these repairmen, and then just as before he makes a heroic exit by flying off into the night. His third appearance occurs when Tuttle and his commandos help rescue Sam from the torture chamber. This time, however, instead of repairing his ducts, the renegade heating engineer leads Sam out to the front of the Ministry of Information, where he allows Sam the privilege of detonating explosive charges he has placed inside the building, thus "setting off a series of enormous explosions that tear the Ministry from top to bottom and fill the sky with tons of liberated paperwork" (Mathews, 330). Tuttle's exit from this scene is even more dramatic than his previous two. In a scene that uncannily evokes the ascent into heaven of Remedios the Beauty in Gabriel García Márquez's *One Hundred Years of Solitude*, Tuttle is enveloped in a cloud of paperwork while standing on the sidewalk and literally disappears into thin air.[25]

Of course, Tuttle's final appearance never really happens; it is simply a figment of Sam's imagination and functions as part of *Brazil*'s traditional false ending. Recognizing this fact certainly helps explain away Tuttle's poetic—if marvelously impossible—exit from the scene. But what about his other two appearances? Can we read them as any "more real" than this final commando sequence? Most viewers would probably argue that we can. But if (as I have suggested in my previous apocryphal reading) *Brazil*'s false ending actually begins with Sam's first arrest at the shopping mall, then Tuttle's second appearance outside of Sam's apartment shortly before Jill mysteriously arrives would also have to be read as a figment of Sam's imagination. It too simply functions as the product of Sam's unconscious desire to be rescued from the bureaucracy once he is under arrest. This leaves us, then, with nothing but Tuttle's first appearance, and since I have not suggested (at least yet) that the film's false ending begins prior to the explosion at the shopping mall, we are obliged to accept this first "Tuttle scene" as a bona fide representation of reality. Tuttle really is a renegade heating engineer who swoops down into people's apartments and performs unauthorized repairs on ducts jealously "owned" by Central Services. As such, he can legitimately be considered a "terrorist" (at least according to the ideological definition used by the Ministry of Information) who should be brought to justice, and who remains at-large only because of the typographic error that has caused the unfortunate arrest and death of Archibald Buttle.

Still, can viewers be sure that Tuttle really does exist? The answer to this question, I think, is quite simply no. For, despite Tuttle's unmistakable resemblance to the actor who plays him, *Brazil* suggests that there is, in fact, no such person; at least, not one whose legal existence could be established using the documentation provided by a film so overwhelmingly preoccupied with bureaucratic paperwork. The whole Buttle/Tuttle debacle begins, as previously noted, when a dead fly falls into the workings of a typewriter and causes Archibald "Tuttle" to become Archibald "Buttle." Close inspection of this typographic error in its original context, however, reveals that the series of unfortunate events that subsequently transpire could not have resulted from this putative typo. The scene in which this error occurs includes a close-up of the teletype-in-question producing multiple copies of a form labeled "MINISTRY OF INFORMATION / DEPT OF INFORMATION RETRIEVAL / SUBJECT FOR DETENTION AND INTERVIEW" At the crucial moment when the dead fly drops into the machine, causing it to malfunction, the correct version of the form (the second copy we have actually seen) is clearly visible on the screen and reads as follows:

SURNAME: TUTTLE
CHRISTIAN NAME(S): ARCHIBALD
CODE NO: B/58/732
OCCUPATION: SHOE REPAIR OPERATIVE
ADDRESS: 412 NORTH TOWER (00:03:19)

Two more still-correct versions of this form flash on the screen, followed by a single erroneous version that has changed the crucial "T" to a "B" in Tuttle's surname, followed again by one more correct version in which the name "Tuttle" has been restored. Shortly thereafter, the storm troopers invade Buttle's home and arrest him, invoking the following bureaucratic formula:

> I hereby inform you under powers entrusted to me under Section 476 that Mr. Buttle, Archibald, residing at 412 North Tower, Shangri La Towers, has been invited to assist the Ministry of Information with certain inquiries and that he is liable to certain financial obligations as specified in Council Order RB-stroke-C-Z-stroke-nine-O-seven-stroke-X. (Mathews, 191)

Setting aside the issue of what ultimately happens to the (at least) five correct versions of this form produced by the teletype machine, the essential problem remains: all the information listed on the "correct" versions of the form is, in fact, correct, *except* for the surname of the individual arrested. The innocent and unsuspecting Archibald "Buttle" does live at 412 North Tower, he is a "shoe repair operative," and his code number is "B/58/732."[26] (Notice too that, despite an early scene between Sam and Mr. Kurtzmann in which they discuss the mistake, there is simply no mention anywhere on the "correct" form of a "heating engineer.") The only actual "mistake" on the form is that the wanted man's surname is listed as "Tuttle" (not "Buttle"!). And, astonishingly, this "mistake" seems to have been "corrected" by the dead fly. Thus, when the storm troopers arrive at Buttle's home to arrest him, all the information on the "erroneous" form they carry is correct, including his surname.

Now, this illogical coincidence can easily (and logically) be attributed to the film's production staff, just as Sancho's disappearing and reappearing donkey can be attributed to a printer's error.[27] To shoot the "fly in the typewriter" scene, someone on Gilliam's staff had to physically produce a series of forms that would be visible in the typewriter's carriage. We can naturally assume that this person simply opened the script and filled in the necessary information by following the dialogue delivered by the storm troopers when they come to arrest Buttle a few pages later. But this explanation—however logical—remains somewhat unsatisfying (at least to me) because it requires us not only to second-guess Gilliam's original authorial intent (a dicey prospect, given his wild imagination) but also to willfully disregard what is clearly—if only fleetingly—visible on the screen. As Slavoj Žižek reminds us in contextualizing the title of his Duke University Press series, SIC: "SIC stands for psychoanalytic interpretation at its most elementary: no discovery of deep, hidden meaning, just the act of drawing attention to the litterality [*sic!*] of what precedes it. A 'sic' reminds us that what was said, inclusive of its blunders, was effectively said and cannot be undone" (Salecl and Žižek, iii; original exclamation). As with Sancho's "quantum" donkey (and in saying this I acknowledge my profound philosophical disagreement with various editors who have rearranged Cervantes's novel so that it makes sense), we must set aside *Brazil*'s real world explanation if we are to read Gilliam's text—"inclusive of its [possible] blunders"—as it exists, not as we think it should exist. Keeping this in mind, Buttle apparently is the right man, as Jack Lint unwittingly reveals when he later says, "I did not get the wrong man. *I* got the right man. The wrong man was delivered to me as the right man" (Mathews, 284). Yet, if Buttle is the right man, who exactly is Archibald "Harry" Tuttle?

One way of reading the identity of Harry Tuttle is as just another projection of Sam's fertile imagination. Sam is, after all, a man who already dreams that he is a flying knight who fights giant samurai warriors and saves goddesslike damsels-in-distress. Is it not possible that Gilliam, perhaps unwittingly anticipating Chuck Palahniuk by more than a decade, has created a timid bureaucrat who conjures up an alter ego in the guise of a friendly superhero who does all the subversive things he wishes he could do? Can we not read "Harry Tuttle" as Sam Lowry's own "Tyler Durden?" Two things support this apocryphal reading. First, throughout the film, no one but Sam ever sees Harry, and we have no independent confirmation that he comes to the aid of anyone else but Sam.[28] Moreover, whenever Tuttle does appear (whether inside or outside of Sam's dreams) he always performs the immediate task Sam would (or should) perform if only he had the courage. When Central Services initially proves uncooperative in sending repairmen to resolve Sam's heating problem, Tuttle is suddenly there to help; when Spoor and Dowser take over Sam's apartment, Tuttle is suddenly there to fill their heated suits with sewage; when Sam has been arrested and is about to be tortured by Jack Lint, Tuttle not only rescues Sam but effectuates the destruction of the Ministry of Information by blowing it up. Second, just as there are a number of embedded discursive clues in *Fight Club* that portend the connection between Jack and Tyler Durden, there are several linguistic clues that suggest a link between Sam and Tuttle. When Tuttle initially bypasses Sam's ducts and Sam says, "Are you telling me that this is illegal?" (as if he didn't already know), Tuttle responds "Well, yes . . . and no. Officially, only Central Service operatives are supposed to touch this stuff. . . . Could you hold these, please?" (Mathews, 226), thus implicating Sam by arranging to have his fingerprints on the equipment. Likewise, when Tuttle blows up the Ministry of Information, he actually hands the plunger to Sam, thus allowing Sam to perform the terrorist act. And on at least two occasions, Tuttle leaves these scenes cheerfully quipping, "We're all in it together" (Mathews, 232, 316), a leitmotiv that can be read as a general expression of solidarity, as well as a specific description of the true nature of Sam and Harry's relationship to each other: they are "in it together" because they represent two sides of the same psyche.[29]

Yet, if Harry Tuttle is nothing but a projection of Sam's fertile imagination—one that has also created a second alter ego in the form of a winged Don Quixote/Icarus figure—two troublesome questions remain. First, since Sam imagines Dream Jill long before he ever actually encounters her at the Ministry of Information (where he sees her in the security monitor when she comes to help sort out the issue of Archibald Buttle's unfortunate death by torture), how can we account for this temporal discrepancy? In other words, at what point and through what mechanism does Jill impact Sam's psyche to the degree necessary to explain his mental transformation of her into the Dulcinea of his dreams? Second, since Harry Tuttle is supposedly the key to Buttle's "erroneous" arrest and torture, what is the connection between Sam and Archibald "The Right Man" Buttle? The answers to these questions, I think, suggest a final apocryphal reading of *Brazil*.

As I note earlier, *Brazil* opens with a cloud scene that evokes Sam's visions of his search for Dream Jill (in the persona of his winged knight). This scene is immediately followed by the terrorist explosion scene that evokes Sam's desire to bring down the entire system (in the persona of his renegade heating engineer). And these two scenes are immediately followed first by the fly-in-the-teletype scene and then by the scene in which the storm troopers burst into Jill's apartment only to cut a hole in her floor in order to descend into the residence below, where they arrest Archibald Buttle. The sequence of this montage is significant, especially for how it begins and how it ends. Over the course of this chapter, I have suggested several places in *Brazil* where its false ending can be shifted to an earlier moment. Because Sam's dream sequences occur not only inside the "real" segments of the film but within the "false" segments as well, the fact that *Brazil* begins with a dream sequence (and then proceeds to articulate a narrative montage that ends with Jill witnessing Buttle's arrest) implies an unavoidable—if coincidental—interpretive "con-sequence": the entire film can be read as one long dream sequence in which the various overlapping characters and intersecting plot lines function as a kind of mise-en-abîme of reflections all leading back to a single arrest that occurs sometime prior to the beginning of the film. What this final apocryphal reading suggests is that the entire film can be read as a 143-minute "false ending" in which the character sitting in the torture chair at the end is actually the one correctly listed on the arrest form: Archibald Buttle. Having been arrested and tortured for reasons known only to Gilliam's Orwellian bureaucrats at the Ministry of Information (perhaps Buttle really is a terrorist who routinely blows up buildings and innocent shoppers), his mind cracks under the pressure and he imagines a surrealistic series of overlapping narratives that collectively seek to explain (and possibly justify) his unbearable situation. Within this stress-induced vision he alternately dreams that he is a lowly shoe repair operative who has been mistakenly arrested because of a typographic error; that he is a winged knight who comes to the rescue of an idealized damsel-in-distress (who not coincidentally resembles his young and attractive upstairs neighbor, and for whom he has perhaps—like Alonso Quixano toward Aldonza Lorenzo—long been pining); that he is a Ministry of Information bureaucrat who hacks into the computer system to right all wrongs, winning Jill's heart in the process; and finally, that he is a renegade heating repairman—a happy-go-lucky superhero—who rescues the unfortunate man sitting in the torture chamber, giving that unfortunate man the chance to bring down the entire establishment, after which he and his ladylove can drive off into a bucolic sunlit valley where they can finally settle down together and live happily ever after.

Aside from simply laying out the arguments as I do here, there is no definitive way to establish the validity of this final apocryphal reading. But, then again, as Cervantes's quixotic narrator repeatedly reminds us, what makes a text "apocryphal" is the impossibility of conclusively determining its veracity or lack thereof. As it stands, "you, wise reader, must make up your own mind, because I should not and cannot do more than this" (2.24:648).[30] Still, because this final apocryphal reading largely depends on positing a narrative event that exists outside the confines of the text itself (that is, an arrest that supposedly occurs prior to the very first frame of the film), perhaps I should end this chapter by backing off slightly from an exploration of these interpretive "con-sequences" to return to a more quixotic (and decidedly less "Cidehametian") conclusion.

Figure 18: Prominently featured in the lobby of the Ministry of Information building, this inverted "pietà" —whose inscription reads "The Truth Shall Make You Free"— suggests that in the end Sam's Dulcinea is actually dead. (*Brazil*, Universal, 1985)

The one fact that seems relatively certain at the end of *Brazil* is that Jill is dead (doubly so, as is appropriate for a film in which mirroring plays such a crucial role).[31] If Jill functions as a specular image of Aldonza Lorenzo/Dulcinea del Toboso, and Sam functions as a reflection of Alonso Quixano/Don Quixote, then Jill's death at the end highlights one of the central dilemmas raised by Cervantes's novel: Don Quixote's well-intentioned quest to change the world often results in his doing more harm than good. After one particularly memorable episode in which Don Quixote rescues a young apprentice who is being beaten by his master, Don Quixote runs into the boy a few chapters later and discovers that the master was so angered by Don Quixote's meddling that he beat the boy with a renewed vengeance as soon as Don Quixote had left the scene (1.31:287). Likewise, when Don Quixote comes upon Ginés de Pasamonte's chain gang and then frees the duly convicted prisoners on the grounds that their freedom has been taken away from them against their will, these convicts repay his kindness (as I note in the previous chapter) by beating him and then stealing Sancho's donkey before they head off into the countryside presumably to commit a whole series of crimes about which Cervantes simply gives us no further information (1.22:185–86).

The discursive significance of Jill's death should perhaps be read accordingly. Despite Sam's good intentions in attempting to do for Real Jill what he successfully does for Dream Jill (that is, rescue his idealized damsel-in-distress), his best efforts result only in her violent and untimely demise; hence, the significance of the statue we see several times during the film prominently situated in the lobby of the Ministry of Information building (Figure 18). Gilliam does not spend a great deal of time focusing on this statue, but it has crucial symbolic value. The statue—whose inscription reads "THE TRUTH SHALL MAKE YOU FREE" (00:12:36)—exists as a kind of inverted pietà in which a winged masculine figure holds in its arms the limp body of a dead woman. This statue is in many ways the key to unlocking the entire Cervantine subtext of the film. In the end, as Sam sits in the torture chair imagining his happy ending with Jill, all the while smiling blithely as "Brazil" echoes endlessly inside his head, this statue reminds us that in Gilliam's dystopic reading of *Don Quixote*, it is Dulcinea who dies and Don Quixote who remains permanently "enchanted." Within an overtly Orwellian text Gilliam asks his audience to ponder the following Cervantine hypothetical questions: What would happen if Don Quixote somehow managed to make Dulcinea an unwitting accomplice to his lunatic assault on the Hapsburg empire and she wound up getting blamed for it all? What would happen if the members of the Holy Brotherhood who pursue Don Quixote throughout the novel somehow managed to track down Aldonza Lorenzo in their search for the man who does so much mischief in her name? How would a dying Don Quixote react if Sansón Carrasco entered his bedchamber and said not that "the lady Dulcinea has been disenchanted" (2.74:977) but something akin to "the Queen, My Lord, is dead?"[32] If Orwell's *Nineteen Eighty-Four* is the story of Winston Smith's loss of self through his acceptance of the "truth" that "2 + 2 = 5" (409), Gilliam's *Brazil* is the story of Sam Lowry's denial of self through his inability to accept the truth that Jill is dead, that she simply does not exist. In the end, Jill really is an absence that can only be filled by a Baudrillardian simulacrum. Sam's escape from "MOI"—and, in particular, from MOI's department of "information retrieval"—is essentially an escape from memory itself.

Chapter 7

The Matrix: Reflected

No film has attracted such immediate and overwhelming critical attention as *The Matrix*. In addition to the kind of amateur analysis provided inside various Internet chat rooms and Web logs, where fans routinely dissect such popular texts, Andy and Larry Wachowski's landmark trilogy has generated critical attention from a great number of serious scholars.[1] Cornel West, for instance, whose critical interest in the film earned him a speaking role in the second and third installments, has noted that the Wachowski Brothers' terrain is so vastly dense that it provides for a nearly endless contemplation. In this regard, scholars from disciplines as diverse as philosophy, theology, gender studies, and queer theory have written extensively on what West calls the Wachowski Brothers' brilliant amalgamation of "so-called high culture, so-called middle brow, so-called low culture in a composite art form" (*The Matrix Reloaded*, supplemental disk, "Preload," 00:04:45–59). The body of critical knowledge related to what could perhaps be called "*Matrix* studies" includes examinations of nihilism, Utopianism, existentialism, genre theory, gender, Walter Benjamin's notion of "aura" in the age of mechanical reproduction, Jacques Lacan's theory of the "big Other," and even pedagogical theory within the U.S. public school system.

The first film in the trilogy, *The Matrix* (1999), tells the story of an alienated office worker named Thomas Anderson (Keanu Reeves)—a character not unlike Jack in *Fight Club* and Sam Lowry in *Brazil*—who spends much of his free time surfing cyberspace under the hacker name "Neo," looking for some kind of confirmation that "there is something wrong with the world" (*Matrix*, 00:27:15). This confirmation comes in the form of a demonstration by Morpheus (Laurence Fishburne) that the world as Neo knows it is simply a complex illusion—"the Matrix"—created by a powerful mainframe computer that stimulates Neo's cerebral cortex to create a virtual reality inside his head. In "real" reality, Neo (along with nearly all the rest of humanity) is actually living in an isolated pod (reminiscent of those seen in *Invasion of the Body Snatchers*) where the heat and electrical impulses produced by his body provide energy for a civilization of machines who have created this elaborate system in order to convert the entire human race into nothing more than a collection of batteries, what the film calls "coppertops." Leading a resistance movement made up of people who have managed to "unplug" themselves from the Matrix, Morpheus frees Neo because he believes Neo is the messianic "One" (note the deliberate anagram) who will help liberate all of humanity. Throughout the film these "unplugged" humans (who have established a vast underground city called Zion) constantly "jack" themselves back into the Matrix from the outside to engage in an ongoing battle with the "Agents," whose job it is, as programs, to police the Matrix and destroy threats to its existence. The climax of the first film occurs when Agent Smith (Hugo Weaving) kills Neo inside the Matrix world, which means that according to the logic of the film he dies in the real world as well. Neo, however, is subsequently "resurrected" through the power of a real-world kiss from Trinity (Carrie-Anne Moss), after which he goes on to defeat Agent Smith before finally becoming a kind of Superman who flies around the Matrix world harassing its cybernetic masters.

The Matrix Reloaded (2003) and *The Matrix Revolutions* (2003) essentially follow the struggle between the machines and the humans but in the process add a couple of significant permutations to the narrative. First, the machines decide that the mere existence of Zion is unacceptable and thus set out to destroy this last human city by sending an army of "sentinels" (squidlike killing robots) to exterminate every man, woman, and child left "unplugged." Second, Agent Smith somehow disconnects himself from the system—becoming what can only be called a "computer virus"—and spends most of the second and third installments taking over the identity of other individuals within the Matrix world, thus effectively replicating himself millions of times over. Where Neo is the *Matrix* trilogy's "One," Smith becomes its "Many." Finally, Neo himself becomes increasingly disconnected from both the real world and the Matrix world as he struggles to discover whether he is the "One," and if so, just what this means.[2]

As this very simplified overview reveals, the *Matrix* trilogy (along with its associated intertexts) is not just the most immediately studied cinematic text in history; it is also, perhaps, the most deliberately self-conscious of its place within our system of contemporary critical theory. For, just as the Wachowski Brothers posit a symbiotic relationship between the humans and the machines within the films, their trilogy itself depends to a very real extent on the fertile symbiosis that exists between the a priori critical intertextualities they have deliberately woven into their cinematic texts and the subsequent criticism these texts have generated. In fact, it would not be an exaggeration to suggest that the Wachowski Brothers' trilogy—mirroring the work of Miguel de Cervantes and Jorge Luis Borges, both of whom famously wrote fiction as a critical endeavor—can be read as critical texts in their own right, disguised as summer blockbusters. Character names drawn from ancient Greek mythology, such as Morpheus, the Oracle, and Persephone, carry with them a considerable semantic value that plays itself out over the course of the trilogy. The same is true of the Biblical terminology that permeates these films—Thomas Anderson ("Doubting Thomas/Son of Man"), Trinity, Zion, and the *Nebuchadnezzar*—not to mention the discourse of contemporary critical theory itself—the Logos, "the desert of the real," and the Merovingian (a character who can be read as an amalgam of French philosopher-critics such as Jacques Derrida, Michel Foucault, Roland Barthes, Jean Baudrillard, and Paul de Man)— that has managed to seep into the Wachowski Brothers' imaginative world. It is far from coincidental that Cornel West (as "Councillor West") serves as an outspoken member of Zion's governing body.

As several other critics have pointed out, the most obvious philosophical trope informing the *Matrix* trilogy is the analogy of Plato's cave borrowed from the *Republic* (book VII). In the Wachowski Brothers' postmodern retelling of this trope, the vast majority of humans are trapped within the cave of their individual pods, while the "life" they believe themselves to be living is merely a virtual reflection generated by the machines who have created what Morpheus calls a "prison for your mind" (*Matrix*, 00:28:25). But if the Matrix is a version of Plato's cave, the Wachowski Brothers update the trope in two significant ways. First, as Gerald J. Erion and Barry Smith point out, the *Matrix* incorporates Descartes's baroque argument that what we take to be "reality" might be nothing more than an illusion created by a "malicious deceiver" in order to trick us (18). But as Erion and Smith also note, the *Matrix* updates even this second Cartesian trope for postmodern audiences by incorporating Peter Unger's twentieth-century transformation of the "malicious demon" into an "evil scientist"—"a super-neurologist who uses a computer to generate electrical impulses that are then transmitted to electrodes fastened to the relevant parts of our central nervous systems"—and Hilary Putnam's disembodied "brain in a vat" (17–22). Or, as Morpheus points out to Neo during their first (virtual) encounter, "What is 'real'? How do you define 'real'? If you're talking about what you can feel, what you can smell, what you can taste and see, then 'real' is simply electrical signals interpreted by your brain" (*Matrix*, 00:40:10). Having escaped from this computer-generated prison, Morpheus sees it as his duty to return to the cave of the Matrix as often as possible to liberate those individuals willing to accept a higher (if unpleasant) reality: that every human still plugged into the Matrix is a "slave" of the machines, despite all appearances to the contrary.

What humanity needs, according to the text, is some kind of savior. And in this the *Matrix* trilogy's second important intertext comes into play. Neo (a.k.a. Thomas Anderson, a.k.a. the messianic "One")—whose death and resurrection in the first film, whose representation as a kind of enlightened healer in *The Matrix Reloaded*, and whose ultimate self-sacrifice in *The Matrix Revolutions* brings about the redemption of all humanity—is a Christ figure. Likewise, Morpheus (despite his symbolic function within a discourse derived from Greek mythology) is a figure of John the Baptist: he is the voice crying in the wilderness preparing the way for the arrival of the prophesied messiah. Trinity, whose name cannot be disassociated from the traditional Christian concept of the triune God, has been seen by at least one critic as a figure of Mary Magdalene (Ford, paragraph 8). And Cypher (Joe Pantoliano)—whose name not only evokes notions of an ambiguously encoded text desperately needing to be "deciphered" but also partially echoes the name of Lucifer—is the Judas Iscariot of this postmodern gospel: he betrays Neo to the Agents in the first film in exchange for being reinserted back into the Matrix.

Alongside its obvious Christian references, the *Matrix* trilogy also incorporates elements of Buddhism, Gnosticism, and even Hinduism.[3] These various religious traditions (along with the racial diversity of the film's cast) not only supply an important sense of "multiculturalism" for an audience raised on the "United Colors of Benetton" but also provide parallel and supporting subtexts for many of the films' philosophical positions. Still, given the importance of the Asian martial arts and wire-fighting techniques so crucial to the Wachowski Brothers' cinematic universe, Buddhist thought (even if only as a compromised version, as Michael Brannigan argues [108–10]), is the logical complement to the *Matrix* trilogy's overt Christianity.[4] Within this parallel reading, Neo functions as a kind of "Buddha or bodhisattva who comes to reveal to humanity its state of ignorance and, presumably, the way out" (Ford, paragraph 15). He is "an enlightened being who forsakes nirvana to stay behind and help humanity" (Fielding, paragraph 5). But while the *Matrix* only obliquely represents Neo as a Buddha figure (in part because of his overshadowing function as a Christian messiah), the film includes at least one overt connection to the Buddhist tradition in the form of a young boy whom Neo meets on his first trip to consult the Oracle. While waiting in an anteroom for his turn to see the Oracle, Neo notices that one of his fellow "potentials," a boy with a shaved head and dressed in the trappings of a Buddhist monk, displays the miraculous ability to bend a spoon with his mind. When the young boy invites Neo to also attempt this feat, he offers the following advice: "Do not try and bend the spoon. That's impossible. Instead, only try to realize the truth. [...] There is no spoon" (*Matrix*, 1:11:42). This is, of course, the central Buddhist metaphor of the film, and it provides the perfect complement to the platonic metaphor of the cave.

Beyond the philosophical and religious issues, two political readings—both related to Marxian theory—are worth noting. The first of these two political intersections relates to the theories of simulation and hyperreality proffered by Baudrillard, who explicitly "appears" twice within *The Ma-*

trix. His first cameo appearance occurs during an early scene in which Neo uses a hollow copy of *Simulacra and Simulation* [*sic*] to hide the illegal software programs he sells like so many packets of heroin. (This inclusion of *Simulacra and Simulations* may seem very au courant, especially since the book functions only as a simulacrum of the book, but Cervantes essentially achieved the same thing in *Don Quixote* four hundred years ago as part of his very baroque self-referential literary game.) Baudrillard's second appearance in the Wachowski Brothers' film happens through Morpheus's designation of the Matrix as "the desert of the real," a phrase explicitly taken from "Simulacra and Simulations" to describe what Baudrillard calls the "generation by models of a real without origin or reality" (169). The problem, however, is that Baudrillard's notion of simulation, as the previous quotation makes abundantly clear, effaces any notion of a Platonic essence; which in turn tends to undermine the cave trope upon which the film is based. As William Merrin points out, "not once does Neo consider whether this 'real world' he is shown might not be just another level of virtual reality—perhaps this 'reality' is one created for the machines by another intelligence to keep the machines themselves in happy slavery?"

This brings us, however, to the second of the two Marxian-inflected issues. In a brilliant essay entitled "*The Matrix*, Marx, and the Coppertop's Life," Martin A. Danahay and David Rieder trace the ways in which Marx's ideas on labor, capital, dialectical materialism, and commodity fetishism play themselves out in the film, especially as they relate to the machines' enslavement of nearly all of humanity for the sole purpose of providing electrical power for their own existence. In this regard, Danahay and Rieder argue that "the Matrix is the sum total of the human 'labor power' that produces it, every day and every hour. Every sight and smell in the Matrix is a product of human labor" (222–23). Nevertheless, as they also note, *The Matrix* cannot really be read as a Marxian critique of this inequitable situation given the way in which the Matrix itself is represented within the minds of those still plugged into it. Stressing the importance of "surplus value" for Marxian theory, Danahay and Rieder argue that the computer-generated dream world of the Matrix—one that is "relatively hip and urban" and that offers " 'really good noodles,' steady work, and a cool club scene"—does not show us what humanity is "missing" when plugged in. "Humanity has to work to generate BTUs, but the Matrix has unlimited bandwidth and full color!" (224). For *The Matrix* to make a genuine "Marxist" statement, Danahay and Rieder argue, the film would have to present the Matrix in black and white, with the real world existing in living color: "humanity works, and they are paid exactly what they are worth" (224). Only "counterrevolutionaries" like Morpheus and Neo are unhappy with the situation.

But it is in this discrepancy between theory and experience that the

Matrix trilogy confronts head on one of the thorniest issues of Marxian political thought. The major dilemma facing Marxist thinkers during much of the twentieth century was what to do about those members of the proletariat who identified with their capitalist oppressors and thus violently opposed a socialist revolution that promised to improve the material conditions of their lives. In other words, how can a worldwide communist revolution ever come to pass without the active support of the very people it is designed to liberate? Thinkers such as Antonio Gramsci grappled with these issues and came to the conclusion that simply pointing out the material oppression of the masses is insufficient. The problem, contrary to what Neo claims in one crucial scene in *The Matrix Reloaded*, is not "choice" but what Gramsci calls "hegemony," which, as I note in Chapter 1, makes no distinction between "force" and "consent" (*Prison Notebooks*, 271). And Gramsci's notion of hegemony is brought to the fore by none other than Morpheus when he explains to Neo the dangers inherent in trying to overthrow a Matrix world that resembles Gramsci's working definition of hegemonic capitalism:

> The Matrix is a system, Neo. That system is our enemy. When you're inside, you look around, what do you see? Businessmen, teachers, lawyers, carpenters. The very minds of the people we are trying to save. But until we do, these people are still a part of that system, and that makes them our enemy. You have to understand, most of these people are not ready to be unplugged. And many of them are so inured, so hopelessly dependent on the system, that they will fight to protect it. (*Matrix*, 00:56:35)[5]

Robert Fiander asks whether individuals like Neo and Morpheus who have escaped the Matrix have any ethical right "to disrupt the somnambulistic trance of the human beings who have nice 'lives' in the [virtual reality] scenario" created for them by the machines (47). Cypher, for one, is quite unhappy with his decision to become "unplugged," and thus his central act of Judas-like betrayal in the first film is nothing more than his desperate attempt to reassert his preference for the pleasantries of virtual reality over the hardships of the real world. But since his reinsertion into the Matrix involves a real-world attack on several of Morpheus's unplugged crew members, including Tank (the "100% pure, old fashioned, home-grown human," a "genuine child of Zion," who was never plugged-in in the first place [*Matrix*, 00:47:00]), Cypher's demise at the hands of Tank (who manages to survive the attack) is appropriate (*Matrix*, 01:30:40). But what about the "collateral" death of so many other individuals for whom the Matrix remains their only reality, not simply one of two from which they might choose? Whenever an Agent takes over the identity of these "normal" people they become a dangerous "enemy" to those who have jacked themselves into the Matrix to bring about its destruction. Hence, one might argue that the responsibility for the deaths of these individuals rests with the Agents themselves, because Neo, Morpheus, and Trinity are simply defending themselves against what amount to unwitting enemies possessed by cyber-demons. But can we make this same argument for the many people inside the Matrix—the numerous policemen and security guards—who are just doing their jobs? A number of critics condemn Neo, Morpheus, and Trinity for their excessive use of violence. But given the magnitude of their endeavor to liberate humanity from a slavery in which they unknowingly find themselves, can we say that the ends somehow justify the means? Can we excuse what Brannigan characterizes as "outright slaughter" (108) and what Gregory Bassham calls "the needless killing of the innocent" (114)? In other words, should we view Neo, Morpheus, and Trinity as the moral equivalent of Harriet Tubman and the Underground Railroad? Or, should we see them as the cyber equivalent of Joseph Stalin and Pol Pot? What the *Matrix* ultimately demonstrates is that fighting for the "greater good" can frequently become a problematic venture because an exact definition of what constitutes the "greater good" is often difficult to pin down. But, of course, this is one of the central dilemmas explored by *Don Quixote*, and it is in this that the Wachowski Brothers demonstrate their profound (if unacknowledged) debt to baroque writers such as Cervantes.

Like so many of the contemporary texts already examined in this book, the *Matrix* trilogy can also be read as a recapitulation of *Don Quixote*. This recapitulation originates primarily within both Cervantes's and the Wachowski Brothers' reinscriptions of Plato's cave metaphor into their respective texts. Neo's discovery of a higher reality—in which he not only recognizes the "true nature" of the world but also finds his true calling within it—mirrors Don Quixote's own voyage of self-discovery. In fact, it is no coincidence that both protagonists begin their narratives with names other than those with which they end their tales. In each instance, the act of self-discovery involves the deliberate invention of a "higher" self, cut loose from the mundane realities of the lower world. Alonso Quixano's dissatisfaction in chapter 1 with his life as a poor hidalgo in barren La Mancha provides the well-known foundation for his desire to recreate the golden age of chivalry culled from his voracious reading of the romances of chivalry. Neo's disillusion with his life is represented concretely in two scenes that mirror similar moments in Cervantes's baroque *Don Quixote*, as well as in other postmodern texts such as *Fight Club* and *Trainspotting* in which the protagonists confront the demoralizing realities of the prosaic world.

In the first of these two scenes, Neo is taken to task by his Matrix-world boss for arriving late at the office one too many times:

You have a problem with authority, Mr. Anderson. You believe that you are special, that somehow the rules do not apply to you. Obviously, you are mistaken. This company is one of the top software companies in the world because every single employee understands that they are part of a whole. Thus, if an employee has a problem, the company has a problem. The time has come to make a choice, Mr. Anderson. Either you choose to be at your desk, on time, from this day forth, or you choose to find yourself another job. Do I make myself clear? (*Matrix*, 00:12:13–00)

Neo responds affirmatively to his boss's final question, but just in case there is any lingering doubt in his mind about the imperatives of subjectivity, Agent Smith soon presents him with a more profound choice than simply whether he will be a "team player" within the corporate culture of "Metacortex" (the highly significant name of his software firm):

As you can see, we've had our eye on you for some time now, Mr. Anderson. It seems that you've been living two lives. In one life, you're Thomas A. Anderson, program writer for a respectable software company. You have a social security number, you pay your taxes, and you help your landlady carry out her garbage. The other life is lived in computers, where you go by the hacker alias "Neo" and are guilty of virtually every computer crime we have a law for. One of these lives has a future. One of them does not. (*Matrix*, 00:17:48)

Like Don Quixote before him, Neo chooses the more interesting and politically engaged of these two optional identities. He gives up the creature comforts of his bourgeois life to depart on a quest that promises to change the world for him and for those around him. When Neo seems to vacillate in his resolve while on his way to his first meeting with Morpheus (who will present Neo with the choice one final time in the form of blue and red pills), Trinity reminds him that there is no real future for Thomas Anderson: "Because you have been down there, Neo. You know that road. You know exactly where it ends. And I know that's not where you want to be" (*Matrix*, 00:23:36).

Changing the world, however, means much more than simply trading a mundane life for something more exciting. The decisions made by Alonso Quixano and Thomas Anderson to radically alter the roads they travel involve more than just changes of scenery. The differences between Alonso Quixano and Don Quixote on the one hand and Thomas Anderson and Neo on the other are essentially differences of perception. As *The Matrix* explicitly notes, the world becomes different for Neo because he sees it for the first time through a different set of eyes, a set of eyes not plugged into the system. And by gaining this additional perspective, he is able to measure the world inside the Matrix against a set of standards provided by the higher reality that has been made available to him by his decision to set aside his identity as Thomas Anderson and give himself fully to his life as Neo. Neo is able to distinguish between "appearances" and "reality" in ways that Thomas Anderson could not have imagined. By creating a cognitive distance between himself and the Matrix, Neo (like everyone else no longer plugged into the system) is able to stand back and "read" it as the encoded text it really is.

The notion of reality as an encoded text is implicit in Plato's metaphorical cave, since those individuals trapped inside it must interpret the world outside the cave by reading the shadows on the wall. The film self-consciously underlines this fact by constantly presenting viewers with streaming images of the Matrix code dribbling down various screens (including the silver screen on which the film itself is projected). And because the signs on which this code is based consist of a strange amalgam of Arabic numerals, mathematical symbols, and Asian characters (all inverted as if reflected in a mirror), this code is literally illegible as far as the film's exterior audience is concerned in ways that Plato's shadows are not. For those privileged characters inside the film, however, reading the Matrix code is as easy as reading musical notation is for a musician or as easy as reading a book is for most literate people in the industrialized world. When Neo encounters one of these screens for the very first time, Cypher explains to him that achieving what could be called a basic "Matrix literacy" makes it possible to decipher the gist of what's occurring on screen: "You get used to it. I don't even see the code. All I see is blonde, brunette, redhead" (*Matrix*, 01:01:35). Ultimately, Neo is able to transcend the Matrix because (unlike Cypher) he can stop seeing blondes, brunettes, and redheads within its code. Neo's greatest success, as will become apparent, is his ability to perceive the Matrix as nothing but code.

Compare this to Don Quixote's own talents as a "reader" of reality. Despite the general prevalence of this baroque preoccupation with appearances and reality throughout Cervantes's novel—whose most famous example, of course, is the windmills episode—Cervantes highlights this juxtaposition in two specific interrelated moments that occur in part 1. The first moment occurs when Don Quixote comes into possession of what he insists is Mambrino's famous golden helmet. When Sancho protests that his master has done nothing more than rob a poor itinerant barber of his brass basin, Don Quixote replies:

> Do you know what I think, Sancho? I think that this famous piece of this enchanted helmet must, by some strange accident, have fallen into the hands of a person who did not understand or appreciate its value, and, not knowing what he was doing, he must, on seeing that it is made of the purest gold, have melted down the other half to sell it, and with the remaining half made this, which seems, as you say, like a barber's basin.

> *But let it be what it will; for me, who knows it well, its transformation is*
> *of no consequence.* (1.21:168; my emphasis)[6]

For Don Quixote, the object's physical appearance is quite literally mean-ingless. It is nothing more than a superficial consideration that masks a deeper reality. Like the virtual reality of the Matrix, Mambrino's helmet exists as nothing more than a text to be read (and thus appreciated) by readers like Don Quixote who are privileged enough to be able to decipher its hidden code.

So important is this notion for Cervantes that Don Quixote returns to his insistence on this point one final time in part 1. When Sancho later expresses skepticism over the reality of Mambrino's helmet, Don Quixote chides him with a reply that could just as easily have fallen from Mor-pheus's lips in one of his several teaching moments with Neo inside the "construct":

> Is it possible that in all the time you have been with me you have failed to
> realize that all things appertaining to us knights errant seem like chi-
> meras, follies and nonsenses, because they have all been turned on their
> head? Not because that is their real state, but because we are always
> attended by a crew of enchanters who keep transforming everything and
> changing it into whatever they like, according to whether they have a
> mind to help us or destroy us; and so what looks to you like a barber's
> basin looks to me like Mambrino's helmet and will look like something
> else to another person. (1.25:209)[7]

In contrast to other moments in the text, where Don Quixote insists that these enchanters have transformed one object into another, he plainly ac-cepts the fact here that Mambrino's golden helmet might very well look like the mundane object Sancho claims it to be. This change of appear-ance, however, does not affect its true essence. As he rightly points out, an object made of gold can easily be melted down by someone ignorant of its true value in order to make it assume a different exterior shape, but this re-formation does not affect its molecular structure. The object con-tinues to be the same object. Its malleability is simply one of the properties of metals. Like linguistic signs themselves, metals are not only infinitely pliable but are also—for all intents and purposes—nearly indestructible. Thus, "readers" of Mambrino's helmet have to learn to look beyond the surface value of this sign in much the same way "readers" of the Matrix have to learn to look beyond the pixels that constitute the trickling code.

This perspectivism is the essence of Plato's lingering influence in these texts. But this perspectivism raises a definite problem regarding one of the major differences between *Don Quixote* and the *Matrix*. In Cervantes's text, Don Quixote stands well inside Plato's cave and must look beyond the surface meaning of its reflected shadows to catch a glimpse of the higher reality that lies just beyond the purview of those ignorant "readers" that surround him. Although he is one of the cave's few privileged readers, he remains nonetheless trapped inside it, and thus his act of "reading" is nothing less than a genuine leap of faith (one Sancho is not yet willing to make). Neo, in contrast, has escaped from Plato's cave entirely (except during those brief incursions when he deliberately goes back inside to help rescue others) and thus he stands outside the cave's entrance looking in. For him, the surface meaning of the encoded Matrix communicates no higher reality beyond that which he has already achieved. In fact, the Matrix does just the opposite: it obscures the nasty realities of the world by deliberately creating a false reflection. Neo's privileged reading requires no act of faith.

What is particularly important about Don Quixote's second statement regarding Mambrino's helmet is just how effectively it ties Cervantes's quixotic world to that of the Wachowski Brothers. Immediately following Don Quixote's encounter with the giants who have suddenly been transformed into windmills, he advises Sancho that "Affairs of war, even more than others, are subject to continual change" (1.8:64). Rutherford's translation of this passage, though clear enough for most purposes, does not quite do justice to the audacity of Cervantes's original rhetoric. In the original Spanish, Don Quixote insists that these affairs of war are subject to "continua mudanza" (1.8:130); more like "continuous mutation." Thus, what Don Quixote acknowledges is not simply that circumstances constantly change (in the kind of mundane sense we all accept daily); rather, he recognizes that reality literally mutates around him: his library inexplicably disappears from the face of the earth, giants suddenly become windmills, strange knights become neighborly bachelors, Sancho's wife is slowly transformed over the course of the novel from "Juana Gutiérrez" into "Juana Panza" before finally becoming "Teresa Panza," while a letter supposedly written during the autumn months of an unnamed year prior to 1605 is dated July 20, 1614. Many of these mutations are deliberate, of course, and form part of Cervantes's exploration of appearances and reality. Others, however, are genuine errors that have managed to find their way into his novel. Still, as I argue in the previous chapter with respect to the "errors" embedded within the text of *Brazil*, these incongruities are all part of the shifting reality that makes up *Don Quixote*'s La Mancha. Cervantes's text—however erroneous—"was effectively said and cannot be undone" (Salecl and Žižek, iii); hence, its blunders should not be separated into "real" and "apparent" categories.

In the *Matrix* trilogy, because the world inside the Matrix is posited as nothing more than a computer-generated virtual reality, the Agents who police this world—like the enchanters Don Quixote evokes in the windmills episode—have powers beyond those of the mere mortals who inhabit it because they can manipulate the code for their own designs. This point is driven home to Neo during the so-called Red Dress training program when Morpheus demonstrates to his young protégé the dangers of accepting reality inside the Matrix as a stable entity. During the training program Neo steals a glance at an attractive blonde in a red dress who passes him on a sidewalk full of pedestrians. But when he turns back to look at her a second time, she has suddenly become one of the male Agents and is now pointing a gun directly at his head. In fact, this ability of the Agents to take over the identity of anyone still plugged into the Matrix is their most formidable weapon, and over the course of the three films we see dozens of people suddenly mutate into Agents just in time to thwart the plans of those who have jacked back in.

This dangerously effective metamorphosis by the Agents, however, is only the most obvious way in which the world of the Matrix is also subject to a continual mutation. There are many others. Midway through the first film, for instance, when Cypher has betrayed Morpheus and the others, Neo experiences what he at first thinks is déjà vu. But Trinity explains to him that moments of "déjà vu" are really computer glitches that frequently occur when the Agents have changed the code. Almost immediately upon saying this, Morpheus, Neo, and Trinity find themselves locked inside a room whose windows and doors (uncannily mirroring the door of Don Quixote's absent library) have been bricked up. At the same time, Morpheus and his band of unplugged hackers have also learned to manipulate the code of the Matrix and thus they perform a number of superhuman feats that include jumping across vast expanses, flying through windows, and stopping bullets in mid-air. Moreover, the "potentials" we meet in the waiting room of the Oracle's kitchen demonstrate a number of impossible talents, including bending spoons with their minds and levitating blocks in the air. And finally, in the second film, the ghostly albino twins are able to materialize and dematerialize at will to avoid being hit by bullets, and when they are hit, they can instantly "heal" themselves by returning their "wounded" limbs back to a pristine state.

In fact, one of the vignettes of *The Animatrix* (entitled "Beyond") plays with this notion of the mutability of life inside the Matrix by narrating the story of a group of children who sneak into a "haunted house" to entertain themselves with the "odd occurrences" that happen inside. As rain falls from a clear blue sky into a single open courtyard, the children practice levitating just inches above the ground in another open (and perfectly dry) space, all the while smashing bottles that immediately reconstitute themselves. Not surprisingly, the strange occurrences that make this house seem "haunted" are due not to some other metaphysical dimension that exists "beyond" the realities of the physical world but to a major glitch in the Matrix's programming code. And when the Agents discover what is happening, they quickly seal off the block in order to repair the glitch. The vignette ends with the children returning to the location a few days later only to be disappointed by the normalcy they encounter there. The Agents have effectively smoothed over the mutating reality that had previously existed at that particular location, and in doing so, have plugged a cognitive hole that could easily have led to more humans questioning the Matrix.

In this regard, there is something distinctly "inquisitorial" about these Agents. If what is at stake in the *Matrix* is the question of perspective, then the Wachowski Brothers' Agents are nothing less than enforcers of a single, official point of view. It is not coincidental, of course, that these figures wear the traditional uniform of the U.S. Secret Service or the FBI. They represent a kind of national police force who patrol the boundaries of the *Matrix*'s virtual platonic cave. As such, their enforcement of the machines' official ideology evokes the bureaucratic function of the Orwellian "thought police" featured in Terry Gilliam's *Brazil*, as well as that of the Spanish Inquisition, whose original mandate was the (often violent) imposition of Catholic orthodoxy on the Iberian Peninsula between its founding in 1478 and its official demise in 1834. Agent Smith's previously noted threat to Neo that only one of his "two lives" has a future, exemplifies the violence inherent in this system.[8] Like that of the Spanish inquisitors before them, the job of the *Matrix*'s Agents is to root out the "heresy" of what can only be called "Zionism" (defined within the context of the films' plot lines as a social movement—with Jewish rhetorical overtones— to establish a safe haven for those humans who do not wish to live under the "catholic" [i.e., "universal"] control of the machines).[9]

The Spanish Inquisition came into being in the late fifteenth century as a response to growing suspicion over the religious loyalty of the Iberian Peninsula's historically prominent Jewish population in the wake of the *Reconquista* and was related to the "blood purity" statutes I discuss in Chapter 1. Fearing that too many *conversos* were, in fact, Crypto-Jews who secretly practiced their outwardly abandoned faith, Ferdinand and Isabella received papal permission to establish the Consejo de la Suprema y General Inquisición. Over the course of the next three and a half centuries, the mission of the Spanish Inquisition was incrementally expanded to include the prosecution of various heresies, including Lutheranism and Illuminism, all of which contributed in no small way to the development of what has come to be called Spain's "Black Legend." As J. H. Elliott remarks, "The Holy Office was essentially the product of fear—and inevitably, being the product of fear, it was on fear that it flourished. In the 1530s and the 1540s it transformed itself into a great apparatus operating through delation and denunciation—a terrible machine that would eventually escape from the control of its own creators and acquire an independent existence of its own" (218).

Although the Inquisition does not make an explicit appearance in *Don Quixote*, Cervantes does assign its function as enforcer of Catholic orthodoxy to Don Quixote's friends and relatives. In part 1, following Don Quixote's first sally, his niece gives the keys to his library to the priest, who—along with the barber, the housekeeper, and the niece herself—conducts what has tellingly come to be called the "Inquisition of the Books," in which this small group of "inquisitors" pass judgment on the various tomes of Don Quixote's collection, burning the vast majority of them to prevent their use as proof of Don Quixote's "heretical" perspective on the realities of chivalry. When this textual auto-da-fe fails to keep the old man from venturing forth on his second sally, the priest and the barber follow him into the Sierra Morena armed with a plan to trick him into coming back to his village, where they hope to sequester him until his delusions have subsided. After numerous permutations, this plan results in Don Quixote's conveyance back home, locked inside a cage, after the priest and barber pointedly gain jurisdiction over him from the troopers of the Holy Brotherhood, who have finally caught up with him.

In part 2, Cervantes assigns this inquisitorial imposition of perspective to the bachelor, Sansón Carrasco, who then becomes Don Quixote's self-appointed Grand Inquisitor. Unlike the priest and the barber of part 1, however, who mistakenly think that they can enforce their orthodox view of reality by imprisoning Don Quixote's body (in effect, physically removing him from his chivalric matrix), Sansón—like O'Brien in Orwell's *Nineteen Eighty-Four* and Agent Smith in the *Matrix* trilogy—knows that imprisoning the mind is a much more effective control mechanism. Hence, Sansón's plan involves getting Don Quixote to "voluntarily" abandon his heretical perspective by attacking its ideological support head on. When he enters Don Quixote's chivalric matrix hidden behind his reflective masks, Sansón lures the knight-errant into combat by insisting that his own lady (first called "Casildea de Vandalia" [2.14:569] and later "whoever she happens to be" [2.64:926]) is superior in every way to Dulcinea del Toboso.[10] Such a challenge, of course, strikes at the heart of Don Quixote's chivalric ideology and cannot go unchecked. But because it strikes at the heart of his vision of self (especially because this identity is self-invented), Sansón's eventual defeat of Don Quixote has serious repercussions beyond those stipulations imposed by Sansón as part of the rules of their combat (which are that Don Quixote must return home and forswear his chivalric profession for one year). Ultimately, Alonso Quixano dies along with Don Quixote just as surely as the characters in the *Matrix* die in the real world if mortally wounded inside the virtual one. As Morpheus explains to Neo when his protégé asks what happens if you die inside the Matrix: "The body cannot live without the mind" (*Matrix*, 00:55:30). Or so we think.

After their initial encounter during the inquisition scene in which Agent Smith delivers his ultimatum to Neo regarding the "future" of his two lives, the two do not meet again until nearly the end of the film, at which point they face each other twice in battles that once again replicate the basic structure of Don Quixote's two jousts with Sansón. The first of these two encounters takes place on a subway platform and is clearly meant as a homage to the final showdown between the good guy and the bad guy of Hollywood westerns such as *High Noon* and *Stagecoach* (a trope that is, itself, taken from the jousting duels of the romances of chivalry).[11] In the opening moment of this encounter, Neo turns to run away from Smith, but he then decides to stay in order to stand his ground. And as he turns to face his nemesis, whirlwinds of litter blow around like so many tumbleweeds along a western Main Street, while the soundtrack provides a tapping that clearly evokes the menace of a rattlesnake. (The soundtrack's musical score has virtually disappeared at this point, but viewers familiar with the western can almost hear the theme from *The Good, the Bad, and the Ugly* echoing in their heads.) Neo and Smith draw their guns, shooting until each is empty (although neither character inflicts a single wound on the other), after which the battle discourse returns to that of the Asian martial arts film so prevalent throughout the rest of the trilogy. At this point, Neo and Smith engage in a highly choreographed fight that ends with Smith holding Neo in a headlock on the subway tracks while the metallic squeal of an oncoming train provides what Smith calls the "sound of inevitability, [...] the sound of [Neo's] death" (*Matrix*, 01:57:50).

Two things tie this scene to Don Quixote's initial battle with Sansón. First, because of Smith's overwhelmingly superior strength as an Agent who can literally bend the Matrix code to suit his combat needs, Neo quite unexpectedly defeats Smith by jumping some twenty vertical feet into the ceiling of the subway tunnel to free himself from Smith, who then is struck by the train as it speeds by. (This, of course, merely kills the vagrant whose identity Smith, as an Agent, has opportunistically assumed in order to fight Neo; Smith walks away unscathed from the encounter by transmorphing himself into yet another person.) Second, and more importantly, however, what is at stake between Neo and Smith at this point in the film is precisely what is at stake between Don Quixote and Sansón. As I have already remarked, Smith's previous arrest and interrogation of Neo is designed to make him abandon his assumed hacker identity. Hence, when Neo chooses his hacker identity over his respectable one, Smith's function throughout the trilogy becomes that of enforcing his previous threat regarding Neo's "two" lives; which is to say, if Neo will not willingly accept his status as Thomas Anderson, Smith will compel him to accept it. Smith's relentless pursuit of Neo is analogous to Sansón's project throughout the second part of *Don Quixote* to force Cervantes's knight-errant to abandon his self-constructed chivalric self in favor of his original identity as Alonso Quixano. Thus, throughout Neo's subway encounter with Smith, the inquisitorial Agent continues to tauntingly refer to his foe as "Mr. Anderson," because this is the official perspective the Agent wishes to impose on Neo, irrespective of whether he has managed to unplug himself from the Matrix. Significantly, then, when Neo literally makes his Herculean leap upward to loosen himself from Smith's grasp, his biggest gesture of defiance is not so much the leap itself as the phrase he utters while performing it: "My name is Neo" (*Matrix*, 01:58:05). For, just as Don Quixote insists, "I know who I am" [1.5:50],[12] when confronted by those who challenge his chivalric identity, Neo's defeat of Smith in this scene is more than just physical. It is an ideological victory that resists the hegemony the gatekeepers of the Matrix seek to impose on all those wishing to opt out.

Neo's second face-to-face encounter with Smith also mirrors Don Quixote's second encounter with Sansón. Having escaped from Smith's literal clutches in the subway, Neo races to a telephone in one of the upper floors of a nearby building while dodging a myriad of Agents who constantly assume the identities of various pedestrians along the way. As he opens the door to answer the ringing telephone—through which he can return to the safety of the real world—he unexpectedly finds himself staring down the barrel of Smith's gun. Smith fires a single shot into Neo's heart, which seems to surprise him more than wound him, after which the Agent empties at least ten more rounds into Neo's chest. This massive assault instantly kills Neo inside the Matrix, which also means that it kills him in the real world as well. (Throughout this scene the film cuts back and forth between the Matrix and the flight deck of the *Nebuchadnezzar* to show us the link between Neo's two deaths.) As it would appear to turn out, neither of Neo's two lives has a future. Smith drives home this point by saying, "Goodbye, Mr. Anderson" (*Matrix*, 02:03:37). And just as "Alonso Quixano the Good" meets his end surrounded by loved ones who beg him not to give up the ghost quite yet, "Neo the Unplugged" dies sitting in a chair on board the *Nebuchadnezzar* surrounded by Morpheus, Tank, and Trinity, none of whom can believe what they have just witnessed, none of whom can believe that Neo is not the "One."

It is in this moment, however, that *The Matrix* moves beyond *Don Quixote*. In order to head off any more unauthorized sequels like Avellaneda's, Cervantes is quite explicit about leaving his protagonist "dead and buried" at the end of his 1615 second part (2.Prologue to the Reader:486).[13] The Wachowski Brothers, however, need the Christ-like Neo to be resurrected at the end of their first film not only so that he can become the "One" but so that he can also move the *Matrix* narrative into the two sequels that will follow. And what, ironically, provokes Neo's very "un-Cervantine" resurrection is a reinscription of a fundamentally Cervantine mechanism: Dulcinea's function as an ideological inspiration for her knight-errant. Immediately following Neo's two deaths (both of which are confirmed first by an Agent in the Matrix world who checks Neo's pulse and declares him dead and then by a heart monitor in the real world clearly showing Neo's cardiographic flat line), Trinity whispers into Neo's real-world ear that he simply cannot die because the Oracle told her that the man with whom

Figure 19: Neo discovers his true strength only when he finally realizes that the trickling streams of Matrix code are nothing more than the shadows on the wall of a virtual platonic cave. (*The Matrix*, Warner Bros., 1999)

she would fall in love would be the "One." And with this, she gives him a kind of inverted "Sleeping Beauty" kiss that revives him in the real world, as well as within the Matrix world, despite the several gunshot wounds that still ooze virtual blood from his virtual chest. Turning to confront the Agents who have just declared him dead, Neo—like the enlightened prisoners of Plato's cave—can suddenly see the Matrix code for what it is (Figure 19). His death and resurrection as the "One" have forever solidified the unorthodox ideological perspective Agent Smith has sought to annihilate with his virtual auto-da-fe. Neo literally jumps into Smith's virtual body, causing the Agent to explode into thousands of luminous shards. Neo ends the film as something of a Superman figure whose ability to fly is the ultimate symbol of his defiance of the orthodox laws set down by the machines and their virtual inquisitors.

Of course, as Neo himself reminds us in the film's epilogue: this is not the end; it is just the beginning. Thus, in true Cervantine fashion, Neo must face Agent Smith again two more times in the third film of the trilogy.[14] As with their two meetings in the first film, the two battles between Neo and Smith in the third film again recapitulate the Don Quixote/Sansón Carrasco encounters. This time, however, Neo and Smith's function as Cervantine mirror images of each other is made quite explicit. The first of these two meetings actually occurs in the real world itself. As I note earlier, Neo's total emersion within Smith's virtual body at the end of the first film has somehow freed the Agent from his own constraints within the Matrix code, allowing him to assume the identities of more than one virtual human at a time. In *The Matrix Reloaded* Smith also manages to transform himself into one of the unplugged humans at the precise moment when this character, having jacked into the Matrix as part of a reconnaissance mission, is about to be "phoned" back into the real world. In this way, Smith manages to escape the Matrix world and pursue Neo into his own real world territory. In this, Smith's "dressing up" in a human body that mirrors the frailties of Neo's own physical body can be read as a reinscription of Sansón's pursuit of Don Quixote into the Sierra Morena and beyond dressed as a knight-errant.

Their second and final encounter occurs inside the Matrix itself, a world now dominated by the rogue Agent who has successfully turned every virtual man, woman, and child into a carbon copy of himself, including the Oracle whose prophetic eyes Smith has long coveted. Neo meanwhile has traveled to the real world "machine city" to offer his services to the machines as the only person who can stop Smith's takeover of the entire Matrix. Plugged back into the Matrix by the machines themselves, Neo finds Smith waiting for him on an urban street lined with thousands upon thousands of identical Smiths who stand as witnesses to this final confrontation. If the Smith of the previous encounter mirrored Neo in his physical limitations, the Smith of this final encounter mirrors Neo's "supernatural" capabilities. Like Neo, he can now fly, and their final battle self-consciously invokes the epic struggle between Superman and General Zod in the 1980 installment of the *Superman* film franchise starring Christopher Reeve. Although the special effects of this final confrontation between Neo and Smith are visually impressive (even by the very high standards set by the previous two *Matrix* films), very little of this thirteen-minute battle is intellectually engaging. What matters, especially for a culminating film whose tag line is "Everything that has a beginning has an end," is the way its ends. Standing inside an enormous crater in the middle of the street (created by their very battle), and having nearly beaten Neo to death, Smith demands to know why Neo keeps fighting when his defeat is so clearly inevitable:

> Why, Mr. Anderson, why? Why? Why do you do it? Why? Why get up? Why keep fighting? Do you believe you are fighting for something, for more than your survival? Can you tell me what it is? Do you even know? Is it Freedom? Or Truth? Perhaps, Peace? Could it be for Love? Illusions, Mr. Anderson, vagaries of perception. Temporary constructs of a feeble human intellect trying desperately to justify an existence that is without meaning or purpose. And all of them as artificial as the Matrix itself. Although, only a human mind could invent something as insipid as Love. You must be able to see it, Mr. Anderson. You must know it by now. You can't win. It's pointless to keep fighting. Why, Mr. Anderson? Why? Why do you persist? (*Revolutions*, 01:48:44)

Neo's response to this question—"Because I choose to" (*Revolutions*, 01:49:54)—is extremely significant. In the first place, it goes to the heart of the entire *Matrix* trilogy's philosophical preoccupation with the issue of free will. Neo has arrived at this point in time (despite his famed predestination as the "One") because he chose the red pill instead of the blue pill when Morpheus offered him the choice between finding out "how deep the rabbit hole goes" and returning to his quiet life as "Thomas Anderson," virtual software engineer oblivious to the real world and all its problems. In essence, Neo persists in fighting Smith because that is his purpose as Neo, as the "One." Ironically, having chosen to be Neo instead of Mr. Anderson when he accepted Morpheus's red pill, Neo can now do nothing else. He might just as well have answered Smith here in the past tense rather than the present tense: "Because I chose to."

In the second place, Neo's response to Smith (in its present tense) can be read nearly four hundred years after the fact as a brilliantly succinct summation of Don Quixote's own raison d'être. Smith's indictment of what he calls Neo's "illusions" and "vagaries of perception" perfectly describe Don Quixote's own temporarily self-constructed worldview. In this regard, Neo is more than just a Christ figure who triumphantly redeems the world after its fall from grace. He is also a Quixote figure who, like his Cervantine predecessor, chooses to battle evil enchanters against insurmountable odds in order to attempt to restore the world to its long-lost golden age that existed before the machines took control of it.[15] Thus, Smith's inquisitorial skepticism echoes that of the churchman, guest of the Duke and Duchess in the second part of the novel, who calls Don Quixote "Don Idiot" and admonishes him to abandon his own illusions: "go back home [...] and stop wandering about the world frittering your time away and turning yourself into the laughing-stock of all who know you and all who do not know you" (2.31:700).[16]

Of course, Cervantes's protagonist does fight for something more than just his own survival. In fact, if survival were the only issue Alonso Quixano would never have left home in the first place. It is because he does conceive of a higher purpose that he has ventured out into the world. Still, the question implicit in the churchman's criticism is exactly that uttered by Smith at the end of his own harangue: Why does Don Quixote persist in fighting for what people like the churchman consider nothing more than illusions? And Don Quixote's response to this churchman's inability to comprehend the values of chivalry amounts to nothing less than Neo's elegant statement of free will directed at an artificial intelligence who, despite spending much of the *Matrix* trilogy vainly attempting to practice it, proves utterly incapable of understanding the concept:

> For which of the idiocies that you have observed in me do you condemn me and insult me [...]? Is it appropriate to go bursting into other men's houses to rule their lives, or for certain people, brought up in the narrow confines of some hall of residence [...] to take it upon themselves

to lay down the laws of chivalry and pass judgement on knights errant? Is it perchance an empty nonsense or a waste of time to wander about the world in search not of pleasure but of the rough and rutted footpath up which the virtuous climb to the heights of immortality? [...] I have redressed outrages, righted wrongs, punished insolence, vanquished giants and felled monsters; I am a lover, merely because it is obligatory for knights errant to be lovers, yet I am not one of those debauched lovers but one of the platonic and continent sort. My intentions are always directed towards worthy ends, that is to say to do good to all and harm nobody; and whether the man who believes this, puts it into practice and devotes his life to it deserves to be called a fool is something for Your Graces, most excellent Duke and Duchess, to determine. (2.32:701)[17]

Don Quixote's succinct statement of his free will and the self-constructed identity that flows from it can be found halfway through this speech when he says, "a knight I am and a knight I shall die" (2.32:701).[18]

Don Quixote's insistence on the connection between free will and identity, however, demonstrates why Neo's final choice is so important, and why it so perfectly mirrors Don Quixote's final choice after his defeat at the hands of the Knight of the White Moon. The terms of combat that Sansón Carrasco imposes on Don Quixote essentially amount to Don Quixote's acceptance of the churchman's prior criticism: "and if you fight and I defeat you, the only satisfaction I demand is for you to put aside your arms, stop looking for your adventures, go back to your village for a year and stay there without ever touching your sword" (2.64:927).[19] Thus when Sansón finally defeats Don Quixote, the weary knight prefers death to a renunciation of his profession: "Drive your lance home, sir knight, and take away my life, since you have taken away my honour" (2.64:928).[20] He fully intends to die a knight-errant. And even though Sansón refuses to accommodate this death wish, Don Quixote soon dies nonetheless. For Neo, this relationship between death and defeat is inverted. At the end of their long struggle, Neo comes to realize that Smith has been right all along, that his defeat is inevitable. But in this very recognition comes Neo's greatest moment of triumph. He chooses to stop fighting and thus allows Smith to assimilate him (at this point, the last nonassimilated individual within the entire Matrix construct). Smith extends his hand into Neo's virtual corporeal space, as we have seen him do so many times before, and with this action Neo becomes a Smith (Figure 20). Shortly thereafter, the Matrix crashes, destroying the entire cadre of renegade Smiths in the process, and then reboots itself, thus returning the system back to square one for what the film suggests is the seventh time. Where Sansón defeats Don Quixote by becoming a mirror image of the knight-errant, Neo ultimately defeats Smith not just by reflecting his enemy but also by allowing himself to be turned into an exact replica. (And here the linguistic mirror-

Figure 20: Where Sansón Carrasco defeats Don Quixote by becoming a mirror image of the knight-errant, Neo defeats Agent Smith not just by reflecting his enemy but by allowing himself to be turned into an exact replica. (*The Matrix Revolutions*, Warner Bros., 2003)

ing of the Spanish words for friend and enemy ["amigo" and "enemigo"] is significant.) In this, Neo ironically succeeds against Smith by abandoning all pretenses to subjectivity, paradoxically choosing to give up his free will in order to accept his fate (something he initially resisted before being unplugged: "I don't like the idea that I am not in control of my life" (*Matrix*, 00:26:52).

Smith's dialogue leading up to this culminating moment of assimilation is crucial for an understanding of its ultimate Cervantine significance: "Wait, I've seen this. This is it, this is the end. Yes, you were laying right there, just like that. And I . . . I . . . I stand here, right here, and I am supposed to say something. I say, 'everything that has a beginning has an end, Neo'" (*Revolutions*, 01:51:30). This is the only time in the entire *Matrix* trilogy where Smith refers to Neo as "Neo" (rather than calling him "Mr. Anderson"), and Smith is completely perplexed by the words he unexpectedly hears coming out of his own mouth. We, of course, have heard these words before. This near-exact turn of phrase is used by the Oracle (Gloria Foster/Mary Alice) when she informs Neo that the end is near.[21] Thus, when we hear these words coming out of Smith's mouth, we realize (as he does not) that this particular "Smith" is not the one we have been following throughout the trilogy, not the one we initially meet in the first film. The Smith who defeats Neo at the end of the third film is the Smith who emerged when the Oracle was, herself, assimilated (a reading confirmed by the fact that, once the system reboots itself, the Oracle's inert body lies in the mud where this particular Smith had previously stood). And just prior to this assimilation, when Neo asks the Oracle about Smith's function within what is clearly a Biblically inspired postmodern morality play,

Figure 21: In a scene that evokes Buzz Lightyear's encounter with his televised mirror image, Neo finds himself surrounded (during his interview with the Architect) by an infinite number of Neos who collectively suggest an ever-bifurcating series of realities all revolving around discrete Neos. (*The Matrix Reloaded*, Warner Bros., 2003)

she tellingly replies, "He is you: your opposite, your negative, the result of the equation trying to balance itself out" (*Revolutions*, 00:29:39). The Oracle's words deliberately echo those of the Architect (Helmut Bakaitis), who responds in the second film to Neo's question about his own functionality by saying: "Your life is the sum of a remainder of an unbalanced equation inherent to the programming of the Matrix. You are the eventuality of an anomaly which, despite my sincerest efforts, I have been unable to eliminate from what is otherwise a harmony of mathematical precision" (*Reloaded*, 01:50:53).

But this takes us back to what is essentially the central moment of the *Matrix* trilogy, both cinematically and philosophically. In a scene simultaneously evoking Miguel de Unamuno's novel *Mist* (in which, again, Augusto Pérez confronts his godlike author in order to engage in a discussion about his free will or lack thereof) and Borges's stories "The Aleph" and "The Garden of Forking Paths" (in which Borges explores the notion of self-enclosed and infinitely bifurcating universes, respectively), Neo's interview with the Architect deliberately reduces all of the *Matrix*'s complex themes to a single conversation that takes place in a unique space apart (neither inside the Matrix world nor inside the real world) where Neo finds himself infinitely surrounded by his own reflection displayed on thousands of television screens that set up a visual mise-en-abîme in which an infinite number of Neos demonstrate an ever-bifurcating series of realities (Figure 21). In fact, to underscore the infinite multiplicity of this visual mise-en-abîme, the camera seems to pass through various screens—from one parallel reality to another—as this scene progresses. And the crux of this scene—indeed the crux of the entire *Matrix* trilogy, since everything that happens from this point on flows from it—comes down to the following piece of dialogue uttered by the Architect as he sends Neo on his final journey:

> Which brings us at last to the moment of truth, wherein the fundamental flaw is ultimately expressed and the anomaly revealed as both beginning and end. There are two doors. The door to your right leads to the source and the salvation of Zion. The door to your left leads back to the Matrix, to her [to Trinity, whose death the Architect insists is inevitable], and the end of your species. As you adequately put: the problem is choice. (*Reloaded*, 01:56:20–47)

Not surprisingly, Neo chooses the door on the left, in part because at this point he still labors under the illusion that he has free will, and in part because a Hollywood blockbuster—however philosophically engaged and postmodern—cannot allow its quixotic hero to abandon his Dulcinea to her untimely demise (a fact that, in an ironically Unamunian way, further calls into question Neo's very subjectivity, since his "choice" is always already overdetermined not just by the Wachowski Brothers' screenplay but by the studio moguls who have financed its production and thus who control all final decisions). Nevertheless, Neo's overdetermined choice of doors does result in a double paradox. On the one hand, his choice of the "left" door does not result, as the Architect erroneously predicts, in the end of humanity. On the other hand, however, as with Neo's final confrontation with Smith, his avoidance of the "right" door does not allow him to escape the fate the Architect has in store for him. But this leads us to one, final Cervantine intertextuality.

In *The Order of Things* Foucault famously says the following of Cervantes's gangly protagonist: "He never manages to escape from the familiar plain stretching out on all sides of the Analogue, any more than he does from his own small province. He travels endlessly over that plain, without ever crossing the clearly defined frontiers of difference, or reaching the heart of identity" (46). Substitute the words "Matrix" for "plain" and "Digital" for "Analogue" in the preceding quotation, and Foucault's comments emerge as equally apropos of Neo. Try as he might, Neo can never escape his inscription within the Matrix code. (Or, as Derrida might say, for Neo "there is nothing outside of the text" [158].) Moreover, since Neo is described in the *Matrix* trilogy as a numerical sign—the remainder of an unbalanced equation—he is not only the anagrammatical, messianic "One," he is also the integer "1," a mathematical sign whose existence, as the Architect so accurately reveals, cannot be separated from the symbolic system within which it is embedded: "The function of the One is now to return to the source, allowing a temporary dissemination of the code you carry, reinserting the prime program" (*Reloaded*, 1:54:51–59). Neo's ultimate function is to simply reboot the system. And in this regard, Neo, the "1," is the quintessential postmodern reflection of Don Quixote: "he is himself like a sign, a long, thin graphism, [whose] whole being is nothing but language [and who wanders] through the world among the resemblances of things" (Foucault, 46). Neo—the remainder, the "unbalancer," the 1 among 0s—is the ultimate embodiment of the Cervantine baroque. He is not just a Christ figure; he is quite simply asymmetry incarnate, a postmodern Don Quixote whose function—first and last—is to always upset the ideological balance that exists within the system.

Conclusion

One of the more prominent themes I touch on in this book, specifically in Chapters 6 and 7, is the baroque preoccupation with "being" versus "seeming." No writer, perhaps, captures this critical obsession better than Sor Juana Inés de la Cruz (1651–95) in a well-known sonnet within which she contemplates the significance of her own portrait.

> This that you gaze on, colorful deceit,
> that so immodestly displays art's favors,
> with its fallacious arguments of colors
> is to the senses cunning counterfeit,
>   this on which kindness practiced to delete
> from cruel years accumulated horrors,
> constraining time to mitigate its rigors,
> and thus oblivion and age defeat,
>   is but an artifice, a sop to vanity,
> is but a flower by the breezes bowed,
> is but a ploy to counter destiny,
>   is but a foolish labor, ill-employed,
> is but a fancy, and, as all may see,
> is but cadaver, ashes, shadow, void. (169)[1]

This poem exists as a direct intertextual response to a sonnet written in 1582 by Luis de Góngora within which Spain's most famously (some would say, excessively) baroque writer contemplates the fugacity of life through an exploration of the fleeting nature of beauty itself.

> While burnished gold shines vainly
> in the sun, a rival to your hair,
> while your white forehead spitefully
> regards the fields' fair lily;
>   while more eyes seek each lip of yours
> than look to find the early carnation,

and while your stately neck with proud
disdain conquers shining crystal,
    enjoy neck, hair, lip and forehead,
before what years of glory made
gold, lily, carnation, shining crystal,
    not only turns to silver or lopped pansy,
but it and you together turn
to clay, smoke, dust, shadow, naught.
       (*Selected Shorter Poems*, 135)[2]

Yet, where Góngora's admonition to seize the day focuses on the unstoppable passage of time, Sor Juana's caution against the deceptions of portraiture deconstructs a symbolic representation that not only seeks to stop time in its tracks but that does so by doing violence to the very "reality" it seeks to capture. What is at stake in this poem is not simply Sor Juana's recognition that the apparent mirror image she sees reflected in her portrait belies the passage of time and thus becomes increasingly divergent from the "real" image it supposedly reflects. What is at stake is the notion that the image itself exists as nothing more than a text to be deciphered (somewhat like Mambrino's helmet or the Matrix) and that its meaning as a reflective code is ultimately determined by the viewer rather than the subject. Sor Juana sees her portrait as "void" because—like Neo—she refuses to look beyond the code of paint and brush strokes that make up its text. For Sor Juana, it is not just that beauty inevitably fades; it is that beauty itself is an artificial construct.

Compare Sor Juana's sonnet to the portrait published on the dust jacket of Patricia Heaton's 2002 autobiography, *Motherhood and Hollywood: How to Get a Job Like Mine* (Figure 22). The front cover of this dust jacket—designed by Robbin Schiff, with photographs by Dana Fineman-Appel—depicts Heaton, the Emmy Award–winning star of the long-running television sitcom *Everybody Loves Raymond*, standing alongside a sporty red convertible somewhere on a lush Los Angeles suburban street. Heaton is shown in this picture posing in a full-length black evening gown and pearl necklace, as if she just stepped out of the car and onto a red carpet laid out for the attendees of one of Hollywood's many annual awards ceremonies. At the same time, however, she is also shown wearing a pair of yellow dishwashing gloves (that evoke the kinds of formal gloves worn by starlets during Hollywood's golden age) and holding aloft a plastic scrub brush (as one might hold an Emmy Award statuette during an acceptance speech).[3] This sartorial juxtaposition is directly related to the book's stated theme of the difficulties inherent in juggling motherhood and a high-power acting career, a theme Heaton explores further in a series of satirical Albertson's grocery store commercials in which we are led to believe that not only does she do all her own shopping (that is, without the help of the ubiquitous Hollywood "personal assistant") but she is supremely interested in finding good bargains just like any other "normal" mom, one not making the kind of money paid to stars of top-rated television series. *Motherhood and Hollywood*'s portrait of Heaton subtly plays with the notion of "being" and "seeming" by implicitly arguing that, while she may seem to be one of America's aristocratic "glitterati," she is in fact just another working mom from Cleveland, Ohio. In a discursive move reminiscent of Góngora's reminder that the "gold, lily, carnation, [and] shining crystal" of our prime years will inevitably turn to "clay, smoke, dust, shadow, [and] naught," Heaton's rubber gloves and scrub brush remind the viewer of this particular dust jacket that her Hollywood glamour is nothing more than the veneer of an artificial lifestyle that will eventually evaporate (as it does for nearly all aging celebrities), and that one day she will no doubt be back to washing her own dishes.

But the visual rhetoric of *Motherhood and Hollywood*'s engagement with "being" and "seeming" does not end with this front cover. Turning the book over, we find that the back cover of the dust jacket displays a visual companion to the front image highly reminiscent of Sor Juana's poetic response to Góngora (Figure 23). Here the portrait from the front cover is apparently reversed in order to give us a "behind the scenes" look at its composition and material production. Heaton is again shown in her full-length evening gown and rubber gloves (this time from behind), but what we now see in the background is the camera and lighting equipment supposedly used in the creation of the front cover's image. More importantly, this picture claims to make us privy to all the "behind the scenes" tricks used by the photographer to create the illusion of beauty depicted on the front cover. Heaton's hair is held in place by several large metal clips, and her dress is held together by a system of fasteners that include bright blue electrical tape and an enormous clamp that bears more than just a passing resemblance to the working end of a set of automotive jumper cables. Like Sor Juana's sonnet, this reversed image of Heaton's formal portrait makes explicit the fact that photographic portraiture itself—especially in the early twenty-first century, where publicity shots are routinely retouched using digital technology—is inherently unreliable, despite photography's popular reputation for "mirroring" reality in exact detail. What the back cover of Heaton's book does is to call into question the front cover's own visual rhetoric by reminding us that the "Hollywood glamour" peddled by contemporary, multinational media corporations (including Random House, publisher of *Motherhood and Hollywood*) is nothing more than a "cunning counterfeit" (Juana, 169) designed to sell a product.

This reversed portrait of Patricia Heaton on the back cover of her book is also highly—one might argue, deliberately—evocative of Diego Velázquez's *Las Meninas* (Figure 24). For, it is hard not to read Fineman-Appel's rather clever image as a kind of homage (however unconscious) to

EMMY®
AWARD—
WINNING STAR
—of—
*Everybody
Loves
Raymond*

Motherhood & Hollywood

how to get a job like mine

Figure 22: The photo on the cover of Patricia Heaton's autobiography is designed to evoke Heaton's double-life as a Hollywood star and working mother. (Photo by Dana Fineman-Appel. Book cover, copyright © 2002, from *Motherhood and Hollywood* by Patricia Heaton. Used by permission of Villard Books, a division of Random House, Inc.)

Spain's most famous baroque painting created by someone professionally trained to think in visual terms. On a thematic level, both works exist as deliberate contemplations on the very medium of their own production (painting and photography, respectively) in much the same way that *Don Quixote* serves as a study in the writing of fiction or Lope de Vega's "Impromptu Sonnet" overtly functions as a playful meditation on the generic conventions of the Italian sonnet.[4] *Motherhood and Hollywood*'s

Figure 23: The photo on the back cover of Heaton's book continues to explore the baroque notion of "being" versus "seeming" by demonstrating that the glamour posited on the front cover can be sustained only by an intricate network of hidden realities. (Photo by Dana Fineman-Appel. Book cover, copyright © 2002, from *Motherhood and Hollywood* by Patricia Heaton. Used by permission of Villard Books, a division of Random House, Inc.)

visible collection of tripods, cameras, electrical cables, and floodlights are contemporary analogues to *Las Meninas*' visible palette, paints, brushes, and canvas (whose exposed "back side" is reflected both by Heaton's own exposed "back side" on the back cover of her book and by her formal portrait on the front cover, an image that provides the privileged viewer of *Motherhood and Hollywood* a perspective on Heaton unavailable to the viewer of *Las Meninas*, for whom a glimpse of the Spanish monarchs' formal portrait is forever denied).

It is in its composition, however, where Heaton's dust jacket uncannily "quotes" Velázquez (to borrow Mieke Bal's turn-of-phrase). For instance, just left of center (at the painting's vanishing point, as so many art historians have remarked) Velázquez famously places a mirror image of his royal patrons, reflected outward toward the viewer as the king and queen pose for this very portrait; Fineman-Appel, for her part, positions Heaton also just left of center (again, at the convergence of the picture's many geometric lines), standing next to the driver's side door of the sports car, in front of a rearview mirror that obliquely reflects a small portion of Heaton's image back toward us as she apparently poses for the photograph seen on the front cover. To the immediate right of (and just slightly below) Velázquez's reflected monarchs stands the young blond Infanta, Doña Margarita, who demurely looks out toward the painting's viewer; to the immediate right of (and just slightly below) the reversed Heaton stands a small blond boy (presumably her son) who grimaces at us as he bounces on the driver's seat of the open convertible. To the immediate left of (and, again, just slightly below) Velázquez's reflected monarchs we see the artist holding the paints and brushes he is supposedly using to create their portrait; to the immediate left of (and, again, just slightly below) the reversed Heaton we see the camera supposedly used to capture the image seen on the front cover of her book. (Conspicuously absent from this picture is any image of Fineman-Appel, who—unlike Velázquez and for a variety of obvious reasons—has evidently preferred not to turn this playful meta-photograph into a self-portrait. In this regard, Fineman-Appel is a postmodern absence whose camera substitutes for what José Antonio Maravall calls Velázquez's subject position as a "painter in the first person" [*Culture*, 174].)

I conclude this book with a discussion of the pictures published on Heaton's dust jacket not because these interrelated images represent a high point in Western art (and certainly not because *Motherhood and Holly-wood* is a particularly profound piece of literature) but because they open up a window on a wider set of intellectual preoccupations, especially when viewed against the reflection provided by Sor Juana's sonnet and *Las Meninas*. The preoccupation with "being" versus "seeming" inscribed within these various texts represents something of an intellectual crisis of faith common to both the seventeenth and twenty-first centuries. I began this book by suggesting that the Spain of the sixteenth and seventeenth centuries and the United States of the past two hundred years can be seen as bookends of Western cultural expansion, mirroring each other in significant ways. Energized by their numerous scientific, economic, and military successes, both societies went about marking their newfound geopolitical status—at least in part—by producing a series of symbolic

Figure 24: Diego Velázquez's *Las Meninas* provides the baroque mirror against which the image on Heaton's back cover is reflected. (Museo del Prado, Madrid. Reproduced by permission)

texts that exude a deep-seated cultural confidence directly related to each nation-state's burgeoning imperial accomplishments. Our customary designation of specific historical periods as the "Spanish Golden Age" and the "American Century" reflects (in both instances) the ongoing conquest of the Americas and the recurrent political domination of the world by a "superpower," as well as the writing of *Don Quixote* and *Moby-Dick* and the construction of El Escorial and the Empire State Building. The "great works" of baroque Spain and twentieth-century Anglo-America—whether architectural, sculptural, musical, or literary—project a distinct rhetorical self-assurance through which the seemingly boundless potential of Spanish and Anglo-American hegemony is emblematically acclaimed to the rest of the world.

The problem with this hegemonic triumphalism, however, is that the cultural ascendancy of both Spain and the United States occurred during a five-hundred-year period of constant and ever-accelerating societal change. These changes—impelled by the cultural revolutions first of the Renaissance and then of the Enlightenment—profoundly undermined the philosophical foundations on which each society was traditionally built. The same social forces that produced Erasmus and Fray Luis de León also gave rise to Martin Luther and John Calvin; the same forces that produced René Descartes and Blaise Pascal eventually gave rise to Charles Darwin and Sigmund Freud. (This is not to mention all the ways in which the European "encounter" with the "foreign" realities of the New World severely called into question many of the received ideas that had seemed irrefutable since the Middle Ages.) Projects that began with the straightforward desire to release people from the superstitions and blind dogmas of the past ultimately resulted in a kind of intellectual second "fall from grace." By the seventeenth century, the once "catholic" Church was no longer so "universal," the once divine right of kings was no longer so divine. By the twentieth century, humans had been moved from the center of all creation to just one branch among many on the Darwinian family tree, the once preeminent marker of our ultimate reflection of God's image—consciousness—rendered little more than an evolutionary accident. (In this regard, the adversarial stance of contemporary Christian fundamentalism against the "evils" of secular humanism ironically mirrors the Counter-Reformation's preoccupation with the "heresies" of Protestantism.) All the certainties that at one time seemed so certain finally began to crumble under the constant onslaught of the Renaissance and Enlightenment reworking of essential cultural forms. And the seventeenth- and twentieth-century responses to these dizzying changes—embodied in what have come to be called the "baroque" and "postmodernism," respectively—represent parallel moments of what could perhaps be called a recurrent "cultural vertigo."

Thus, while many of the texts produced during Spain's "Golden Age" and the United States' "American Century"—particularly those I examine in this book—certainly exhibit an overtly imperial zeitgeist, they also inscribe a distinct (if only secondary) tone of underlying philosophical skepticism toward the whole idea of greatness. The once illustrious heroes of the past—from the demigods of the ancient Greek epic to the superhuman saints of medieval hagiography—have become the reluctant antiheroes of the picaresque novel and punk rock. The once utopian desire to unify the nation under one flag and one faith—whether during the medieval *Reconquista* of the Iberian Peninsula or the nineteenth-century taming of the

American wilderness—has given way to the dystopian visions of Mateo Alemán, Francisco de Quevedo, Terry Gilliam, and Chuck Palahniuk. The eager attempts by Don Quixote and Buzz Lightyear to do genuine good in the world are called into question by the problematic dementia of the very figures who perform these heroic acts; the decisive triumphs of Don Quixote and Neo in their respective confrontations with authority are undermined not only by their apparent lack of free will but also by their ultimate reinscription within the very authoritarian system they sought to overturn. What each of the texts examined in this book ultimately suggests is that whatever surface meaning we may read into any particular narrative, there nevertheless remains a subterranean quality that challenges the value of this superficial interpretation.

It is a cliché (not to mention largely inaccurate) to say that history repeats itself. Each generation inherits a distinct set of historical circumstances and each generation must navigate its way through the world by inventing its own unique present through its own unique interpretation of the past. (In this regard, *Tilting Cervantes* is the distinct product of my own contemporary effort to understand the present through a particular rereading of the past as I currently encounter it.) Nevertheless, I do not think that the co-incidental analogies—the interreflected cultural patterns—I have uncovered in this book are entirely coincidental. They are a product of each epoch's similar attempts to reinterpret the past according to present philosophical needs and of the radical doubt this discursive move eventually inspires. The historical periods we have come to call the "baroque" and "postmodernism" are a product of the overripening of the utopian desires present at the beginning of the Renaissance and the Enlightenment. And these desires can never be fulfilled (at least adequately) in an imperfect world hostile to utopias of any kind, whether pastoral, theological, political, or scientific.

Early in the first part of *Don Quixote*, the knight and his squire happen upon a cluster of goatherds' huts whose owners proceed to invite the pair to spend the night in their company, eating roasted acorns while sitting around a campfire. Inspired by the pastoral setting, Don Quixote begins to wax poetic and philosophical as he evokes a utopian past conjured up for him by such Renaissance poets as Garcilaso de la Vega and Juan Boscán:

> Happy the age and happy the centuries were those on which the ancients bestowed the name of golden, not because gold (so prized in this our age of iron) was then to be obtained with ease, but because men living in such times did not know those two words *yours* and *mine*. In that blessed age all things were held in common; no man, to gain his daily sustenance, had need to take any other pains than to reach up and pluck

it from the sturdy oaks, liberally inviting him to taste their sweet and toothsome fruit. [...] All then was peace, all was friendship, all was harmony. (1.11:84)[5]

As Miguel de Cervantes's narrator ironically notes, Don Quixote's "long harangue" leaves his hosts "bemused and bewildered" (1.11:85–86).[6] This is true, as Sancho later comments, because Don Quixote's "useless arguments" do not adequately reflect the real world inhabited by these working goatherds whose demanding vocation leaves them no time to perform the conventions of pastoral literature.[7] Superficially, this juxtaposition of the rural "being" with the pastoral "seeming" is meant to be humorous because it once again demonstrates Don Quixote's basic disconnection from reality in much the same way Sor Juana's sonnet exposes the great rift between her portrait and her self. But what it exposes on a much deeper philosophical level is the central dilemma of Cervantes's entire novel, whose protagonist eventually disavows his own chivalric project. Lost "golden ages" (assuming they ever existed to begin with) are not only irrecoverable; they are decidedly unwelcome because they inevitably get in the way of all the worldly business that must be attended to in modern society. A society in which the daily procurement of food required nothing more than our simply reaching upward to pluck it off the communal trees would be met with swift opposition by those who have an economic stake in the buying and selling of fruit. Ultimately, while poets and troubadours like Joni Mitchell might repeatedly insist that "we got to get ourselves back to the garden" ("Woodstock"), we are far too invested—economically, emotionally, philosophically—in the sweat of our brow to actually return to Eden even if we could. Don Quixote's "impossible dream" is just that.

And with this I arrive at one final baroque reflection. In the first installment of the *Matrix* trilogy Agent Smith describes for Morpheus the design flaws inherent in the machines' original attempt to create a virtual human world:

> Did you know that the first Matrix was designed to be a perfect human
> world, where none suffered, where everyone would be happy? It was
> a disaster. No one would accept the program. Entire crops were lost.
> Some believe that we lacked the programming language to describe your
> perfect world. But I believe that, as a species, human beings define their
> reality through misery and suffering. The "perfect world" was a dream
> that your primitive cerebrum kept trying to wake up from; which is why
> the Matrix was redesigned to this: the peak of your civilization. (*Matrix*,
> 01:31:55)

The Architect later reiterates these design limitations during his one and only encounter with Neo in *The Matrix Reloaded*:

> The first Matrix I designed was, quite naturally, perfect. It was a work of art. Flawless. Sublime. A triumph equaled only by its monumental failure. The inevitability of its doom is apparent to me now as a consequence of the imperfection inherent in every human being. Thus, I redesigned it—based on your history—to more accurately reflect the varying grotesqueries of your nature. However, I was again frustrated by failure. I have since come to understand that the answer eluded me because it required a lesser mind, or perhaps a mind less bound by the parameters of perfection. (*Reloaded*, 01:52:42)

Over the course of this book I have cited various baroque texts and then used them to project forward through time a commentary on our own contemporary culture. I conclude here by suggesting that these two Wachowskian observations on the relationship between art and life— informed as they are by so much poststructuralist theory—can be read backwards as commentaries on the function of the baroque itself. In sharp contrast to a medieval world view that posited tangible reality as nothing more than a vale of tears to be endured by those hoping to inherit a paradise in the afterlife, the Renaissance sought to articulate—in a fundamental way—a heaven on earth in which the most profound crisis was either unrequited love or the forced separation of the lover from his or her beloved. Yet, as Sor Juana's sonnet makes clear, this kind of utopian imaginary is increasingly difficult to maintain because "imperfect" readers will fail to recognize themselves in the reflected parameters of such simple perfection. Thus, in recognizing the lack of correspondence between reality and its artistic representation (again, between "being" and "seeming"), the baroque responds not by concealing this rift but by reveling in it. Much of what we call the "baroque" is really a celebration of the inherent distortions that undermine the "flawless sublimity" of art. The baroque holds a mirror up to life not to accentuate the image reflected but to celebrate the mirror itself. And no culture since the seventeenth century has been as actively engaged in this critical reflection as our own.

Notes

Introduction

1. Where possible, I have cited published translations of non-English texts. Where no published English translations exist, I have created my own English translations. In those instances where I have cited only the title of a non-English work, I have made no attempt to distinguish between my own titles and those I have borrowed from someone else.

Chapter 1

1. *Reconquista* refers to the eight-hundred-year military campaign by Spanish Christians to "reconquer" the Iberian Peninsula following the Muslim invasion of 711 CE.
2. The Siglo de Oro (historically called the Golden Age in English) actually comprises some two hundred years between 1500 and 1700.
3. Throughout the *Reconquista*, the ever-shifting boundary between Muslim and Christian territories on the Iberian Peninsula encouraged the development of a vocabulary to describe the ethnicity of those populations that found themselves stranded, as it were, "behind enemy lines." The term *mozárabe*, for instance, describes a Christian living within the boundaries of a Muslim territory; conversely, the term *mudéjar* describes a Muslim living in a Christian territory. After the fall of Granada in 1492, those Muslims who chose conversion over exile were then called Moriscos (although they too were expelled in 1609).
4. The Spanish term *comedia* is not semantically equivalent to its English cognate "comedy." It is a generic term that denotes any early modern Spanish three-act play written in verse, including those that could only be considered "tragedies" in English. Thus, the term *comedia histórica* refers to a particular subset of the generic form whose plot and themes are taken from Spanish history, especially from the history of the *Reconquista*.
5. As recent comments made by prominent televangelists such as Jerry Falwell and John Hagee demonstrate, the "Treacherous Moor" has once again become Christianity's ultimate enemy (see Ron Brown; Moore; and Russell).
6. "bravo espectáculo" (3:659).
7. Following English lexical custom, Pagden translates Cortés's Spanish *mezquitas* (mosques) as "temples" (Cortés, *Letters*, 35).
8. Defining Muslims as "pagan" demonstrates a clear lack of understanding among medieval Christians concerning the foundations of Islam.
9. See also Sullivan.
10. "Entendió también que lejos de allí había hombres de un ojo y otros con hocicos

de perros que comían los hombres y que en tomando uno lo degollaban y le bebían su sangre y le cortaban su natura"; "aquellos indios [la] llamaban *Bohío*, la cual decían que era muy grande y que había en ella gente que tenía un ojo en la frente, y otros que se llamaban caníbales, a quien mostraban tener gran miedo" (Columbus, *Cuatro viajes*, 54, 66).

11. Barbara Simerka points out that Lope's *Arauco Tamed* "also alludes to cannibalism and devil-worship on the part of the colonized subjects" (123).

12. For a detailed discussion of Ford's cinematic treatment of American Indians, see Maltby; and Pye.

13. To make it easier for viewers to scan directly to a particular scene I have provided DVD time codes (where possible).

14. "De la antigua casa y nobleza de vuestra merced propuse a las musas la historia en acto cómico [...] y así, entre tanto, quise ofrecer a vuestra merced esta historia, que escribí en *lenguaje antiguo* para dar mayor propiedad a la verdad del suceso, y no con pequeño estudio, por imitarla en su natural idioma" (1:336; my emphasis).

15. For more on this ancient dialect, see Zamora Vicente.

16. "Old Christians" (*cristianos viejos*) defined their own ethnic superiority by supposedly tracing their "untainted" bloodlines to before the time of the Muslim invasion.

17. For a superb discussion of the richness and importance of Islam in the cultural history of Spain, see Menocal.

18. Although Mauregatus is a historical figure, Lope's *comedia* elides many of the details that surround his life. Mauregatus is said to be the son of Alfonso I of Asturias and a Muslim peasant. He held the Asturian throne briefly between 783 and 789 CE. Legend attributes to Mauregatus the agreement to pay an annual tribute of one hundred damsels to Abderramán I, the Emir of Cordoba, in exchange for Abderramán's help in gaining the Asturian throne. Lope's Mauregato is represented more as a bureaucratic functionary of the Moors than as the uncle (not to mention political rival) of the play's Asturian king, Alfonso II. Ironically, Mauregato's historically accurate name contributes to the discursive dehumanization of the Muslims of this play, since his Spanish name essentially amounts to "Moor-cat."

19. "Parióme mi madre / una noche escura, / cubrióme de luto, / faltóme ventura. / Cuando yo nací, / hora fué menguada; / ni perro se oía, / ni gallo cantaba; / ni gallo cantaba, / ni perro se oía, / sino mi ventura, / que me maldecía" (1:355).

20. "Al pensar en tí, / Tierra en que nací, / Qué nostalgia siente mi corazón. / En mi soledad, / con este cantar, / Siento alivio y consuelo en mi dolor. / *Ahora, muchachos, ¡váyanse!* [whispered aside] / Las notas tristes de esta canción / Me traen recuerdos de aquel amor. / Al pensar en él, / Vuelve a renacer / La alegría en mi triste corazón" (00:45:33).

21. Following the Mexican-American War (1846–48), the Treaty of Guadalupe Hidalgo gave the United States ownership of what are now California, Nevada, Utah, and parts of Colorado, Arizona, and New Mexico.

22. Teresa Kirschner notes that in *Arauco Tamed* Lope positions the Spanish caballero, Don García, against an Amerindian counterpart in the figure of "the godlike King Caupolicán" (34).

23. Maravall argues that while chivalry was a particularly Germanic institution this did not keep late medieval writers from tracing the concept all the way back to the ancient Greeks and Romans (*Utopía*, 60).

24. See also Díaz Roig, 148–49.

25. *Amadís de Gaula* is the chivalric novel upon which Don Quixote bases his entire life as a knight-errant.

26. "Tienes, Señor, un vasallo / de quien lo son quatro Reyes. [...] el gran Rodrigo llegó, / peleó, rompió, mató, / y vencióme a mí el primero" (*Las mocedades del Cid*, 137).

27. "la doy a Osorio, y él la lleva al moro" (1:357).

28. Profoundly informed as it is by both Freudian theory and poststructuralist linguistics, Jacques Lacan's theory of desire and the unconscious is much more complex than Girard's. For Lacan, as Terry Eagleton succinctly puts it, "All desire springs from a lack, which it strives continually to fill. Human language works by such lack [...]. To enter language is to be severed from what Lacan calls the 'real,' that inaccessible realm which is always beyond the reach of signification, always outside the symbolic order" (167–68).

29. "Atiende, Osorio cobarde, / afrenta de homes, atiende, / porque entiendas la razón / si non entenderla quieres. / Las mujeres non tenemos / vergüenza de las mujeres; / quien camina entre vosotros / muy bien desnudarse puede, / porque sois como nosotras, / cobardes, fracas y endebres, / fembras, mujeres y damas; / y así, no hay por qué non deje / de desnudarme ante vos, / como a fembras acontece. / Pero cuando vi los moros, / que son homes, y homes fuertes, / vestíme; que non es bien / que las mis carnes me viesen" (1:363).

30. "[...] todos somos / homes, de Dios por la gracia. / Non soy yo fembra; ma, Dios, / magüer que Casto me llaman, / que el Casto fué por virtud, / non porque el brío me falta" (1:367).

31. "furia[,] muerte [y] rayo" (3:662).

32. It is significant that the damsel warrior calls herself "Don Martín *el* de Aragón" not just "Don Martín de Aragón." The addition of the masculine article doubly enhances her masculine gender performance.

33. Harriet Boyer reads Doña Sancha's sexually charged act as "the embodiment of the spirit of the Reconquista" and as an expiation for the legendary culpability of Florida, whose rape at the hands of the last Visigothic king, Rodrigo, supposedly precipitated the Muslim invasion in the first place (481).

34. The Spanish word *tonto* means "stupid."

35. The "Tale of Inappropriate Curiosity" (as Rutherford translates the title of *El curioso impertinente* [Cervantes, *Don Quixote*, 295]) is one of several short exemplary novels written by Cervantes. Unlike the rest of this collection, which Cervantes published together in 1613 under the title *Novelas ejemplares* (*Exemplary Stories*), the "Tale of Inappropriate Curiosity" was inserted as an intercalated text within *Don Quixote*. For more on the exemplary novels, see Chapter 3.

Chapter 2

1. Throughout this chapter, for reasons I explain later, I refer to the authors of these two books by the names listed on the copyright pages. Both texts were produced with the help of ghostwriters whose contributions I do not attempt to analyze in detail.

2. Significantly, the image located on page vi opposite Manson's table of contents— which can be interpreted as a kind of alternative schema for reading the book— is a map of hell taken from Allen Mandelbaum's 1980 translation of the *Divine Comedy*.

3. Ironically, because the work was published anonymously, many early readers

mistakenly assumed that *Lazarillo de Tormes* was a genuine autobiography in much the same way that some original viewers of *This Is Spinal Tap* mistook Rob Reiner's "mockumentary" for the genuine "rockumentary" it claimed to be.

4. See Bjornson; Blackburn; Brownlee; Friedman; Kaler; Miller; Monteser; Parker; Rico; Sieber; Spadaccini; Stone; Whitbourn; and Wicks.

5. As far as generic specifications are concerned, I am largely uninterested in approaches to literature that categorize texts the same way biologists organize various plant species using the Linnaean system of classification. Literary texts simply cannot be treated as genetic organisms delimited by some inherent DNA sequence that predetermines their form. In this regard, Ulrich Wicks is entirely right in saying that what is called "genre theory" (dependent as it often is on rigid categories) can become quite "tiresome," especially when it "undermines literature by squelching what we most admire in literary texts: the innovative, the unpredictable, the experimental" (4).

6. As Eisenberg notes: "There is, in fact, only *one* work which all agree to be picaresque novel, Part I of the *Guzmán de Alfarache* [...]. This is for a reason which is logical, consistent, and dramatically simple: the work contains a *pícaro*. Mateo Alemán used the word in the work, and the *Guzmán* was to contemporaries the *Libro del pícaro*. Since the book is a novel, what better reason could there be for calling it a picaresque novel?" (207).

7. The term "novel" has evolved somewhat since Cervantes first published his collection *Novelas ejemplares* in the early seventeenth century. Some translators render this word as "novels"; others prefer "novellas"; still others use the term "stories." In deference to Cervantes, I generally use the phrase "exemplary novels" when discussing them, even though I consider them to be more like short stories. For the convenience of the reader, I have used C. A. Jones's title *Exemplary Stories*, which can be found in the Works Cited under Cervantes.

8. For more on Dickens's debt to Cervantes, see Dowling; and Long.

9. For a detailed discussion of this period of rock history, see Bacon.

10. "tal alteración sintió mi estómago, que le dio con el hurto en ella, de suerte que su nariz y la negra mal maxcada longaniza a un tiempo salieron de mi boca" (*Lazarillo*, 40).

11. "Y yo, según lo que echaron sobre mí de sus estómagos, pensé que por ahorrar de médicos y boticas aguardan nuevos para purgarse" (Quevedo, 143).

12. "Al triste de mi padrastro azotaron y pringaron" (*Lazarillo*, 20).

13. "Amaneció y, antes que él despertase, yo me levanté y me fui a una posada, sin que me sintiese; torné a cerrar la puerta por defuera, y échéle la llave por una gatera. [...] Déjele en el aposento una carta cerrada, que contenía mi ida y las causas, avisándole que no me buscase, porque eternamente no lo había de ver" (Quevedo, 205).

14. Unlike more traditional picaresque narratives, which begin with a discussion of the narrator's own birth, Lydon's first chapter begins with a "death" of sorts; that is, with the demise of "Johnny Rotten," the founding lead singer of the band. Chapter 1 begins: " 'Ever get the feeling you've been cheated?' My famous last words on stage. The Sex Pistols ended the way they began—in utter disaster. Everything between was equally disastrous" (1). The final chapter recapitulates this sentiment: "That last moment on stage in San Francisco was the truth. I had felt cheated. I felt that my life had been stolen from me by lesser beings. Our inabilities ruined something truly excellent" (326).

15. In the original Spanish, Lazarillo says, "Mi nascimiento fue dentro del

río Tormes, por la cual causa tomé el sobrenombre; y fue desta manera" (*Lazarillo*,12). Alpert has ignored the literality of *dentro* ("within") and has instead chosen "*on* the River Tormes," thus granting Lazarillo a social respectability he does not actually claim to possess (Alpert, 25; my emphasis).

16. See also Davis and Womack on "pseudo-families" in *A Clockwork Orange*.

17. "Criado te he y con buen amo te he puesto; válete por ti" (*Lazarillo*, 22).

18. "Parescióme que en aquel instante desperté de la simpleza en que, como niño, dormido estaba. Dije entre mí: 'Verdad dice éste, que me cumple avivar el ojo y avisar, pues solo soy, y pensar cómo me sepa valer'" (*Lazarillo*, 23).

19. "Pablos, abre el ojo que asan carne. Mira por ti, que aquí no tienes otro padre ni madre" (*Quevedo*, 145).

20. See also Miller, 70–77.

21. Lydon criticizes Mick Jagger's self-fashioned working-class persona ("The Rolling Stones did live in a hovel, but wasn't Mick Jagger from a nice wealthy family?" [87]) before turning his text over to Caroline Coon, who drives the point home: "During the sixties, it was rock 'n' roll that saw the class system breaking down. It was rock 'n' roll that served as counterculture class politics and therefore instrumental in breaking things down. *Mick Jagger faked his accent to sound more working class.* His view of what it was to be working class was that you should be thick and stupid, yet another conceit about the English class system" (Lydon, 87; my emphasis).

22. Again, Lydon derisively notes that Mick Jagger and the rest of the Rolling Stones "became like little royal families unto themselves. They carted themselves around the country, waving to us occasionally. They bought immense houses, joined the stockbrokers' belt, and sent their kids to—*public schools!* See? The system! They became it" (196; original emphasis).

23. Alice Cooper's interview with Terry Gross reveals the full extent to which shock rock is as much a part of the history of American theater as of American music. At one point during the interview Cooper states that Groucho Marx (who was an apparent fan of Cooper's concerts) once told him that "Alice Cooper" was the "last hope for Vaudeville" (00:22:49). Moments later in this same interview, Cooper himself characterizes his act as a kind of "strange, dark cabaret" (00:23:38).

24. Manson's single opaque contact lens reflects Bowie's famously damaged pupil, his Goth make-up and his gender-bending name reflect Alice Cooper's own performance, and his overt Satanism reflects that of Black Sabbath.

25. See also Hickey-Moody on the relationship between Manson and Antonin Artaud's Theater of Cruelty and the ways in which Manson—whom she calls a "somewhat sexist businessman, heavily disguised as a transgressive performer"— pushes the "limits of gendered transgression" but not so much as to jeopardize his "inclusion in popular, mass media."

26. Temple's *Filth and the Fury* also underlines the distinction between "Johnny Rotten" and John Lydon by never showing Lydon's current face, which Temple hides (along with those of the rest of his interviewees) in the dark shadows of a silhouette.

27. For more on Borges and infinite narrative loops, see Chapter 5.

28. Alpert's English translation—one assumes for reasons of consistency of style— removes all traces of Quevedo's elusive original "letter" addressed to "Your Grace," both of which have been entirely replaced by the "book" and its "reader" (as happens—although inconsistently— in Quevedo's final pages).

Chapter 3

1. "Y fueme peor, como v. m. verá en la segunda parte, pues nunca mejora su estado quien muda solamente de lugar, y no de vida y costumbres" (308).

2. In the book, we never actually learn the name of this narrator, but both David Fincher's film crew and a number of later critics have taken to calling him "Jack" because of one of the text's rhetorical leitmotivs. At one point, this narrator comes across a series of pop-cultural health or medical articles in which various body parts describe themselves and their functions to the reader from within the perspective of a first-person narrative: "I am Jack's medulla oblongata." (In the book, the name associated with this leitmotiv is actually "Joe.") This becomes a running joke for the narrator of *Fight Club*, who frequently comments on his own narration by issuing such off-handed remarks as "I am Jack's complete indifference" and "I am Jack's cold sweat." Hence, Palahniuk's nameless narrator has become known as "Jack." For the sake of clarity, I too use this name.

3. Regarding Marla as a reflective "tourist," Don Quixote also finds himself surrounded by all sorts of people who have escaped into the forests of the Sierra Morena to pretend to be shepherds clearly drawn from their own reading of pastoral literature, thus becoming what could only be called "literary tourists."

4. Ironically, thanks to the litigious nature of corporate America—of which Fox Studios is a major player—the film actually had to drop the trademarked name IKEA and substitute in its place an entirely fictitious Scandinavian entity called "Fürni."

5. Wolff's 1970 play stages the social conflict between a bourgeois woman and a lower-class vagrant whom she has allowed to enter her apartment on the pretext of carrying her groceries for her. When this vagrant refuses to leave, Wolff's allegory becomes all too clear as the vagrant methodically tears the apartment and all its furniture to shreds, making handfuls of little paper flowers in the process.

6. For more on *Fight Club*'s various explorations of gender and sexuality, see Boon; J. Michael Clark; Suzanne Clark; Friday; Giroux; and Peele.

7. Because there are so many editions of *Don Quixote* available to readers, my parenthetical documentation includes the part and chapter from which I quote, as well as the page number from the particular edition I am citing.

8. "Estaba en el primero cartapacio pintada muy al natural la batalla de don Quijote con el vizcaíno, puestos en la mesma postura que la historia cuenta" (1.9:144).

9. A few more significant embedded clues can be found in the following passages from the novel: "Tyler worked part-time as a movie projectionist. Because of his nature, Tyler could only work night jobs. [...] Some people are night people. Some people are day people. I could only work a day job" (25). "I don't know how long Tyler had been working on all those nights I couldn't sleep" (27). "The manager of the Pressman Hotel very gently took the receiver out of my hand. The manager said he didn't want me working here anymore, not the way I looked now. I'm standing at the head of the manager's desk when I say, what? You don't like the idea of *this*? And without flinching, still looking at the manager, I roundhouse the fist at the centrifugal force end of my arm and slam fresh blood out of the cracked scabs in my nose. For no reason at all, I remember the night Tyler and I had our first fight." (116).

10. See also Ambrosini.
11. In light of *Fight Club*'s cinematic ending, Baudrillard's earlier reference to the World Trade Center is eerily prescient.
12. Although Rutherford renders Cervantes's original "Caballero de los Espejos" (2.14:140) not incorrectly as the "Knight of the Spangles" (2.14:575), I prefer to use the more literal translation of "mirrors."
13. "Caballero de los Leones" (2.17:166).
14. "Alonso Quijano el Bueno" (2.74:589).
15. *Stranger Than Fiction*, which rearticulates Unamuno's text for contemporary cinema audiences, undermines the "author's" decision to kill her protagonist by having Karen Eiffel (Emma Thompson) change her mind at the last moment, thus sparing the life of her protagonist Harold Crick (Will Ferrell).
16. *Jekyll and Hyde* makes no explicit appearance in Palahniuk's text, although both *Sybil* (the television movie starring Sally Field as a woman with several distinct personalities) and *Psycho* (Alfred Hitchcock's masterpiece) do. Jim Uhls's screenplay evokes Stevenson explicitly when Marla calls Jack/Tyler "Dr. Jekyll and Mr. Jackass."
17. "¿Cómo puede estar acabado [...] si aún no está acabada mi vida?" (1.22:272).
18. I refer to the fact that the dialogue between Scipio and Berganza is actually a narrative continuation of "The Deceitful Marriage" (the immediately preceding story in Cervantes's *Exemplary Stories*), whose first-person narrator recounts the conversation he overheard outside his hospital window while spending a delirious night recuperating from a head injury.

Chapter 4

1. "[La historia] es tan trillada y tan leída y tan sabida de todo género de gentes, que apenas han visto algún rocín flaco, cuando dicen: 'Allí va Rocinate.'" (2.3:64).
2. As I note throughout this book, Cervantes's work has had such a profound impact on world literature that a direct causality is often unnecessary when tracing Cervantine intertextualities. Nevertheless, in an attempt to discern whether Lasseter and company had deliberately based *Toy Story* on *Don Quixote*, I looked for textual evidence of this influence within the film itself. Part 1, chapter 6, of *Don Quixote* consists of what has come to be called the "Inquisition of the Books," in which various characters go through Don Quixote's library and comment on its collection—including books written by Cervantes himself—before burning virtually all of the knight's books. Knowing that not a single element of a computer-generated film like *Toy Story* could arise casually, I conducted my own "Inquisition of the Books." Carefully manipulating the pause button on my DVD player, I examined every visible book on Andy's bedroom bookshelf, looking for a copy of *Don Quixote* that would be my "smoking gun." Unfortunately, no such title appears on the bookshelf, which is apparently stocked with the Pixar animators' own favorite childhood books. But there is one extremely Cervantine book among all those on the shelf: *Tin Toy* by "Lasseter."
3. "baciyelmo" (1.44:540).
4. "Yo nací libre, y para poder vivir libre escogí la soledad de los campos" (1.14:186).
5. "Y aun creo que estamos ya tan de su parte que, aunque su retrato nos muestre

que es tuerta de un ojo y que del otro le mana bermellón y piedra azufre, con todo eso, por complacer a vuestra merced, diremos en su favor todo lo que quisiere" (1.4:100).

6. "una moza asturiana, ancha de cara, llana de cogote, de nariz roma, del un ojo tuerta y del otro no muy sana. Verdad es que la gallardía del cuerpo suplía las demás faltas: no tenía siete palmos de los pies a la cabeza, y las espaldas, que algún tanto le cargaban, la hacían mirar al suelo más de lo que ella quisiera" (1.16:198).

7. As part of his ongoing literary response to the publication of the unauthorized sequel to *Don Quixote* written by the pseudonymous Avellaneda, Cervantes includes a chapter late in his own second part in which Don Álvaro Tarfe—a character original to Avellaneda's narrative—meets Don Quixote at an inn and, after some conversation, agrees to sign an affidavit swearing that of the two Don Quixotes, Cervantes's is the true one (Rutherford, 2:72, 969 [Murillo, 2:72, 579]).

8. Between chapters 30 and 57 of the second part of Cervantes's novel, the Duke and Duchess invite Don Quixote and Sancho into their castle so that they can amuse themselves at the expense of Don Quixote and Sancho.

9. "¡Bravo, mi señor Don Quijote, bravo! La ley no se hizo para ti, ni para nosotros tus creyentes; nuestras premáticas son nuestra voluntad. Dijiste bien; tenías bríos para dar tú solo cuatrocientos palos a cuatrocientos cuadrilleros que se te pusieran delante, o por lo menos para intentarlo, que en el intento está el valor" (*Vida*, 133).

10. "que la muerte no triunfó / de su vida con su muerte" (2.74:592).

11. Sansón Carrasco informs Don Quixote and Sancho of the existence of part 1 as a published book in the opening chapters of part 2. This revelation leads to a whole discussion about the nature of literary representation.

12. In her comparison of *Toy Story* and Harriet Beecher Stowe's *Uncle Tom's Cabin*, Gina Camodeca reads Andy's mark of "ownership" as analogous to the kind of "branding" a slave master might effectuate upon the body of a slave (52).

13. "Para mí sola nació don Quijote, y yo para él; él supo obrar y yo escribir; solos los dos somos para en uno" (2.74:592).

14. "que deje reposar en la sepultura los cansados y ya podridos huesos de don Quijote" (2.74:593).

15. "¿Cómo puede estar acabado [mi libro] si aún no está acabada mi vida?" (1.22:272).

Chapter 5

1. See Hundley; "Iran FM Reasserts Rushdie Death Sentence amid Conservative Clamour"; "Iran Group Reaffirms Rushdie Death Edict"; "Iran's Revolutionary Guards Say Fatwa Against Rushdie Irrevocable"; and "Islamists in Iran Again Insist That Rushdie Fatwa Should Stay."

2. "Si a ésta se le puede poner alguna objeción cerca de su verdad, no podrá ser otra sino haber sido su autor arábigo, siendo muy propio de los de aquella nación ser mentirosos" (1.9:144).

3. "habiendo y debiendo ser los historiadores puntuales, verdaderos y no nada apasionados" (1.9:144).

4. We cannot forget that the narrative segments of *The Satanic Verses* that precipitated the charges of blasphemy for which Rushdie was condemned were part of a dream sequence that, like the Montesino's Cave episode in *Don Quixote*, was intended to be read as both apocryphal and ambiguous.

5. The opening sentences of *Don Quixote* are as well known as Herman Melville's opening in *Moby-Dick*: "In a village in La Mancha, the name of which I cannot quite recall, there lived not long ago one of those country gentlemen or hidalgos who keep a lance in a rack, an ancient leather shield, a scrawny hack and a greyhound for coursing. [...] His surname's said to have been Quixada, or Quesada (as if he were a jawbone, or a cheesecake): concerning this detail there's some discrepancy among the authors who have written on the subject, although a credible conjecture does suggest he might have been a plaintive Quexana" (1.1:25). ("En un lugar de la Mancha, de cuyo nombre no quiero acordarme, no ha mucho tiempo que vivía un hidalgo de los de lanza en astillero, adarga antigua, rocín flaco y galgo corredor. [...] Quieren decir que tenía el sobrenombre de Quijada, o Quesada, que en esto hay alguna diferencia en los autores que deste caso escriben; aunque por conjeturas verosímiles se deja entender que se llamaba Quejana" [1.1:69–71].)

6. Rushdie's use of the term "cross-breed" comes from Américo Castro's prominent theory that Cervantes was motivated by his social status as a *converso* (i.e., of Jewish origin) on his father's side. Rushdie's evocation of Erasmus relates to the fact that Erasmus's *Praise of Folly* has been thoroughly studied as a source for *Don Quixote*.

7. The "boom" refers to the period of Latin American literary history between the late 1940s and the early 1980s when the work of such important writers as Alejo Carpentier, Juan Rulfo, Carlos Fuentes, Julio Cortázar, Mario Vargas Llosa, and Gabriel García Márquez exploded onto the world scene.

8. Hispanists are likely to balk slightly at Henighan's assertion here, because most would probably locate the "foundations" of the Hispanic tradition at least in the twelfth-century *Poema de Mio Cid*, if not in the preceding Hispano-Arabic *jarchas* of the eleventh century.

9. Cervantes's exemplary novel "The Glass Graduate" tells the story of a law student who, having been given a poisonous love potion by a spurned admirer, descends into a fit of madness such that he comes to believe that he is made entirely of glass, and that if anyone were to touch him he would shatter into pieces.

10. For more on Monipodio's criminal significance, see Johnson, 37–50.

11. In one well-known episode of *Don Quixote* (examined in Chapter 4), the knight stops a group of Jewish silk merchants on their way to Murcia and refuses to let them pass until they confess that Dulcinea is the most beautiful woman in the world. Critics have frequently read this episode as Cervantes's commentary on forced conversion (with Dulcinea functioning as an analogue of the Virgin Mary). When one of the merchants asks to see proof of her beauty before he is willing to make such a declaration, Don Quixote chides him for requiring proof of such an obvious truth and insists that the whole point is to make this confession without proof.

12. Rushdie has also established other important intertextualities here with the work of E. M. Forster: Raman Fielding shares his surname with one of the central characters from *A Passage to India*, while "Moraes" is the surname of one of the central figures in Forster's story "The Other Boat." The importance of this connection to Forster is discussed later.

13. I refer, as does Rushdie himself, to Dulcinea del Toboso whose "real" name is Aldonza Lorenzo.

14. "Recordé también esa noche que está en el centro de las *1001 Noches*, cuando la reina Shahrazad (por una mágica distracción del copista) se pone a referir

textualmente la historia de las *1001 Noches*, con riesgo de llegar otra vez a la noche en que la refiere, y así hasto lo infinito" ("El jardín," 111).

15. "palabra por palabra y línea por línea" ("Pierre Menard, autor," 52).

16. See Holzapfel and Rodríguez; Incledon; Rodríguez Monegal; Steiner; and Wreen.

17. "infinitamente más rico" ("Pierre Menard, autor," 56–57).

18. As I note in Chapter 4, Sansón Carrasco is Don Quixote's chief nemesis in part 2, appearing first as the "Knight of the Mirrors" and later as the "Knight of the White Moon."

19. "Crueles estrellas y propicias estrellas / presidieron la noche de mi génesis; / debo a las últimas la cárcel / en que soñé Quijote" (*Gold of the Tigers*, 66).

20. Rushdie borrows this second citation from John Ford's *Man Who Shot Liberty Valance*.

21. "Pierre Menard, autor," 56.

22. This story's epigraph consists of a citation taken from the *Qur'an*: "And God made him die during the course of a hundred years and then He revived him and said: / 'How long have you been here?' / 'A day, or part of a day,' he replied." ("The Secret Miracle," 143). ("Y Dios lo hizo morir durante cien años y luego lo animó y le dijo: / —¿Cuánto tiempo has estado aquí? / —Un día o parte de un día—respondió." ["El milagro secreto," 165])

Chapter 6

1. Radford's *Nineteen Eighty-Four* was indeed released in 1984.

2. For a detailed analysis of the connections between *Nineteen Eighty-Four* and *Brazil*, see Rogers; and Williams.

3. *Brazil* does, in fact, end this way in the Universal Studios ninety-seven-minute cut shown on television in 1989.

4. See Chapter 4.

5. "sobre las bellas bella Dulcinea" (1.4:99).

6. "—Bien la conozco—dijo Sancho—, y sé decir que tira tan bien una barra como el más forzudo zagal de todo el pueblo. ¡Vive el Dador, que es moza de chapa, hecha y derecha y de pelo en pecho, y que puede sacar la barba del lodo a cualquier caballero andante, o por andar, que la tuviere por señora! ¡Oh hideputa, qué rejo que tiene, y qué voz! Sé decir que se puso un día encima del campanario del aldea a llamar unos zagales suyos que andaban en un barbecho de su padre, y aunque estaban de allí más de media legua, así la oyeron como si estuvieran al pie de la torre. Y lo mejor que tiene es que no es nada melindrosa, porque tiene mucho de cortesana: con todos se burla y de todo hace mueca y donaire" (1.25:312).

7. Compare, for instance, the moral dissonance between "court" and "countryside" in Shakespeare's *As You Like It*.

8. The idea that enchanters—principally, Frestón—pursue Don Quixote is actually an excuse invented by his friends after they burn his books and seal up his library in an attempt to put an end to his unhealthy preoccupation with chivalric novels. When Don Quixote awakens to find his library mysteriously gone, these friends blame its "disappearance" on an evil enchanter, thus undermining their own strategy for bringing the old man back down to earth (Rutherford, 1.6:59–61).

9. It is difficult, for instance, not to see a connection between Mr. Kurtzmann's attempts to keep Sam from accepting a promotion and Sam's fifth dream

sequence in which his insecure boss—in the surrealistic guise of a cobblestone street with stone hands—reaches up and grabs Dream Sam's ankles, saying "Sam, don't go, please," as Sam attempts to catch Dream Jill's cage before it floats away.

10. *Don Quixote* also includes a dream sequence in which the somnambulant protagonist defeats a "giant" (which turns out to be a wineskin) and awakens to find that his efforts have metaphorically restored "Princess Micomicona's" kingdom to her, which turns out to be Don Fernando's real-world acceptance of his previous promise to marry Dorotea (Rutherford, 1:35–36; 330–46).

11. "—Yo no veo, Sancho—dijo don Quijote—, sino a tres labradoras sobre tres borricos" (2.10:109).

12. Jill's line about Sam's paranoia occurs in the film but not the published screenplay.

13. "A esta sazón ya se había puesto Don Quijote de hinojos junto a Sancho, y miraba con ojos desencajados y vista turbada a la que Sancho llamaba reina y señora, y como no descubría en ella sino una moza aldeana, y no de muy buen rostro, porque era carirredonda y chata, estaba suspenso y admirado, sin osar desplegar los labios" (2.10:109–10).

14. "—Apártense nora en tal del camino, y déjennos pasar; que vamos de priesa" (2.10:110).

15. "Así que, Sancho, por lo que yo quiero a Dulcinea del Toboso, tanto vale como la más alta princesa de la tierra. [...] ¿Piensas tú que las Amariles, las Filis, las Silvias, las Dianas, las Galateas, las Alidas y otras tales de que los libros, los romances, las tiendas de los barberos, los teatros de las comedias, están llenos, fueron verdaderamente damas de carne y hueso, y de aquellos que las celebran y celebraron? No, por cierto, sino que las más se las fingen [...]. Y así, bástame a mí pensar y creer que la buena de Aldonza Lorenzo es hermosa y honesta; [pues] me hago cuenta que es la más alta princesa del mundo. [...] Y para concluir con todo, yo imagino que todo lo que digo es así, sin que sobre ni falte nada, y píntola en mi imaginación como la deseo" (1.25:313).

16. "ha puesto nubes y cataratas en mis ojos" (2.10:110).

17. Because Efron sees the "rejection of Dulcinea" as a "joyous imaginative act of liberation," he would probably see Sam's loss of faith in Jill as the first step on the road to freedom (144).

18. For a detailed discussion of the complex narrative structure of *Don Quixote*, see Parr.

19. "Llegando a escribir el traductor desta historia este quinto capítulo, dice que le tiene por apócrifo, porque en él habla Sancho Panza con otro estilo del que se podía prometer de su corto ingenio, y dice cosas tan sutiles, que no tiene por posible que él las supiese; pero que no quiso dejar de traducirlo, por cumplir con lo que a su oficio debía, y así, prosiguió" (2.5:73).

20. The Cave of Montesinos is a real geographical formation located in La Mancha. It is named for a character from the medieval romances of chivalry who, as legend has it, was born in France but was forced to flee to Spain.

21. I refer to the fact that, for a number of reasons (including Cervantes's carelessness), time varies greatly over the course of *Don Quixote*. The year and month in which the narrative is supposed to occur fluctuates radically from the distant past to the near future, while also progressing from July to November and then back again. For more on this issue, see Murillo, *Golden Dial*.

22. "No me puedo dar a entender, ni me puedo persuadir, que al valeroso don Quijote le pasase puntualmente todo lo que en el antecedente capítulo queda escrito: la razón es que todas las aventuras hasta aquí sucedidas han sido contingibles y verisímiles; pero ésta desta cueva no le hallo entrada alguna para tenerla por

verdadera, por ir tan fuera de los términos razonables. [...] Tú, letor, pues eres prudente, juzga lo que te pareciere, que yo no debo ni puedo más; puesto que se tiene por cierto que al tiempo de su fin y muerte dicen que se retrató della, y dijo que él la había inventado, por parecerle que convenía y cuadraba bien con las aventuras que había leído en sus historias" (2.24:223–24).

23. "que parte de las cosas que vuesa merced vio, o pasó, en la dicha cueva son falsas, y parte verisímiles" (2.25:238).

24. Here the transition from "reality" to "dream" occurs so swiftly that the viewer is not even aware that it has taken place. But to be sure, this ambiguity in and of itself is part of the logic of a false ending; if we suspect that we are being duped, we are less likely to be astonished by the surprise real ending.

25. In one of the more famous scenes from García Márquez's book, Remedios la Bella ascends into heaven while hanging sheets out to dry: "Amaranta felt a mysterious trembling in the lace on her petticoats and she tried to grasp the sheet so that she would not fall down at the instant in which Remedios the Beauty began to rise. Úrsula, almost blind at the time, was the only person who was sufficiently calm to identify the nature of that determined wind and she left the sheets to the mercy of the light as she watched Remedios the Beauty waving good-bye in the midst of the flapping sheets that rose up with her, abandoning with her the environment of beetles and dahlias and passing through the air with her as four o'clock in the afternoon came to an end, and they were lost forever with her in the upper atmosphere where not even the highest-flying birds of memory could reach her" (222–23). ("Amaranta sintió un temblor misterioso en los encajes de sus pollerinas y trató de agarrarse de la sábana para no caer, en el instante en que Remedios, la bella, empezaba a elevarse. Úrsula, ya casi ciega, fue la única que tuvo serenidad para identificar la naturaleza de aquel viento irreparable, y dejó las sábanas a merced de la luz, viendo a Remedios, la bella, que le decía adiós con la mano, entre el deslumbrante aleteo de las sábanas que subían con ella, que abandonaban con ella el aire de los escarabajos y las dalias, y pasaban con ella a través del aire donde terminaban las cuatro de la tarde, y se perdieron con ella para siempre en los altos aires donde no podían alcanzarla ni los más altos pájaros de la memoria" [313].)

26. A few minutes later the film shows another close-up of Buttle's arrest receipt on which his "C.R.O" number has become "2B/O47/E9." Shortly thereafter, another close-up of a form being examined by Mr. Kurtzmann shows the original number "B/58/732." The discrepancy can only be resolved if one reads the number listed on the arrest receipt either as serving a different bureaucratic function or as simply "apocryphal."

27. Like the issue of time, objects in *Don Quixote* are also problematic. The first edition of the novel, published by Juan de la Cuesta in 1605, apparently failed to include a lengthy narrative segment in which Ginés de Pasamonte steals Sancho's donkey. This segment was later included in the second edition published a few months later, but it was then (apparently) inserted in the wrong place, because Sancho's donkey is still present a few pages after this act of theft supposedly occurs. Some modern editors have attempted to resolve this problem either by deferring to the first edition or by moving the inserted passage of the second edition to the place where they think it belongs. In any event, many readers of *Don Quixote* encounter a text in which Sancho's donkey disappears and reappears several times. For more on the numerous errors embedded in *Don Quixote*, see Baena.

28. There is a fleeting moment when Jill notices him as he flies away from Sam's apartment, but as we have already said, this moment may not be "real" in any event.

29. It has been suggested that Gilliam's use of the name "Tuttle" was inspired by an episode of the sitcom *M*A*S*H* in which Hawkeye (Alan Alda) and his co-conspirators create an entirely fictitious captain named "Jonathan S. Tuttle" in order to funnel army resources to a local orphanage. These resources ultimately include Captain Tuttle's "back pay" after Hawkeye "kills off" his creation by having him "jump" to a heroic—if unfortunate—death without a parachute. Gilliam's leitmotiv of "We're all in it together" echoes Hawkeye's eulogy at Captain Tuttle's funeral: "We can all be comforted by the thought that he's not really gone. There's a little Tuttle left in all of us. In fact, you might say that all of us together made up Tuttle" ("Tuttle").

30. "Tú, letor, pues eres prudente, juzga lo que te pareciere, que yo no debo ni puedo más" (2.24:223).

31. One such reflective moment occurs when Sam and Jill are fighting over the package/bomb in the shopping mall. As the two struggle, leaning against the edge of a large mirror, we see a double set of Sams and Jills.

32. "está desencantada la señora Dulcinea" (2.74:588).

Chapter 7

1. One of the better-known serious academic treatments of *The Matrix* is a collection of critical essays entitled *"The Matrix" and Philosophy* (ed. William Irwin). Alongside this single volume, the Modern Language Association Online Bibliography currently lists more than one hundred entries for the *Matrix*, all of which have been published within the past decade. Compare this to only sixty-six entries for *Citizen Kane* (widely regarded as the most important film in the history of American cinema), which took more than thirty years to accumulate.

2. Closely tied to this trilogy of live action *Matrix* films, the Wachowski Brothers also produced a video game entitled *Enter the Matrix* (2003) and a Japanese anime film entitled *The Animatrix* (2003). The latter consists of nine vignettes, some of which are directly tied to the plotline of the trilogy, while others exist as independent narratives that are only indirectly related to the feature films themselves.

3. See Bassham; Bowman; Brannigan; Flannery-Dailey and Wagner; and Ford.

4. See also Flannery-Dailey and Wagner.

5. See also Beverley.

6. "—¿Sabes qué imagino, Sancho? Que esta famosa pieza deste encantado yelmo, por algún estraño acidente debió de venir a manos de quien no supo conocer ni estimar su valor, y, sin saber lo que hacía, viéndola de oro purísimo, debió de fundir la otra mitad para aprovecharse del precio, y de la otra mitad hizo ésta, que parece bacía de barbero, como tú dices; pero sea lo que fuere, que para mí que la conozco no hace al caso su trasmutación" (1.21:255).

7. "¿Que es posible que en cuanto ha que andas conmigo no has echado de ver que todas las cosas de los caballeros andantes parecen quimeras, necedades y desatinos, y que son todas hechas al revés? Y no porque sea ello ansí, sino porque andan entre nosotros siempre una caterva de encantadores que todas nuestras cosas mudan y truecan, y les vuelven según su gusto, y según tienen la gana de favorecernos o destruirnos; y así, eso que a ti te parece bacía de

barbero, me parece a mí el yelmo de Mambrino, y a otro le parecerá otra cosa" (1.25:306–7).

8. Given Neo's function as a Christ figure within the Wachowski Brothers' trilogy, his interrogation by Agent Smith evokes the well-known scene in Fyodor Dostoevsky's *Brothers Karamazov* where the Grand Inquisitor interrogates Christ himself and ultimately banishes him.

9. See also Lavery.

10. "sea quien fuere" (2.64:532).

11. Although I do not analyze this element of *Stagecoach* in Chapter 1, Ford's film does contain a subplot that ends in a midnight gunfight between Ringo and the Plummer brothers.

12. "Yo sé quien soy" (1.5:106).

13. "muerto y sepultado" (2.Prólogo al lector:37).

14. Neo and Smith engage in various minor skirmishes in the second film, but none of these rises to the level of Cervantine encounter we find in films one and three.

15. Unamuno's entire project in *The Life of Don Quixote and Sancho* and *The Tragic Sense of Life* is to convert Don Quixote into a Christ figure by declaring "quijotismo" to be the true religion of Spain, with Cervantes's knight-errant as its patron saint.

16. "volveos a vuestra casa, [...] y dejad de andar vagando por el mundo, papando viento y dando que reír a cuantos os conocen y no conocen" (2.31:282).

17. "¿Por cuál de las mentecaterías que en mí ha visto me condena y vitupera [...]? ¿No hay más sino a trochemoche entrarse por las casas ajenas a gobernar sus dueños, y habiéndose criado algunos en la estrecheza de algún pupilaje [...] meterse de rondón a dar leyes a la caballería y a juzgar de los caballeros andantes? ¿Por ventura es asumpto vano o es tiempo mal gastado el que se gasta en vagar por el mundo, no buscando los regalos dél, sino las asperezas por donde los buenos suben al asiento de la inmortalidad? [...] Yo he satisfecho agravios, enderezado tuertos, castigado insolencias, vencido gigantes, y atropellado vestiglos; yo soy enamorado, no más de porque es forzoso que los caballeros andantes lo sean; y siéndolo, no soy de los enamorados viciosos, sino de los platónicos continentes. Mis intenciones siempre las enderezo a buenos fines, que son de hacer bien a todos y mal a ninguno: si el que esto entiende, si el que esto obra, si el que desto trata merece ser llamado bobo, díganlo vuestras grandezas, duque y duquesa excelentes" (2.32:283–84).

18. "caballero soy y caballero he de morir" (2.32:283).

19. "y si tú pelearas y yo te venciere, no quiero otra satisfación sino que dejando las armas y absteniéndote de buscar aventuras, te recojas y retires a tu lugar por tiempo de un año, donde has de vivir sin echar mano a la espada" (2.64:532–33).

20. "Aprieta, caballero, la lanza, y quítame la vida, pues me has quitado la honra" (2.64:534).

21. Gloria Foster played the Oracle in the first two *Matrix* films, but she died unexpectedly in 2001. Mary Alice replaced her in the final film. The Wachowski Brothers' incorporated this change of physical appearance into the narrative of *The Matrix Revolutions* by implying that the machines had caused the Oracle's physical transformation to punish her for aiding Neo and Morpheus. In this way, her change of appearance becomes just another accepted aspect of the ever-mutating realities of the Matrix world.

Conclusion

1. "Éste, que ves, engaño colorido, / que del arte ostentando los primores, / con falsos silogismos de colores / es cauteloso engaño del sentido; / éste, en quien la lisonja ha pretendido / excusar de los años los horrores, / y venciendo del tiempo los rigores / triunfar de la vejez y del olvido, / es un vano artificio del cuidado, / es una flor al viento delicada, / es un resguardo inútil para el hado: / es una necia diligencia errada, / es un afán caduco y, bien mirado, / es cadáver, es polvo, es sombra, es nada" (168). The translation quoted in the text was originally published as "She Attempts to Minimize the Praise Occasioned by a Portrait of Herself Inscribed by Truth—Which She Calls Ardor," in *Sor Juana Inés de la Cruz: Poems*, trans. Margaret Sayers Peden (Binghamton, NY: Bilingual Press/ Editorial Bilingüe, 1985), and later appeared in *Poems, Protest, and a Dream: Selected Writings*, trans. Margaret Sayers Peden (London: Penguin, 1997). Copyright © 1985 Bilingual Press/Editorial Bilingüe, Arizona State University, Tempe. Reprinted by permission.

2. "Mientras por competir con tu cabello, /oro bruñido el Sol relumbra en vano, / mientras con menosprecio en medio el llano / mira tu blanca frente al lilio bello; / mientras a cada labio, por cogello, / siguen más ojos que al clavel temprano, / y mientras triunfa con desdén lozano / de el luciente cristal tu gentil cuello; / goza cuello, cabello, labio y frente, / antes que lo que fué en tu edad dorada / oro, lilio, clavel, cristal luciente / no sólo en plata o víola troncada / se vuelva, mas tú y ello juntamente / en tierra, en humo, en polvo, en sombra, en nada" (*Obras completas*, 447). The translation quoted in the text is from Poem XLVIX in *Luis de Góngora: Selected Shorter Poems,* trans. Michael Smith (London: Anvil Press Poetry, 1995). Reprinted by permission.

3. An earlier version of the cover of *Motherhood and Hollywood* shows Heaton wearing her yellow rubber gloves while actually holding her Emmy Award.

4. Lope's charming *ars poetica*, "Soneto de repente," describes the necessary formal requirements of an Italian sonnet while performing them in the process.

5. "Dichosa edad y siglos dichosos aquellos a quien los antiguos pusieron nombre de dorados, y no porque en ellos el oro, que en esta nuestra edad de hierro tanto se estima, se alcanzase en aquella venturosa sin fatiga alguna, sino porque entonces los que en ella vivían ignoraban estas dos palabras de *tuyo* y *mío*. Eran en aquella santa edad todas las cosas comunes; a nadie le era necesario para alcanzar su ordinario sustento tomar otro trabajo que alzar la mano y alcanzarle de las robustas encinas, que liberalmente les estaban convidando con su dulce y sazonado fruto. [...] Todo era paz entonces, todo amistad, todo concordia" (1.11:155–56).

6. "larga arenga"; "embobados y suspensos" (1.11:157).

7. "the work these good people have got to do all day long doesn't let them spend their nights singing" (1.11:88) ("el trabajo que estos buenos hombres tienen todo el día no permite que pasen las noches cantando" [1.11:160–61]).

Works Cited

Alcalá, Manuel. Preliminary Note. In *Cartas de relación*, by Hernán Cortés. Mexico City: Porrúa, 1988.

Alemán, Mateo. *Guzman de Alfarache*. Ed. José María Micó. 2 vols. Madrid: Cátedra, 1994.

Alpert, Michael, trans. *Two Spanish Picaresque Novels: Lazarillo de Tormes (Anon), The Swindler (Francisco de Quevedo)*. London: Penguin, 1969.

Amadís de Gaula. Ed. Edwin B. Place. 4 vols. Madrid: Consejo Superior de Investigaciones Científicas, 1959–69.

Ambrosini, Richard. "Lo specchio come psiche in 'Dr. Jekyll and Mr. Hyde.'" In *Giocó di specchi: Saggi sull'uso letterario dell'immagine dello specchio*, ed. Agostino Lombardo. Rome: Bulzoni, 1999.

The Animatrix. Dir. Peter Chung et al. Screenplay by Andy Wachowski, Larry Wachowski, et al. Warner Bros., 2003. B/W and color, 102 min.

Annie Get Your Gun. By Herbert Fields and Dorothy Fields. Music and lyrics by Irving Berlin. Dir. Joshua Logan. Perf. Ethel Merman. Imperial Theater, New York. May 16, 1946.

Apache. Dir. Robert Aldrich. Screenplay by James R. Webb. Perf. Burt Lancaster, Jean Peters, John McIntire, and Charles (Bronson) Buchinsky. United Artists, 1954. Blackhawk. Color, 91 min.

Apocalypto. Dir. Mel Gibson. Screenplay by Mel Gibson and Farhad Safinia. Perf. Rudy Youngblood, Dalia Hernández, and Jonathan Brewer. Touchstone, 2006. Color, 139 min.

Bacon, Tony. *London Live: From the Yardbirds to Pink Floyd to the Sex Pistols; The Inside Story of Live Bands in the Capital's Trail-Blazing Music Clubs*. San Francisco: Miller Freeman Books, 1999.

Baena, Julio. *Discordancias cervantinas*. Newark, DE: Juan de la Cuesta, 2003.

Baker, Stephen. "You Must Remember This": Salman Rushdie's *The Moor's Last Sigh*." *Journal of Commonwealth Literature* 35.1 (2000): 43–54.

Bakhtin, Mikhail. *Rabelais and His World*. Trans. Hélène Iswolsky. Bloomington: Indiana University Press, 1984.

Bal, Mieke. *Quoting Caravaggio: Contemporary Art, Preposterous History*. Chicago: University of Chicago Press, 1999.

Bartra, Roger. "Arabs, Jews, and the Enigma of Spanish Imperial Melancholy." Trans. Amanda Harris Fonseca. *Discourse: Journal for Theoretical Studies in Media and Culture* 22.3 (2000): 64–72.

Bassham, Gregory. "The Religion of *The Matrix* and the Problems of Pluralism." In *"The Matrix" and Philosophy: Welcome to the Desert of the Real*, ed. William Irwin. Chicago: Open Court, 2002. 111–25.

Bateman, Eric. "Walt Disney vs. Wallace Stegner: Community Leadership and Masculine Myths." In *Community in the American West*, ed. Stephen Tchudi. Reno: Nevada Humanities Committee, 1999. 81–89.

The Battle at Elderbush Gulch. Dir. D. W. Griffith. Perf. Lillian Gish and Lionel Barrymore. Biograph, 1913. B/W, 29 min.

Baudrillard, Jean. *Selected Writings*. Ed. Mark Poster. 2nd ed. Palo Alto: Stanford University Press, 2001.

Beckett, Samuel. *Waiting for Godot: Tragicomedy in Two Acts*. Trans. Samuel Beckett. New York: Grove Press, 1982.

Beusterien, John. "Reading Cervantes: A New Virtual Reality." *Comparative Literature Studies* 43.4 (2006): 428–40.

Beverley, John. "Subaltern Resistance in Latin America: A Reply to Tom Brass." *Journal of Peasant Studies* 31.2 (2004): 261–75.

Bhabha, Homi K. *The Location of Culture*. London: Routledge, 1994.

Bird, Robert Montgomery. *Nick of the Woods; or, The Jibbenainosay: A Tale of Kentucky*. Ed. Curtis Dahl. New Haven: College & University Press, 1967.

Bjornson, Richard. *The Picaresque Hero in European Fiction*. Madison: University of Wisconsin Press, 1977.

Blackburn, Alexander. *The Myth of the Picaro: Continuity and Transformation of the Picaresque Novel, 1554–1954*. Chapel Hill: University of North Carolina Press, 1979.

Blade Runner. Dir. Ridley Scott. Screenplay by Hampton Francher and David [Webb] Peoples. Based on the novel by Philip K. Dick. Perf. Harrison Ford, Rutger Hauer, Sean Young, Edward James Olmos, M. Emmet Walsh, Daryl Hannah, and William Sanderson. Warner Bros., 1982. Color, 117 min.

Bloom, Harold. *The American Religion: The Emergence of the Post-Christian Nation*. New York: Touchstone, 1993.

———. *The Anxiety of Influence: A Theory of Poetry*. New York: Oxford University Press, 1973.

———. *The Western Canon: The Books and School of the Ages*. New York: Harcourt Brace, 1994.

Boon, Kevin Alexander. "Men and Nostalgia for Violence: Culture and Culpability in Chuck Palahniuk's *Fight Club*. *Journal of Men's Studies* 11.3 (2003): 267–76.

Borges, Jorge Luis. "El Aleph." In *El Aleph*. Buenos Aires: Alianza, 1989. 155–74.

———. "The Aleph." Trans. N. T. di Giovanni. In *Borges: A Reader*, ed. Emir Rodríguez Monegal and Alastair Reid. New York: E. P. Dutton, 1981. 154–63.

———. "The Garden of Forking Paths." Trans. Helen Temple and Ruthven Todd. In *Ficciones*, ed. Anthony Kerrigan. New York: Grove Press, 1962. 89–101.

———. *The Gold of the Tigers: Selected Later Poems*. Trans. Alastair Reid. New York: E. P. Dutton, 1977.

———. "El jardín de senderos que se bifurcan." In *Ficciones*. Buenos Aires: Alianza, 1990. 101–16.

———. "Kafka and His Precursors." Trans. Ruth L. C. Simms. In *Borges: A Reader*, ed. Emir Rodríguez Monegal and Alastair Reid. New York: E. P. Dutton, 1981. 242–46.

———. "Kafka y sus precursores." In *Otras inquisiciones*. Buenos Aires: Alianza, 1989. 107–9.

———. "El milagro secreto." In *Ficciones*. Buenos Aires: Alianza, 1990. 165–74.

———. "Pierre Menard, autor del Quijote." In *Ficciones*. Buenos Aires: Alianza, 1990. 47–59.

———. "Pierre Menard, Author of Don Quixote." Trans. Anthony Bonner. In *Ficciones*, ed. Anthony Kerrigan. New York: Grove Press, 1962. 45–55.

———. "The Secret Miracle." Trans. Anthony Kerrigan. In *Ficciones*, ed. Anthony Kerrigan. New York: Grove Press, 1962. 143–50.

Bork, Robert H. *Slouching Towards Gomorrah: Modern Liberalism and American Decline*. New York: ReganBooks, 1996.

Bowman, Donna. "The Gnostic Illusion: Problematic Realized Eschatology in *The Matrix Reloaded*." *Journal of Religion and Popular Culture* 4 (2003): 21 paragraphs, *www.usask.ca/relst/jrpc/art4-matrixreloaded-print.html* (accessed May 2, 2008).

Boyd, Katrina G. "Pastiche and Postmodernism in *Brazil*." *Cinefocus* 1.1 (1990): 33–42.

Boyer, Harriet P. "*Las famosas asturianas* y la mujer heroica." In *Lope de Vega y los orígenes del teatro español: Actas del I congreso internacional sobre Lope de Vega*. Ed. Manuel Criado de Val. Madrid: EDI-6, 1981. 479–84.

Brannigan, Michael. "There Is No Spoon: A Buddhist Mirror." In *"The Matrix" and Philosophy: Welcome to the Desert of the Real*, ed. William Irwin. Chicago: Open Court, 2002. 101–10.

Brazil. Dir. Terry Gilliam. Screenplay by Terry Gilliam, Tom Stoppard, and Charles McKeown. Perf. Jonathon Pryce, Robert De Niro, Katherine Helmond, Ian Holm, Bob Hoskins, Michael Palin, and Kim Greist. Universal, 1985. Color, 142 min.

Broken Arrow. Dir. Delmer Daves. Screenplay by Michael Blankfort. Perf. James Stewart, Jeff Chandler, Debra Paget, and Iron Eyes Cody. 20th Century-Fox, 1950. B/W, 93 min.

Brown, Bill. "How to Do Things with Things (A Toy Story)." *Critical Inquiry* 24.4 (1998): 935–64.

Brown, Ron. "The Rev. John Hagee Gives Warning at Thomas Road." *The News & Advance* (Lynchburg, Virginia), September 3, 2006. *www.newsadvance.com/servlet/ Satellite?pagename=LNA/MGArticle/LNA_BasicArticle&c=MGArticle&cid=1149190407326* (accessed July 26, 2007).

Brownlee, Marina S. "Discursive Parameters of the Picaresque." In *The Picaresque: A Symposium on the Rogue's Tale*, ed. Carmen Benito-Vessels and Michael Zappala. Newark: University of Delaware Press, 1994. 25–35.

Buber, Martin. *I and Thou*. Trans. Walter Kaufmann. New York: Charles Scribner's Sons, 1970.

Burgess, Anthony. *A Clockwork Orange*. New York: W. W. Norton, 1986.

Burningham, Bruce R. *Radical Theatricality: Jongleuresque Performance on the Early Spanish Stage*. West Lafayette, IN: Purdue University Press, 2007.

Burshatin, Israel. "Playing the Moor: Parody and Performance in Lope de Vega's *El primer Fajardo*." *PMLA* 107 (1992): 566–81.

Buscombe, Edward. *Stagecoach*. London: British Film Institute Publishing, 1992.

Byron, George Gordon, Baron. *The Works of Lord Byron*. Ed. Ernest Hartley Coleridge. Vol. 4, *Poetry*. New York: Octagon Books, 1966.

Camodeca, Gina. "Uncle Toy's Cabin: The Politics of Ownership in Disney's *Toy Story*." *Studies in American Culture* 25.2 (2002): 51–63.

Cantor, Paul A. "Tales of the Alhambra: Rushdie's Use of Spanish History in *The Moor's Last Sigh*." *Studies in the Novel* 29.3 (1997): 323–41.

Casas, Bartolomé de las. *Brevísima relación de la destruición de las Indias*. Ed. André Saint-Lu. Madrid: Cátedra, 1989.

Case, Thomas E. "Lope and the Moriscos." *Bulletin of the Comediantes* 44.2 (1992): 195–216.

———. "El morisco gracioso en el teatro de Lope." In *Lope de Vega y los orígenes del teatro español: Actas del I congreso internacional sobre Lope de Vega.* Ed. Manuel Criado de Val. Madrid: EDI-6, 1981. 785–90.

Castro, Américo. *Cervantes y los casticismos españoles.* Madrid: Alfaguara, 1966.

Castro, Guillén de. *Las mocedades del Cid.* Ed. Luciano García Lorenzo. Madrid: Cátedra, 1984.

Cervantes Saavedra, Miguel de. *El ingenioso hidalgo Don Quijote de la Mancha.* Ed. Luis Andrés Murillo. 2 vols. Madrid: Castalia, 1978.

———. *Exemplary Stories.* Trans. C. A. Jones. London: Penguin, 1972.

———. *The Ingenious Hidalgo Don Quixote de la Mancha.* Trans. John Rutherford. Intro. Roberto González Echevarría. New York: Penguin Books, 2001.

———. *Novelas ejemplares.* Ed. Harry Sieber. 2 vols. Madrid: Cátedra, 2001.

Cheyenne Autumn. Dir. John Ford. Screenplay by James R. Webb. Perf. Richard Widmark, Carroll Baker, James Stewart, Karl Malden, Edward G. Robinson, Sal Mineo, Dolores del Río, and Ricardo Montalban. Warner Bros., 1964. Color, 154 min.

Childers, William. *Transnational Cervantes.* Toronto: University of Toronto Press, 2006.

Chrisafis, Angelique. "*Don Quixote* Is the World's Best Book Say the World's Top Authors." *Guardian,* May 8, 2002. *www.guardian.co.uk/Archive/Article/0,4273,4409130,00.html* (accessed May 2, 2008).

Christe, Ian. *Sound of the Beast: The Complete Headbanging History of Heavy Metal.* New York: HarperEntertainment, 2003.

Clark, J. Michael. "Faludi, *Fight Club*, and Phallic Masculinity: Exploring the Emasculating Economics of Patriarchy." *Journal of Men's Studies* 11.1 (2002): 65–76.

Clark, Suzanne. "*Fight Club*: Historicizing the Rhetoric of Masculinity, Violence, and Sentimentality." *JAC* 21.2 (2001): 411–20.

A Clockwork Orange. Dir. Stanley Kubrick. Screenplay by Stanley Kubrick. Based on the novel by Anthony Burgess. Perf. Malcolm McDowell, Patrick Magee, and Michael Bates. Warner Bros., 1971. Color, 137 min.

Cohen, J. M., trans. *The Adventures of Don Quixote.* By Miguel de Cervantes. London: Penguin, 1950.

Cohen, Ralph. "Genre Theory, Literary History, and Historical Change." In *Theoretical Issues in Literary History.* Ed. David Perkins. Cambridge: Harvard University Press, 1991. 85–113.

Columbus, Christopher. *Los cuatro viajes del almirante y su testamento.* Ed. Ignacio B. Anzoátegui. Madrid: Espasa-Calpe, 1986.

———. *The Log of Christopher Columbus.* Trans. Robert H. Fuson. Camden, ME: International Marine Publishing Company, 1987.

Cooper, Alice [Vincent Damon Furnier]. Interview with Terry Gross. *Fresh Air.* National Public Radio. May 17, 2007.

Cortés, Hernán. *Cartas de relación.* Ed. Manuel Alcalá. Mexico City: Porrúa, 1988.

———. *Letters from Mexico.* Trans. Anthony Pagden. Intro. J. H. Elliott. New Haven: Yale University Press, 2001.

Danahay, Martin A., and David Rieder. "*The Matrix*, Marx, and the Coppertop's Life." In *"The Matrix" and Philosophy: Welcome to the Desert of the Real*, ed. William Irwin. Chicago: Open Court, 2002. 216–24.

Davis, Nina Cox. *Autobiography as* Burla *in the "Guzmán de Alfarache."* Lewisburg, PA: Bucknell University Press, 1991.

Davis, Todd F., and Kenneth Womack. " 'O my brothers': Reading the Anti-Ethics of the Pseudo-Family in Anthony Burgess's *A Clockwork Orange.*" *College Literature* 29.2 (2002): 19–36.

Del Río, Carmen M. "Borges' 'Pierre Menard'; or, Where Is the Text?" *Kentucky Romance Quarterly* 25 (1978): 459–69.

Derrida, Jacques. *Of Grammatology.* Trans. Gayatri Chakravorty Spivak. Baltimore: Johns Hopkins University Press, 1974.

Descartes, René. *The Philosophical Writings of Descartes.* Trans. John Cottingham, Robert Stoothoff, and Dugald Murdoch. 2 vols. Cambridge: Cambridge University Press, 1985.

Díaz Balsera, Viviana. "Araucanian Alterity in Alonso de Ercilla and Lope de Vega." In *Looking at the "Comedia" in the Year of the Quincentennial: Proceedings of the 1992 Symposium on Golden Age Drama at the University of Texas, El Paso, March 18–21.* Ed. Barbara Mujica, Sharon D. Voros, and Matthew D. Stroud. Lanham, MD: University Press of America, 1993. 23–36.

Díaz del Castillo, Bernal. *Historia verdadera de la conquista de la Nueva España.* Ed. Carlos Pereyra. Madrid: Espasa-Calpe, 1989.

Díaz Roig, Mercedes, ed. *El Romancero viejo.* Madrid: Cátedra, 1988.

Dowling, Constance. "Cervantes, Dickens, and the World of the Juvenile Criminal." *Dickensian* 82.4 (1986): 151–67.

Eagleton, Terry. *Literary Theory: An Introduction.* Minneapolis: University of Minnesota Press, 1983.

Efron, Arthur. *"Don Quixote" and the Dulcineated World.* Austin: University of Texas Press, 1971.

Eisenberg, Daniel. "Does the Picaresque Novel Exist?" *Kentucky Romance Quarterly* 26 (1979): 203–19.

Elliott, J. H. *Imperial Spain, 1469–1716.* London: Penguin, 1990.

Enter the Matrix. Dir. Andy Wachowski and Larry Wachowski. Sony PlayStation 2. DVD-ROM. Warner Bros. and Infogrames, 2003.

Erion, Gerald J., and Barry Smith. "Skepticism, Morality, and *The Matrix.*" In *"The Matrix" and Philosophy: Welcome to the Desert of the Real*, ed. William Irwin. Chicago: Open Court, 2002. 16–27.

Fernández de Avellaneda, Alonso [pseud.]. *Don Quixote de la Mancha (Part II): Being the Spurious Continuation of Miguel de Cervantes' Part I.* Trans. Alberta Wilson Server and John Esten Keller. Newark, DE: Juan de la Cuesta, 1980.

Fiander, Robert. "At the Movies: The Interpenetration of Cinema and Virtual Reality." *Antigonish Review* 120 (2000): 43–52.

Fielding, Julien R. "Reassessing *The Matrix/Reloaded.*" *Journal of Religion and Film* 7.2 (2003): 18 paragraphs. *www.unomaha.edu/jrf/Vol7No2/matrix. matrixreloaded.htm* (accessed May 2, 2008).

Fight Club. Dir. David Fincher. Screenplay by Jim Uhls. Based on the novel by Chuck Palahniuk. Perf. Brad Pitt, Edward Norton, and Helena Bonham Carter. 20th Century Fox, 1999. Color, 139 min.

The Filth and the Fury. Dir. Julien Temple. Perf. Paul Cook, Steve Jones, Johnny Rotten, Glen Matlock, Malcolm McLaren, and Sid Vicious. DVD. Fine Line Features, 2000. Color, 108 min.

The Fisher King. Dir. Terry Gilliam. Screenplay by Richard LaGravenese. Perf. Jeff Bridges, Robin Williams, Mercedes Ruehl, and Amanda Plummer. Columbia/ Tri-Star, 1991. Color, 137 min.

Fister, Barbara. "Mugging for the Camera: Narrative Strategies in *Brazil*. *Literature/ Film Quarterly* 24.3 (1996): 288–92.

Flannery-Dailey, Frances, and Rachel Wagner. "Wake Up! Gnosticism and Buddhism in *The Matrix*." *Journal of Religion and Film* 5.2 (2001): 40 paragraphs. *www. unomaha.edu/jrf/gnostic.htm* (accessed May 2, 2008).

Ford, James L. "Buddhism, Christianity, and *The Matrix*: The Dialectic of Myth-Making in Contemporary Cinema." *Journal of Religion and Film* 4.2 (2000): 24 paragraphs. *www.unomaha.edu/~wwjrf/thematrix.htm* (accessed June 28, 2004).

Forster, E. M. (Edward Morgan). "The Other Boat." In *The Life to Come and Other Short Stories*. New York: Norton, 1992. 166–97.

———. *A Passage to India*. New York: Knopf, 1992.

Fort Apache. Dir. John Ford. Screenplay by Frank S. Nugent. Perf. John Wayne, Henry Fonda, Shirley Temple, Pedro Armendáriz. RKO Radio Pictures, 1948. B/W, 125 min.

Foucault, Michel. *The Order of Things: An Archaeology of the Human Sciences*. New York: Vintage, 1994.

Fowler, Alastair. *Kinds of Literature: An Introduction to the Theory of Genres and Modes*. Cambridge: Harvard University Press, 1982.

Friday, Kirster. " 'A Generation of Men Without History': *Fight Club*, Masculinity, and the Historical Symptom." *Postmodern Culture: An Electronic Journal of Interdisciplinary Criticism* 13.3 (2003): 38 paragraphs. *www.iath.virginia.edu/ pmc/issue.503/13.3friday.html* (accessed May 2, 2008).

Friedman, Edward H. *The Antiheroine's Voice: Narrative Discourse and Transformations of the Picaresque*. Columbia: University of Missouri Press, 1987.

Fuchs, Barbara. *Mimesis and Empire: The New World, Islam, and European Identities*. Cambridge: Cambridge University Press, 2001.

Fuentes, Carlos. *Aura*. Mexico City: Ediciones Era, 1962.

Garcés, María Antonia. "Zoraida's Veil: 'The Other Scene' of the Captive's Tale." *Revista de estudios hispánicos* 23.1 (1989): 65–98.

García Márquez, Gabriel. *Cien años de soledad*. Ed. Jacques Joset. Madrid: Cátedra, 1987.

———. *One Hundred Years of Solitude*. Trans. Gregory Rabassa. New York: Avon, 1971.

Gilliam, Terry. "Salman Rushdie and Terry Gilliam: A Conversation from the 29th Telluride Film Festival." Telluride Film Festival, 2002. *Lost in La Mancha*. Bonus disc. Dir. Keith Fulton and Louis Pepe. DVD. IFC Films/New Video Group, 2002. Color, 89 min.

Girard, René. *Deceit, Desire, and the Novel: Self and Other in Literary Structure*. Trans. Yvonne Freccero. Baltimore: Johns Hopkins University Press, 1965.

Giroux, Henry A. "Private Satisfactions and Public Disorders: *Fight Club*, Patriarchy, and the Politics of Masculine Violence." *JAC* 21.1 (2001): 1–31.

Góngora, Luis de. *Obras completas*. Ed. Juan Mille y Giménez and Isabel Mille y Giménez. Madrid: Aguilar, 1961.

———. *Polyphemus and Galatea: A Study in the Interpretation of a Baroque Poem*. Trans. Gilbert F. Cunningham. Intro. Alexander A. Parker. Austin: University of Texas Press, 1977.

———. *Selected Shorter Poems*. Trans. Michael Smith. London: Anvil Press Poetry, 1995.

González Echevarría, Roberto. *Celestina's Brood: Continuities of the Baroque in Spanish and Latin American Literatures.* Durham: Duke University Press, 1993.

Gramsci, Antonio. *Selections from Cultural Writings.* Ed. David Forgacs and Geoffrey Nowell-Smith. Trans. William Boelhower. London: Lawrence and Wishart, 1985.

————. *Selections from the Prison Notebooks of Antonio Gramsci.* Trans. Quintin Hoare and Geoffrey Nowell Smith. New York: International Publishers, 1971.

Greenblatt, Stephen. *Renaissance Self-Fashioning: From More to Shakespeare.* Chicago: University of Chicago Press, 1980.

Hall, Sheldon. "How the West Was Won: History, Spectacle, and the American Mountains." *The Book of Westerns.* Ed. Ian Cameron and Douglas Pye. New York: Continuum, 1996. 255–61.

Hall, Stuart, Chas Critcher, Tony Jefferson, John Clarke, and Brian Roberts. *Policing the Crisis: Mugging, the State, and Law and Order.* New York: Holmes & Meier, 1978.

Heaton, Patricia. *Motherhood and Hollywood: How to Get a Job Like Mine.* New York: Villard, 2002.

Hebdige, Dick. *Subculture: The Meaning of Style.* London: Methuen, 1979.

Heidegger, Martin. *The Concept of Time.* Trans. William McNeill. Oxford: Blackwell, 1992.

————. *History of the Concept of Time: Prolegomena.* Trans. Theodore Kisiel. Bloomington: Indiana University Press, 1985.

Hellmann, John M. Jr. " 'I'm a Monkey': The Influence of the Black American Blues Argot on the Rolling Stones." *Journal of American Folklore* 86 (1973): 367–73.

Henighan, Stephen. "Coming to Benengeli: The Genesis of Salman Rushdie's Rewriting of Juan Rulfo in *The Moor's Last Sigh.*" *Journal of Commonwealth Literature* 33.2 (1998): 55–74.

Hickey-Moody, Anna. "Gender Performativity, an Ethics of Self, and the Art of Consuming Marilyn Manson." *Azimuté. members.optusnet.com. au/~robert2600/azimute/music/manson.html* (accessed May 2, 2008).

Hirsch, E. D. Jr. *Cultural Literacy: What Every American Needs to Know.* New York: Vintage, 1988.

Holzapfel, Tamara, and Alfred Rodríguez. "Apuntes para una lectura del *Quijote* de Pierre Menard." *Revista Iberoamericana* 43 (1977): 671–77.

Hombre. Dir. Martin Ritt. Screenplay by Irving Ravetch and Harriet Frank Jr. Perf. Paul Newman, Fredric March, and Richard Boone. 20th Century-Fox, 1967. Color, 110 min.

Hondo. Dir. John Farrow. Screenplay by James Edward Grant. Perf. John Wayne, Geraldine Page, Ward Bond, Michael Pate, James Arness, and Rodolfo Acosta. Warner Bros., 1953. Color, 83 min.

Hundley, Tom. "Rushdie, Britain Stir Muslim World's Fury." *Chicago Tribune,* June 20, 2007, sec. 1, p. 5.

Ibsen, Henrik. *Hedda Gabler and A Doll's House.* Trans. Christopher Hampton. London: Faber and Faber, 1989.

Incledon, John. "La obra invisible de Pierre Menard." *Revista Iberoamericana* 43 (1977): 665–69.

"Iran FM Reasserts Rushdie Death Sentence amid Conservative Clamour." *Agence France Presse.* February 14, 2000. International news. Available from *www. lexis-nexis.com,* September 12, 2002.

"Iran Group Reaffirms Rushdie Death Edict." *New York Times,* February 15, 1999, late ed., A5.

"Iran's Revolutionary Guards Say Fatwa Against Rushdie Irrevocable." *Agence France Presse*. February 13, 1999. International news. Available from *www.lexis-nexis.com*, September 12, 2002.

Irwin, William, ed. *"The Matrix" and Philosophy: Welcome to the Desert of the Real*. Chicago: Open Court, 2002.

"Islamists in Iran Again Insist That Rushdie Fatwa Should Stay." *Deutsche Presse-Agentur*. February 13, 2001. International news. Available from *www.lexis-nexis.com*, September 12, 2002.

Jameson, Fredric. *Postmodernism; or, The Cultural Logic of Late Capitalism*. Durham: Duke University Press, 1991.

Johnny Mnemonic. Dir. Robert Longo. Screenplay by William Gibson. Perf. Keanu Reeves, Dolph Lundgren, Takeshi Kitano, Dina Meyer, and Ice-T. Columbia/Tristar, 1995. Color, 107 min.

Johnson, Carroll B. *Cervantes and the Material World*. Urbana: University of Illinois Press, 2000.

Juana Inés de la Cruz. *Poems, Protest, and a Dream: Selected Writings*. Trans. Margaret Sayers Peden. Intro. Ilan Stavans. London: Penguin, 1997.

Kaler, Anne K. *The Picara: From Hera to Fantasy Heroine*. Bowling Green, OH: Bowling Green State University Popular Press, 1991.

King, B. B., and Eric Clapton. "Riding with the King." By John Hiatt. *Riding with the King*. Reprise Records, 2000.

Kirschner, Teresa J. "Encounter and Assimilation of the Other in *Arauco domado* and *La Araucana* by Lope de Vega." In *Christian Encounters with the Other*, ed. John C. Hawley. New York: New York University Press, 1998. 33–43.

Lacan, Jacques. *The Four Fundamental Concepts of Psycho-Analysis*. Ed. Jacques-Alain Miller. Trans. Alan Sheridan. New York: Norton, 1978.

Lacarra, María Eugenia, ed. *Poema de Mio Cid*. Madrid: Taurus, 1982.

Lavery, David. "From Cinespace to Cyberspace: Zionists and Agents, Realists and Gamers in *The Matrix* and *eXistenZ*." *Journal of Popular Film and Television* 28.4 (2001): 150–57.

Lazarillo de Tormes. Ed. Francisco Rico. Madrid: Cátedra, 1997.

Lestringant, Frank. *Cannibals: The Discovery and Representation of the Cannibal from Columbus to Jules Verne*. Trans. Rosemary Morris. Berkeley: University of California Press, 1997.

Long, Pamela H. "Fagin and Monipodio: The Source of *Oliver Twist* in Cervantes's *Rinconete y Cortadillo*." *Dickensian* 90.2 (1994): 117–24.

Lost in La Mancha. Dir. Keith Fulton and Louis Pepe. IFC Films/New Video Group, 2002. Color, 93 min.

Lydon, John [with Keith Zimmerman and Kent Zimmerman]. *Rotten: No Irish, No Blacks, No Dogs; The Authorized Autobiography of Johnny Rotten and the Sex Pistols*. New York: Picador, 1994.

Maltby, Richard. "A Better Sense of History: John Ford and the Indians." *The Book of Westerns*. Ed. Ian Cameron and Douglas Pye. New York: Continuum, 1996. 34–49.

The Man from Laramie. Dir. Anthony Mann. Screenplay by Philip Yordan and Frank Burt. Perf. James Stewart, Arthur Kennedy, Donald Crisp, John War Eagle. Columbia, 1955. Color, 104 min.

Mann, Charles C. *1491: New Revelations of the Americas Before Columbus*. New York: Random House, 2005.

Manson, Marilyn [Brian Warner]. *Antichrist Superstar*. Prod. Trent Reznor. CD. Interscope, 1996.

———. *Guns, God, and Government World Tour*. DVD. Eagle Vision, 2002. Color, 107 min.

———. [with Neil Strauss]. *The Long Hard Road Out of Hell*. New York: ReganBooks, 1998.

Maravall, José Antonio. *Culture of the Baroque: Analysis of a Historical Structure*. Trans. Terry Cochran. Ed. Wlad Godzich and Nicholas Spadaccini. Minneapolis: University of Minnesota Press, 1986.

———. *Utopía y contrautopía en el "Quijote."* Santiago de Compostela, Spain: Pico Sacro, 1976.

Matar, Nabil. *Turks, Moors, and Englishmen in the Age of Discovery*. New York: Columbia University Press, 1999.

Mathews, Jack. *The Battle of Brazil*. New York: Applause Theatre & Cinema Books, 1998.

The Matrix. Dir. Andy Wachowski and Larry Wachowski. Screenplay by Andy Wachowski and Larry Wachowski. Perf. Keanu Reeves, Laurence Fishburne, Carrie-Anne Moss, Hugo Weaving, and Joe Pantoliano. Warner Bros., 1999. Color, 136 min.

The Matrix Reloaded. Dir. Andy Wachowski and Larry Wachowski. Screenplay by Andy Wachowski and Larry Wachowski. Perf. Keanu Reeves, Laurence Fishburne, Carrie-Anne Moss, Hugo Weaving, Jada Pinkett Smith, and Gloria Foster. Warner Bros., 2003. Color, 138 min.

The Matrix Revolutions. Dir. Andy Wachowski and Larry Wachowski. Screenplay by Andy Wachowski and Larry Wachowski. Perf. Keanu Reeves, Laurence Fishburne, Carrie-Ann Moss, Hugo Weaving, Mary Alice, and Jada Pinkett Smith. Warner Bros., 2003. Color, 129 min.

McDermott, Gerald R. "Jonathan Edwards and American Indians: The Devil Sucks Their Blood." *New England Quarterly* 72.4 (1999): 539–57.

McKendrick, Melveena. *Woman and Society in the Spanish Drama of the Golden Age: A Study of the* mujer varonil. Cambridge: Cambridge University Press, 1974.

McMorran, Will. "From Quixote to Caractacus: Influence, Intertextuality, and *Chitty Chitty Bang Bang. Journal of Popular Culture* 39.5 (2006): 756–79.

McNab, Chris. "Derrida, Rushdie and the Ethics of Mortality." In *The Ethics in Literature*, ed. Andrew Hadfield, Dominic Rainsford, and Tim Woods. New York: St. Martin's Press, 1999. 136–51.

Menéndez Pidal, Ramón, ed. *Flor nueva de romances viejos*. Madrid: Espasa-Calpe, 1976.

Menocal, María Rosa. *The Ornament of the World: How Muslims, Jews, and Christians Created a Culture of Tolerance in Medieval Spain*. Boston: Little, Brown, 2002.

Merrin, William. " 'Did You Ever Eat Tasty Wheat?': Baudrillard and *The Matrix*." *Scope: An Online Journal of Film Studies*, May 2003. *www.scope.nottingham. ac.uk/article.php?issue=may2003&id=257&section=articlewww* (accessed May 2, 2008).

Mighty Morphin' Power Rangers. Fox Television. 1993–96.

Miller, Stuart. *The Picaresque Novel*. Cleveland: The Press of Case Western Reserve University, 1967.

Mitchell, Joni. "Woodstock." *Ladies of the Canyon*. CD. Reprise, 1970; Warner Bros., 1990.

Monteser, Frederick. *The Picaresque Element in Western Literature*. University: University of Alabama Press, 1975.

Montesquieu, Charles Louis de Secondat, Baron de la Brède et, 1689–1755. *The Spirit of the Laws*. Ed. and trans. Anne M. Cohler, Basia Carolyn Miller, and Harold Samuel Stone. Cambridge: Cambridge University Press, 1989.

Monty Python and the Holy Grail. Dir. Terry Gilliam and Terry Jones. Written and performed by Graham Chapman, John Cleese, Terry Gilliam, Eric Idle, Terry Jones, and Michael Palin. DVD. Columbia/Tristar, 1975. Color, 94 min.

Moore, Art. "Evangelist's 'Tone Incited Hatred of Muslims.'" *World Net Daily*, November 5, 2003. *www.worldnetdaily.com/news/article.asp?ARTICLE_ID=35432* (accessed May 2, 2008).

Murillo, Luis Andrés. *The Golden Dial: Temporal Configuration in* Don Quijote. Oxford: Dolphin, 1975.

———. "Introducción biográfica y crítica." *El ingenioso hidalgo Don Quijote de la Mancha*. By Miguel de Cervantes. Madrid: Castalia, 1978.1:9–32.

Ndalianis, Angela. "Baroque Perceptual Regimes." *Senses of Cinema: An Online Film Journal Devoted to the Serious and Eclectic Discussion of Cinema* 5 (2000). *www.sensesofcinema.com/contents/00/5/baroque.html* (accessed May 2, 2008)

Nehring, Neil. "Revolt into Style: Graham Greene Meets the Sex Pistols." *PMLA* 106.2 (1991): 222–37.

———. "The Shifting Relations of Literature and Popular Music in Postwar England." *Discourse: Journal for Theoretical Studies in Media and Culture* 12.1 (1989–90): 78–103.

Nineteen Eighty-Four. Dir. Michael Radford. Screenplay by Michael Radford and Jonathan Gems. Perf. John Hurt, Richard Burton, and Suzanna Hamilton. Atlantic, 1984. Color, 113 mins.

Ocasio, Rafael. "Ethnic Underclass Representation in the *Cantigas*: The Black Moro as a Hated Character." In *Estudios alfonsinos y otros escritos: En homenaje a John Esten Keller y a Aníbal A. Biglieri*, ed. Nicolás Toscano Liria. New York: National Endowment for the Humanities, Alfonso X el Sabio Institute, 1990; National Hispanic Foundation for the Humanities, 1991. 183–88.

Orwell, George [Eric Blair]. *Nineteen Eighty-Four*. Intro. Bernard Crick. Oxford: Claredon, 1984.

Oxford English Dictionary, The Compact. 2nd ed. Oxford: Clarendon Press, 1991.

Pagden, Anthony. *European Encounters with the New World: From Renaissance to Romanticism*. New Haven: Yale University Press, 1993.

Palahniuk, Chuck. *Fight Club*. New York: Henry Holt, 1996.

Parker, Alexander A. *Literature and the Delinquent: The Picaresque Novel in Spain and Europe, 1599–1753*. Edinburgh: Edinburgh University Press, 1967.

Parks, Rita. *The Western Hero in Film and Television: Mass Media Mythology*. Studies in Cinema, no. 10. Ann Arbor: UMI Research Press, 1982.

Parr, James A. Don Quixote: *An Anatomy of Subversive Discourse*. Newark, DE: Juan de la Cuesta, 1988.

Peele, Thomas. "*Fight Club*'s Queer Representations." *JAC* 21.4 (2001): 862–69.

Pérez Firmat, Gustavo. Introduction to *Do the Americas Have a Common Literature?* Ed. Gustavo Pérez Firmat. Durham: Duke University Press, 1990. 1–5.

Pipes, Daniel. *The Rushdie Affair: The Novel, the Ayatollah, and the West*. New York: Birch Lane Press, 1990.

Pinkus, Karen. "Self-Representation in Futurism and Punk." *South Central Review: The Journal of the South Central Modern Language Association* 13.2–3 (1996): 180–93.

Plato. *Republic*. Trans. Robin Waterfield. Oxford: Oxford University Press, 1993.

Prospero's Books. Dir. Peter Greenaway. Screenplay by Peter Greenaway. Based on *The Tempest* by William Shakespeare. Perf. John Gielgud, Michael Clark, and Isabelle Pasco. Miramax, 1991. Color, 129 min.

Pye, Douglas. "Double Vision: Miscegenation and Point of View in *The Searchers*." In *The Book of Westerns*, ed. Ian Cameron and Douglas Pye. New York: Continuum, 1996. 229–35.

Quevedo, Francisco de. *El Buscón*. Ed. Domingo Ynduráin. Madrid: Cátedra, 1996.

Ramírez, Álvaro. "*Don Quijote* and the Age of Simulacra." *Hispania* 88.1 (2005): 82–90.

Reed, Cory. "Scientific and Technological Imagery in *Don Quijote*." In *Don Quijote Across Four Centuries, 1605–2005*, ed. Carroll B. Johnson. Newark, DE: Juan de la Cuesta, 2006. 167–84.

Reed, Helen H. "Theatricality in the Picaresque of Cervantes." *Cervantes* 7.2 (1987): 71–84.

Rico, Francisco. *The Spanish Picaresque Novel and the Point of View*. Trans. Charles Davis and Harry Sieber. Cambridge: Cambridge University Press, 1969.

Riley, Glenda. "Annie Oakley: The Peerless Lady Wing-Shot." In *By Grit and Grace: Eleven Women Who Shaped the American West*, ed. Glenda Riley and Richard W. Etulain. Golden, CO: Fulcrum, 1997. 93–114.

Rodríguez Monegal, Emir. "Borges, the Reader." *Diacritics* 4.4 (1974): 41–49.

Rogers, Richard A. "*1984* to *Brazil*: From the Pessimism of Reality to the Hope of Dreams. *Text and Performance Quarterly* 10 (1990): 34–46.

Rojas, Fernando de. *La Celestina*. Ed. Dorothy S. Severin. Madrid: Cátedra, 1997.

———. *Celestina*. Ed. Dorothy Sherman Severin. Trans. James Mabbe. Warminster, Wiltshire, UK: Aris & Phillips, 1987.

The Rolling Stones. *Forty Licks*. ABKCO, 2002 (CD 1); Virgin, 2002 (CD 2).

Rosaldo, Renato. "Imperialist Nostalgia." *Culture and Truth: The Remaking of Social Analysis*. Boston: Beacon Press, 1989. 68–87.

Rushdie, Salman. *East, West: Stories*. New York: Pantheon, 1994.

———. *The Ground Beneath Her Feet*. New York: Picador, 2000.

———. *Haroun and the Sea of Stories*. London: Granta, 1990.

———. *Imaginary Homelands: Essays and Criticism, 1981–1991*. London: Granta, 1991.

———. *Midnight's Children*. London: Penguin Books, 1991.

———. *The Moor's Last Sigh*. New York: Vintage, 1995.

———. "*The Moor's Last Sigh*: Charlie Rose / 1996." *Conversations with Salman Rushdie*. Ed. Michael Reder. Jackson, Mississippi: University Press of Mississippi, 2000. 199–215.

Russell, Alec. "US Evangelist Leads the Millions Seeking a Battle with Islam." *Daily Telegraph*, May 8, 2006. Available at *www.telegraph.co.uk/news/*

Said, Edward W. *Orientalism*. New York: Vintage Books, 1979.

Salecl, Renata, and Slavoj Žižek, eds. *Gaze and Voice as Love Objects*. Durham: Duke University Press, 1996.

Sayers, Dorothy L., trans. *The Song of Roland*. London: Penguin, 1957.

The Searchers. Dir. John Ford. Screenplay by Frank S. Nugent. Perf. John Wayne, Jeffery Hunter, Vera Miles, Ward Bond, Natalie Wood, Beulah Archuletta, and Chief Thundercloud. Warner Bros., 1956. Cumberland Video. Color, 119 min.

Seed, Patricia. *Ceremonies of Possession in Europe's Conquest of the New World, 1492–1640*. Cambridge: Cambridge University Press, 1995.

Sex Pistols. *Jubilee*. CD. Virgin, 2002.

————. *Never Mind the Bollocks, Here's the Sex Pistols*. Dir. Matthew Longfellow. Perf. Paul Cook, Steve Jones, Johnny Rotten, Glen Matlock, Malcolm McLaren, and Sid Vicious. DVD. Eagle Rock, 2002. Color, 100 min.

The Shining. Dir. Stanley Kubrick. Screenplay by Stanley Kubrick and Diane Johnson. Based on the novel by Stephen King. Perf. Jack Nicholson, Shelly Duvall, and Scatman Crothers. Warner Bros., 1980. Color, 146 min.

Sieber, Harry. *The Picaresque*. London: Methuen, 1977.

Simerka, Barbara. *Discourses of Empire: Counter-Epic Literature in Early Modern Spain*. University Park: Pennsylvania State University Press, 2003.

Simerka, Barbara, and Christopher B. Weimer. "Duplicitous Diegesis: *Don Quijote* and Charlie Kaufman's *Adaptation*." *Hispania: A Journal Devoted to the Teaching of Spanish and Portuguese* 88.1 (2005): 91–100.

Simmons, William S. "Cultural Bias in the New England Puritans' Perception of Indians." *William and Mary Quarterly* 38.1 (1981): 56–72.

Slotkin, Richard. *Regeneration Through Violence: The Mythology of the American Frontier, 1600–1860*. Middletown, CT: Wesleyan University Press, 1973.

Spadaccini, Nicholas "Daniel Defoe and the Spanish Picaresque Tradition: The Case of Moll Flanders." *Ideologies and Literature: A Journal of Hispanic and Luso-Brazilian Studies* 2.6 (1978): 10–26.

Spivak, Gayatri Chakravorty. "Can the Subaltern Speak?" In *Marxism and the Interpretation of Culture*, ed. Cary Nelson and Lawrence Grossberg. Urbana: University of Illinois Press, 1988. 271–313.

Stagecoach. Dir. John Ford. Perf. John Wayne, Claire Trevor, Andy Devine, John Carradine, Chris-Pin Martin, and Elvira Rios. United Artists, 1939. DVD. Warner Home Video, 1997. B/W, 97 min.

Stam, Robert. *Literature Through Film: Realism, Magic, and the Art of Adaptation*. Oxford: Blackwell, 2005.

Star Trek. Perf. William Shatner, Leonard Nimoy, and DeForest Kelly. NBC. 1966–69.

Star Trek: The Next Generation. Perf. Patrick Stewart, Jonathan Frakes, Brent Spiner, Gates McFadden, Marina Sirtis, LeVar Burton, and Michael Dorn. Fox Television. 1987–94.

Stegner, Wallace. "Variations on a Theme by Crèvecoeur." In *Where the Bluebird Sings to the Lemonade Springs: Living and Writing in the West*. New York: Random House, 1992. 99–116.

Steiner, George. *After Babel: Aspects of Language and Translation*. London: Oxford University Press, 1975.

Stevenson, Robert Louis. *The Strange Case of Dr Jekyll and Mr Hyde*. In *The Strange Case of Dr Jekyll and Mr Hyde and Other Tales of Terror*, ed. Robert Mighall. London: Penguin, 2002.

Stone, Robert S. *Picaresque Continuities: Transformations of Genre from the Golden Age to the Goethezeit*. New Orleans: University Press of the South, 1998.

Stranger Than Fiction. Dir. Marc Forster. Screenplay by Zach Helm. Perf. Will Ferrell, Queen Latifah, and Emma Thompson. Sony, 2006. Color, 113 min.

Sullivan, Sherry. "Indians in American Fiction, 1820–1850: An Ethnohistorical Perspective." *Clio* 15.3 (1986): 239–57.

This Is Spinal Tap. Dir. Rob Reiner. Screenplay by Christopher Guest, Michael McKean, Harry Shearer, and Rob Reiner. Perf. Christopher Guest, Michael McKean, Harry Shearer, Fred Willard, and Rob Reiner. Embassy, 1984. Color, 83 min.

Toy Story. Dir. John Lasseter. Story by John Lasseter, Pete Docter, Andrew Stanton, and Joe Ranft. Screenplay by Joss Whedon, Andrew Stanton, Joel Cohen, and Alec Sokolow. Music by Randy Newman. Perf. Tom Hanks, Tim Allen, Don Rickles, Jim Varney, Wallace Shawn, John Ratzenberger, and Annie Potts. Walt Disney/Pixar, 1995.

Toy Story 2. Dir. John Lasseter, Ash Brannon, and Lee Unkrich. Story by John Lasseter, Pete Docter, Ash Brannon, and Andrew Stanton. Screenplay by Andrew Stanton, Rita Hsiao, Doug Chamberlain, and Chris Webb. Music by Randy Newman. Perf. Tom Hanks, Tim Allen, Joan Cusak, Kelsey Grammer, Don Rickles, Jim Varney, Wallace Shawn, John Ratzenberger, Annie Potts, Wayne Knight, Laurie Metcalf, and Estelle Harris. Walt Disney/Pixar, 1999.

Trainspotting. Dir. Danny Boyle. Screenplay by John Hodge. Based on the novel by Irvine Welsh. Perf. Ewan McGregor, Ewan Bremner, Jonny Lee Miller, Kevin McKidd, and Robert Carlyle. Miramax, 1996. Color, 94 min.

Turner, Frederick Jackson. *Rereading Frederick Jackson Turner: "The Significance of the Frontier in American History" and Other Essays.* Ed. John Mack Faragher. New York: Henry Holt and Company, 1994.

Tuska, Jon. *The American West in Film: Critical Approaches to the Western.* Westport, CT: Greenwood Press, 1985.

"Tuttle." *M*A*S*H.* Dir. William Wiard. Screenplay by David Ketchum and Bruce Shelly. Perf. Alan Alda, Wayne Rogers, McLean Stevenson, Loretta Swit, Larry Linville, and Gary Burghoff. CBS. January 14, 1973.

Twelve Monkeys. Dir. Terry Gilliam. Screenplay by Chris Marker and David Webb Peoples. Perf. Bruce Willis, Madeleine Stowe, Brad Pitt, and Christopher Plummer. Universal, 1995. Color, 129 min.

Unamuno, Miguel de. *Mist: A Tragicomic Novel.* Trans. Warner Fite. Urbana: University of Illinois Press, 2000.

———. *Niebla.* Ed. Germán Gullón. Madrid: Espasa-Calpe, 1990.

———. *Our Lord Don Quixote: The Life of Don Quixote and Sancho with Related Essays.* Trans. Anthony Kerrigan. Intro. Walter Starkie. Princeton: Princeton University Press, 1967.

———. *Vida de Don Quijote y Sancho.* Ed. Ricardo Gullón. Madrid: Alianza, 1987.

Vega, Lope de. *Obras escogidas.* Ed. Federico Carlos Sáinz de Robles. 5th ed. 3 vols. Madrid: Aguilar, 1990.

Velázquez, Diego. *Las Meninas.* Madrid: Museo del Prado.

Voigts-Virchow, Eckart. " 'The Lord of the Files': Carnivalising Dystopia (*Nineteen Eighty-Four*) in Terry Gilliam's *Brazil*." In *Text und Ton im Film*, ed. Paul Goetsch and Dietrich Scheunemann. Tübingen, Germany: Guntar Narr Verlag, 1997. 265–84.

Wasserman, Dale. *Man of La Mancha: A Musical Play.* Lyrics by Joe Darion. Music by Mitch Leigh. New York: Random House, 1966.

Wegenstein, Bernadette. "Shooting Up Heroines." In *Reload: Rethinking Women and Cyberculture*, ed. Mary Flanagan and Austin Booth. Cambridge: MIT Press, 2002. 332–54.

Weiss, Timothy. "At the End of East/West: Myth in Rushdie's *The Moor's Last Sigh*." *Jouvert: A Journal of Postcolonial Studies* 4.2 (2000). *http://social.chass.ncsu.edu/jouvert/v4i2/weiss.htm* (accessed September 9, 2001).

Whitbourn, Christine J. *Knaves and Swindlers: Essays on the Picaresque Novel in Europe.* London: Oxford University Press, 1974.

Whitman, Walt. *Leaves of Grass.* New York: Barnes & Noble, 1993.

Wicks, Ulrich. *Picaresque Narrative, Picaresque Fictions: A Theory and Research Guide*. Westport, CT: Greenwood Press, 1989.

Williams, Linda Ruth. "Dream Girls and Mechanic Panic: Dystopia and Its Others in *Brazil* and *Nineteen Eighty-Four*." In *British Science Fiction Cinema*, ed. I. Q. Hunter. London: Routledge, 1999. 153–68.

Wolff, Egon. *Flores de papel*. In *Nueve dramaturgos hispanoamericanos: Antología del teatro hispanoamericano del siglo XX*, vol. 2, ed. Frank Dauster, Leon Lyday, and George Woodyard. Ottawa: Girol, 1979. 145–221.

The Wonder Years. Perf. Fred Savage and Daniel Stern. ABC. 1988–93.

Wreen, Michael J. "Don Quixote Rides Again!" *Romanic Review* 86 (1995): 141–63.

Wright, Robert. " 'I'd Sell You Suicide': Pop Music and Moral Panic in the Age of Marilyn Manson." *Popular Music* 19.3 (2000): 365–85.

Zamora Vicente, Alonso. "Sobre la fabla antigua de Lope de Vega." In *Philologica Hispaniensia in Honorem Manuel Alvar, I: Dialectología*. Madrid: Gredos, 1983. 645–49.

Index

Page numbers in bold indicate illustrations